A Guide to

EUROPEAN COMMUNITY LAW

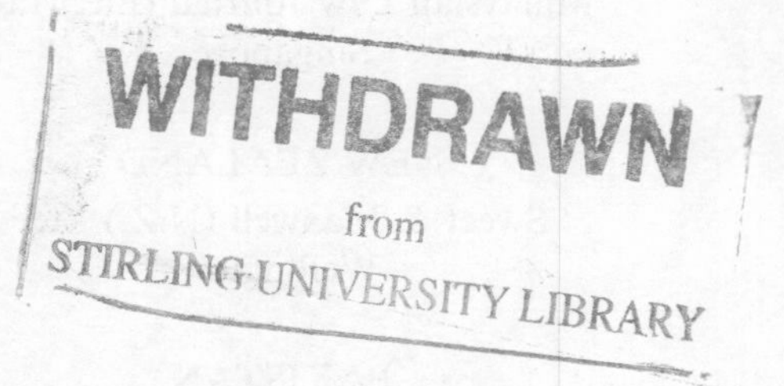

AUSTRALIA
The Law Book Company Ltd.
Sydney : Melbourne : Brisbane

GREAT BRITAIN
Sweet & Maxwell Ltd.
London

INDIA
N. M. Tripathi Private Ltd.
Bombay

ISRAEL
Steimatzky's Agency Ltd.
Jerusalem : Tel Aviv : Haifa

MALAYSIA : SINGAPORE : BRUNEI
Malaysian Law Journal (Pte.) Ltd.
Singapore

NEW ZEALAND
Sweet & Maxwell (N.Z.) Ltd.
Wellington

PAKISTAN
Pakistan Law House
Karachi

U.S.A. AND CANADA
Matthew Bender & Co. Inc.
New York

A Guide to

EUROPEAN COMMUNITY LAW

by

P. S. R. F. MATHIJSEN

Director with the Commission
of the European Communities
Professor of Law, University of Nijmegen

Preface

by

J. D. B. MITCHELL

Salvesen Professor of European Institutions
University of Edinburgh

LONDON
SWEET & MAXWELL

NEW YORK
MATTHEW BENDER

1972

Published in Great Britain by
Sweet & Maxwell Ltd. of
11 New Fetter Lane, London
Published in the U.S.A. by
Matthew Bender & Co. Inc. of
235 East 45th Street,
New York, New York 10017
Printed in Great Britain
by Thanet Press,
Margate, Kent

SBN Hardback 421 17690 3
Paperback 421 17700 4

Library of Congress Catalog Card No. 72—88587

To my daughters Claire
Bénédicte
Stéphanie
Valérie
Olivia
Daphné

ACKNOWLEDGMENT

I HAVE dedicated this book to my children who followed the progress of my writing with awe, annoyance and, I hope, some admiration, but it became a real family affair when my wife Beverly volunteered to read, correct and reread my manuscript. Without all this affectionate interest the writing would have been an impossible task.

I am in deep debt to Mr. J. E. Ferry, barrister, who not only read the manuscript, corrected my English and made valuable suggestions, but helped me understand some of the questions which are bound to be raised on accession by lawyers in the United Kingdom. I am much indebted to Professor John Mitchell who encouraged me to write this book; he also undertook to write the Preface for which I feel honoured. He and Mr. T. C. Daintith read my manuscript and their amendments which were gratefully accepted have helped to make this book readable for English-speaking people.

For tireless typing and retyping I am most thankful to Jenny Keymeulen.

Finally, I am very pleased to mention the effective help given by my daughters Claire, Bénédicte and Stéphanie in compiling the index.

The author is an Official of the European Communities; the views expressed in this book are his and may not be attributed to the institutions of the Community.

PREFACE

THAT British lawyers and law students will need a guide to European Community Law, cannot be denied, and there could be few better qualified than Professor Pierre Mathijsen to produce it. Not only has he many years' experience of the practical working of the system, but that experience is also backed by teaching Community law in Nijmegen. What he has produced is indeed a guide. It does not set out to be an exhaustive treatise, citing all the abundant literature that exists (though hints of the many arguments run all through the book). Nevertheless, the word " guide " should not be taken too lightly. Perhaps because of the background of teaching, he has packed in a great deal of substance. This is no cursory indication simply of main features.

It is particularly to be welcomed for many reasons. Lawyers' disputes about Community law can resemble theological ones. Thus Professor Mathijsen's treatment in his introduction, or in passages dealing with competition law (in the broadest sense), puts the debate on the right footing. The need for the uniform and direct application of Community law ceases to be a matter of dogma; it springs from the economic purposes of the Community. Without this " equality before the law " those purposes will be frustrated. A preface is not the place for contentious statements, but again the realism of his approach should be noted. It is true that the Dutch Constitution helps the acceptance of Community law. Yet, as the Author says " if the sole justification for supremacy of Community law over national law were national law itself, this supremacy would be at the mercy of the next constitutional amendment." This insistence upon the distinctive and autonomous character of Community law is essential. Without a proper understanding of this, the British debates are likely to be conducted in false terms. In substance, British lawyers are going to face no problems which have not already been encountered within the legal systems of the Six, and which have not already found solutions there. At times, even, the shape of those systems presented more difficult problems, at others, as in the Belgian case of the *Fromagerie–Franco Suisse* "*Le Ski*", the problem is almost identical. An unwritten constitution is not so extraordinary after all. Thus this matter of fact approach which the author adopts is the only reasonable one, for law and lawyers exist to serve practical ends. Certainly law and legal theory does not exist solely for lawyers. The argument about the sovereignty of Parliament should be seen in its proper proportion. The "guide" gives, as a guide should, the proper approach.

Not only does the *Guide* avoid the theology, but in other ways it prints the basic principles. It would be wrong in a Preface to such a book, to use words like "teleological," but throughout, the author underlines the purposive elements of this law. This is important in two ways. First, the law must be seen as a whole. State aids and regional policy do march side by side (though the Author carefully points out the distinctions among regional development aids). There is, though, at this point of time, a tendency which is natural enough for British lawyers to pick out those pieces of the law which are of particular interest to them and to forget or ignore the rest. Not only may such an attitude cause a less full understanding of each branch, but unless the whole picture, including this purposive element, is grasped, prediction of patterns of development become much more difficult. Thus the whole picture in sufficient detail is essential. Secondly, this purposive element is important in leading back to the economic background. This link between law and economics is often too little emphasised, but here this link is rightly emphasised throughout.

To many lawyers, institutional questions are of no interest. The importance of such questions can, no doubt, be exaggerated. Yet it is not merely for completeness that they should be treated as they are in this guide. The relationship of Commission and Council is not merely a matter of interest to political scientists. Often it provides the explanation of why the law emerges in the shape that it does, often also it can explain why the law does not emerge. Thus, even at the level of practicality, these passages are, especially at this time, of importance to British lawyers. So too are the passages on the policies made, half made or to be made. As the Author puts it, he has tried to give a photograph of Community law and indeed of the Communities as they now are. For those entering this new legal order such a photograph is essential. It is presented in such a way that those who wish an enlargement of any part can start to make their own. It is a photograph which evokes no fears. Looking at it, all these arguments about the difficulties of mixing common and civil law systems are seen for what, in this context, they are – empty ones.

A guide is meant to help, and not do everything for those being guided. In this book Professor Mathijsen helps not only those who are ignorant of the road but does as much for those who are already some way along the road.

26 *June* 1972 J. D. B. MITCHELL

TABLE OF CONTENTS

TABLE OF COURT OF JUSTICE CASES

Mentioned in this book, of which an English translation exists in C.M.L.R. or which are discussed in C.M.L.Rev.

Case No.	*Case*	*C.M.L.R.*	*C.M.L.Rev.*
42, 49–59	Breedband	1963, 60	
9, 12–60	Vloeberghs	1963, 44	
7–61	Pork Products	1962, 39	
10–61	Radio Valves	1962, 187	
13–61	Bosch	1962, 1	
14–61	Hoogovens	1963, 73	
2, 3–62	Gingerbread	1963, 199	Vol. 1, 211
16, 17–62	Fruit and Vegetables	1963, 160	Vol. 1, 210
24–62	Wine	1963, 347	Vol. 1, 351
25–62	Plauman	1964, 29	Vol. 1, 353
26–62	Van Gend en Loos	1963, 105	Vol. 1, 82
28 to 30–62	Da Costa en Schake	1963, 224	Vol. 1, 213
31, 33–62	Lütticke	1963, 152	Vol. 1, 211
34–62	Sweet oranges	1963, 369	Vol. 1, 351
35–62/16–63	Leroy	1964, 562	
36–62	Aciéries du Temple	1964, 49	
13–63	Refrigerators	1963, 289	Vol. 1, 352
15–63	Lassalle	1964, 259	
23, 24, 52–63	Henricot	1964, 119	
28–63	Hoogovens	1964, 125	Vol. 1, 359
53, 54–63	Lemmerzwerke	1964, 384	
73, 74–63	Rotterdam	1964, 198	Vol. 2, 95
90, 91–63	Milk Products	1965, 58	Vol. 2, 340
100–63	Kalsbeek–van der Veen	1964, 548	
101–63	Fohrmann and Krier	1964, 245	
106, 107–63	Toepfer	1966, 111	Vol. 3, 233
108–63	Merlini	1965, 109	
1–64	Glucoseries	1964, 596	Vol. 3, 231
6–64	Costa v. ENEL	1964, 425	Vol. 2, 197
45–64	Machine parts	1966, 97	Vol. 3, 367
56, 58–64	Grundig Consten	1966, 418	Vol. 5, 209
10–65	Deutschmann	1965, 259	Vol. 3, 232
32–65	Regulation 19/65	1969, 39	Vol. 4, 202
48–65	Lütticke	1966, 378	Vol. 4, 78
54–65	Forges de Châtillon	1966, 525	
56–65	Ulm	1966, 357	Vol. 4, 197
57–65	Lütticke	1971, 674	Vol. 4, 327
61–65	Vaassen	1966, 508	Vol. 4, 440
8 to 11–66	Noordwyks cement accoord	1967, 77	Vol. 5, 71 and 319
2–67	De Moor	1967, 223	
24–67	Parke, Davis	1968, 47	Vol. 6, 129, 217
28–67	Molkerei-Zentrale	1968, 187	Vol. 6, 132
30–67	Molitoria		Vol. 5, 480
6–68	Watenstedt	1969, 26	
13–68	Salgoil	1969, 181	Vol. 6, 478
14–68	Wilhelm	1969, 100	Vol. 6, 488
19–68	De Cicco	1969, 67	
24–68	Statistial	1971, 611	Vol. 7, 72
29–68	Eierkontor	1969, 390	
31–68	Chanel	1971, 403	

Case No.	*Case*	*C.M.L.R.*	*C.M.L.Rev.*
5–69	Völk *v.* Verwaecke	1969, 273	Vol. 7, 8
6, 11–69	Export credits	1970, 43	Vol. 7, 479
15–69	Ugliola	1970, 194	Vol. 7, 343
27–69	Caisse de maladie	1970, 243	Vol. 7, 350
40–69	Bollmann	1970, 141	
43–69	Bilger		Vol. 8, 241
47–69	Aids to textile	1970, 351	Vol. 8, 82
50–69	Stay of execution	1971, 724	
64–69	Compagnie française	1970, 369	
68–69	Brock	1971, 55	
69–69	Alcan	1970, 337	
6–70	Borromeo Arese	1970, 436	
9–70	Grad	1971, 1	Vol. 8, 380
22–70	AETR	1971, 335	Vol. 8, 392
28–70	Otto Witt	1971, 163	
30–70	Otto Scheer	1972, 255	Vol. 8, 250
40–70	Sirena	1971, 260	Vol. 9, 83
78–70	DGG	1971, 631	Vol. 9, 87

TABLE OF EUROPEAN TREATIES

ABBREVIATIONS

J.O. French edition of the *Official Journal of the European Communities.*

Remarks

1. This Official Journal was published under the name "Journal Officiel de la Communauté Européenne du Charbon et de l'Acier" from 1952 to 19 April 1958; on 20 April 1958 the first issue of the "Journal Officiel des Communaués Européennes" appeared, without modifying the structure of the Journal itself; this lasted until 31 December 1967.

References to publications in the Official Journal for the period 1952-1967 are made by mentioning the page and the year: such as J.O. 849/65. Between 1 July and 31 December 1967 each issue is paged separately.

2. After 1 January 1968 (see J.O. L 30, 1968), the Journal was divided into two separate editions designated by the letters "L" and "C."

Legislative texts are published in the edition marked "L" and are again subdivided in two categories:

I. Acts for which publication is a condition for their application (see E.E.C., Art. 191);

II. Acts for which publication is not required.

All other texts appear in the edition marked "C."

References to publications in the Official Journal after 1 January 1968 are made by mentioning the letter "L" or "C," the No. of the issue and the year, for instance J.O. L 31, 1970.

Rec. *Recueil de la Jurisprudence de la Cour.*

Remarks

The roman numeral refers to the volume and the figure to the page. Starting with Volume XV, the "motifs" of judgments are divided into sections; these are indicated by a figure in brackets.

The reader will be interested in knowing that:

- the index of Volumes XIII *et seq.* contains a chronological and a numerical list of all the judgments of the Court of Justice;
- the index of Volume XIII contains an index of all the Community provisions (treaties, protocols, regulations, etc.) referred to in the judgments of the Court.

General Report	General Report on the activities of the Communities, published yearly by the Commission. The year mentioned after the word Report refers to the period covered by the Report.
C.M.L.R.	Common Market Law Reports.
C.M.L.Rev.	Common Market Law Review.
E.C.S.C.	European Coal and Steel Community.
E.E.C.	European Economic Community.
Euratom E.C.A.E.	European Community of Atomic Energy.
Merger Treaty	Treaty of 8 April 1965 establishing a Single Council and a Single Commission of the European Communities.
Budgetary Treaty	Treaty of 22 April 1970 amending Certain Budgetary Provisions of the Treaties establishing the European Communities and of the Treaty establishing a Single Council and a Single Commission of the European Communities.

English Version of Official Texts

Since there exists no authentic English translation of the Court Reports nor of the Official Journal of the European Communities, the English version of the acts of the Community Institutions used in this book were made by the author and based on the French texts. The English texts of the European treaties used for this book are those published by H.M. Stationery Office in 1972, since it is in that form that the English text of the European treaties will become authentic as from the date of accession of the United Kingdom to the European Communities.

Chapter 1

COMMUNITY LAW

I. Existence of Community Law

1–1. As the title of this book suggests, a system of law has existed for the last few years sufficiently original, individualised or characteristic to be considered separately from either municipal law or international law. At first glance, there seems to be nothing particularly new or different in the various treaties concerning the European Communities; all of them: the treaty establishing the European Coal and Steel Community (E.C.S.C.)[1] back in 1952, the two so-called treaties of Rome establishing the European Economic Community (E.E.C.)[2] and the European Atomic Energy Community (Euratom)[3] both effective since 1 January 1958 (and the same applies to the treaty of accession),[4] are classical examples of international treaties under which various sovereign States assume reciprocal duties and obligations in accordance with international law. But are they really?

According to the Court of Justice set up under these European treaties and whose task it is to ensure that law is observed in the interpretation of these treaties,[5] they are not. In a judgment of 5 February 1963 (case 26–62, *Van Gend & Loos*)[6] the Court of Justice held " that the objective of the E.E.C. treaty *i.e.* to establish a common market whose functioning directly affects the citizens of the Community, implies that this treaty is more than an agreement which would only create mutual obligations between the contracting states " and " that this view is confirmed by the Preamble to the treaty which beyond the Governments, addresses itself to the peoples, and more concretely by the creation of organs institutionalising sovereign rights the exercise of which affects both the Member States and their citizens ".[7] From this short passage it can be concluded that two aspects of the European treaties are original enough to

[1] Cmnd. 4863, January 1972.
[2] Cmnd. 4864, January 1972.
[3] Cmnd. 4865, January 1972.
[4] Cmnd. 4862, January 1972.
[5] See E.C.S.C., Art. 31, E.E.C., Art. 164, and Euratom, Art. 136.
[6] See also the judgment of 13 November 1964 in the cases 90 and 91–63, Rec. X, 1232.
[7] Rec. IX, 23.

justify the opinion that they are more than mere classical international agreements: in the first place, the fact that not only the Member States as such, but also the citizens are affected by them and secondly the fact that institutions (organs) were set up which exercise sovereign rights in limited domains.

1–2. International law or law of nations is traditionally the name for " the customary and treaty rules which are considered legally binding by States in their intercourse with each other "[8] and it is therefore generally accepted that individuals can claim no rights nor assume obligations under international law. By signing the European treaties the Member States have, on the contrary, in the opinion of the Court " attributed to Community law an authority which their citizens may invoke in the national courts ".[9] Furthermore, when referring to Community law the Court does not only mean the provisions of the various European treaties (primary Community law) but also the decisions of the Community's institutions (secondary Community law). And this constitutes one more characteristic of the Communities as compared to other international organisations, namely the direct relationship which exists between these institutions and the citizens of the various Member States, without the opportunity for the latter to interfere or the necessity for them to intervene in order to give binding effect to these decisions which, as expressed in the European Communities Bill " are without further enactment to be given legal effect or used in the United Kingdom " (cl. 2(1)). This is what the Court, in the above mentioned judgment meant when it referred to " the creation of organs institutionalising sovereign rights the exercise of which affects . . . [the] citizens."

1–3. These two characteristics need further definition. In regard to the binding effect of the Community rules, there is the fundamental question of which rules have this direct binding effect: all the rules contained in the European treaties and in the implementing acts of the institutions or only certain of their provisions and in the latter case, what determines whether a Community provision is directly binding? And as regards the powers of the institutions, how do they relate to the powers of the national authorities? Answers to all these questions can be found in various judgments of the Court of Justice.

As regards the conditions which must be fulfilled to make a Community provision directly binding, the Court of Justice expressed

[8] Oppenheim, *International Law*, 8th ed., p. 5.
[9] Rec. IX, 23; see also the Court's judgment in the *Enel* case (6–64), Rec. X, 1141.

them most clearly in its judgment of 3 April 1968, *Molkerei-Zentrale* case (28–67)[10]: " that Community law being independent *vis-à-vis* the legislation of the Member States not only imposes obligations upon the citizens, but is also intended to grant them certain rights; that these rights not only exist when explicitly provided for in the Treaty, but also as a result of clearly defined obligations imposed by the Treaty, both upon Member States and upon the Community institutions; that in that respect it is necessary but also sufficient that the provision which is being invoked lends itself by its very nature to produce direct effects in the legal relations existing between the Member States and their citizens; that E.E.C. Art. 95(1), prohibiting discrimination, provides for a clear and unconditional obligation; that this obligation was not made dependent upon any condition nor its implementation or effectiveness upon any act of the Community institutions or of the Member States; that said prohibition therefore is complete and legally perfect, so that it can create direct effects in the legal relations between the Member States and their citizens."[11] In other words, to be directly applicable a Community provision must

(1) impose a prohibition upon a Member State,
(2) be clear,
(3) be unconditional and
(4) be final, *i.e.* not require further implementing provisions to be effective.

The following Community provisions are among those considered by the Court to establish " enforceable Community right," within the meaning of Clause 2(1) of the European Community Bill: E.E.C., Art. 12 in the *Van Gend & Loos* case (26–62)[12]; E.E.C., Arts. 37(2) and 53 in the *ENEL* case (6–64)[13]; the rules concerning competition in the *Grundig* case (56 and 58–64)[14]; E.E.C., Art. 32(1) and (2) in case 13–68[15] and Article 52 of Regulation 3 of 25 September 1958 (case 27–69)[16].

[10] See also the judgments in the *Van Gend & Loos* case (26–62), Rec. IX, 22–23 and in the second *Lütticke* case (57–65), Rec. XII, 293. The judgment referred to above (*Molkerei-Zentrale*) is the more interesting, since the question concerning the direct effect of E.E.C., Art. 95(1), had been raised already by a German court in the case 57–65; another German court raised the same question asking the court whether it still held the same opinion.

[11] Rec. XIV, 226; see also Rec. XII, 302, case 57–65.

[12] Rec. IX, 28.

[13] Rec. X, 1167.

[14] Rec. XII, 500.

[15] Rec. XIV, 677.

[16] Rec. XV, 411.

1–4. The second characteristic of the European treaties which needs to be further examined concerns the " sovereign rights " of the institutions. In the *ENEL* case (6–64), the Court of Justice, referring to the " real powers " of the Community added that these resulted either " from a limitation or a transfer of the powers of the Member States to the Community " and that by establishing the Community, " the Member States have restricted, although in limited domains, their sovereign rights."[17] Such transfers of sovereign rights concern legislative, administrative and judicial powers. As will be seen, these transfers are sometimes provided for in the national constitutions, sometimes they are not, but whatever the case, it has never been disputed by any of the Member States that such transfers indeed took place, the only question being to what extent.

1–5. Once it is recognised, with the Court of Justice, that the treaties establishing the European Communities have indeed transferred certain powers to their institutions and that these institutions have powers in regard both to the Member States and their citizens, the conclusion as to the existence of a new legal order should follow automatically. There are, however, other arguments in favour of this conclusion: as the Court of Justice held in the above mentioned *ENEL* case, " as opposed to ordinary international agreements, the E.E.C. treaty has established its own legal order, which was integrated into the legal systems of the Member States when the treaty became effective and which binds their jurisdictions; that, indeed, by establishing for an unlimited time a Community endowed with its own institutions, with legal personality, capacity in law, with the right of international representation and in particular with real powers resulting from a limitation or a transfer of the powers of the Member States, the latter have restricted, albeit in limited domains, their sovereign rights and thereby created a body of law applicable to their citizens and to themselves."[18]

The Court came to the same conclusion in several of the above mentioned judgments: in the cases *Van Gend & Loos*, second *Lütticke*, and *Molkerei-Zentrale*. Of particular interest is the *Dairy-Products* case (90 and 91–63): the defendants, the Belgian and Luxembourg Governments maintained that since the Commission itself had failed to fulfil some of its obligations under the treaty, it had lost the right to charge them with default before the Court; they based this thesis

[17] Rec. X, 1159.
[18] *Ibid.*

on international law which in their opinion allows a party injured by the failure of another party to carry out its obligations, to dispense with fulfilling its own. The Court held that " such a bond between the obligations of the Community subjects cannot be accepted under Community Law; that the treaty not only creates mutual obligations between the different parties to which it applies, but establishes a new legal order which regulates their powers, rights and obligations and the necessary proceedings for establishing and penalizing violations; that therefore, except in the cases explicitly provided for, the Treaty system implies that Member States are forbidden to take the law into their own hands."[19] The Court of Justice here formally rejects the automatic applicability of international law to the European treaties. As was seen in the *Molkerei-Zentrale* case, the Court had previously also rejected the automatic applicability of municipal law.[20]

1–6. The interpretation thus given by the Court of Justice to the European treaties and the ensuing legal provisions is also confirmed by the opinion of several municipal courts. Italy and the Federal Republic of Germany strongly adhere to the dualistic theory (International law or Municipal law) and furthermore their constitutional Courts are competent to examine the constitutionality of national laws. Since, according to the dualistic theory the norms of international law are by ratification of international agreements incorporated in the national body of laws and become thereby the equivalent of a national law, national judges can request their constitutional court to examine the constitutionality of Community law for instance. This was, at least, the thesis of the Tribunale di Torino which asked the Corte Costituzionale whether E.C.S.C., Arts. 33(2), 41 and 92 were compatible with the Italian Constitution.

In its judgment of 27 December 1965, the Corte Costituzionale held that " the legal order of the Coal and Steel Community is clearly distinct from the Italian legal order. . . . The E.C.S.C. legal order is accepted by the Italian order, not to be incorporated in the national legal order, but so that the international co-operation which is the objective of the Community can be implemented in the national order and so that the Community's powers can be circumscribed when they extend into the national legal order." The Italian

[19] Rec. X, 1231–1232.
[20] Rec. XIV, 226, case 28–67

Constitutional Court in this case thus rejected a too strict application of the dualistic theory to Community law.

In another decision (7 March 1964)[21] the same Court while recognising the possibility of limiting national sovereignty by an international treaty, seemed to imply that since the E.E.C. treaty had been ratified by a law, this law would be automatically modified by a subsequent conflicting law; since the Italian Constitution " does not confer greater effect upon the ordinary law that gives effect to a treaty."[22]

1–7. In the Federal Republic a similar question was raised before the Bundesverfassungsgericht. Several German undertakings asked the Court to examine the constitutionality of regulations of the Council and of the Commission which, according to the undertakings, were to be considered as being issued by the German Administration. In its judgment of 18 October 1967,[23] the constitutional Court held that " Regulations of the Council and of the Commission are acts of a special public authority created by the treaty and clearly distinct from the authorities of the Member States. The institutions of the E.E.C. exercise sovereign rights which the Member States have abandoned in favour of the Community they established. The Community is not a State, nor a Federal State. It is a Community of a special nature, which is in the process of progressive integration, an interstate creation . . . to which the Federal Republic – as the other Member States – have transferred certain sovereign rights. Thus was established a new public authority, which is independent *vis-à-vis* the State authority of the various Member States; the measures of this Community do not therefore need to be confirmed (ratified), neither can they be abolished by them. The E.E.C. treaty contains some of the administrative law of the Community. The legal measures enacted by the institutions of the Community within the framework of their treaty powers, the secondary Community law, constitutes a separate legal order, whose provisions neither belong to international law nor to the municipal law of the Member States. The Community law and the National Law of the Member States constitute two independent and separate legal orders; Community law finds its origin in an autonomous legal source." This German Constitutional Court decision neatly sum-

[21] See also [1964] C.M.L.R. 435 and C.M.L.Rev. 1964, 224.
[22] Brinkhorst/Schermers, *Judicial Remedies in the European Communities*, 1969, 167.
[23] See also C.M.L.Rev. 1967, 483.

marises the main points discussed above on the existence of a " Community law."

II. Community Law and National Law

1–8. Once it is admitted that Community Law is an independent legal order existing within the Community, several questions arise as to the relations between this Community law and the national legal orders. Since it is established that certain Community provisions are directly applicable and so can be invoked by the citizens in their national Courts, it appears necessary to examine the application of Community law, its interpretation, the possibilities of conflict with national law and the simultaneous application of national and Community law.

1. Application of Community law by the national courts

1–9. In its judgment of 5 February 1963 in the first *Tarief Commissie* or *Van Gend & Loos* case (26–62), the Court of Justice held that " article 12 of the Treaty establishing the European Economic Community has direct effect and confers upon the citizens of the Community individual rights which the national jurisdictions must uphold."[24] The fact that a Community provision has legal effect in the Member States implies therefore the obligation of the national courts to enforce the provision in question when requested to do so by a party in a case before them. This obligation also follows from E.E.C., Art. 5 (Euratom, Art. 192) under which the Member States must " take all appropriate measures, whether general or particular, to ensure fulfilment of the obligations arising out of this Treaty."

1–10. In the United Kingdom the obligation for the Courts to apply Community law follows from clause 2 of the European Communities Bill; this provision refers to the " rights, powers, liabilities, obligations and restrictions " which " in accordance with the Treaties are without further enactment to be given legal effect or used in the United Kingdom " and provides that those " shall be

[24] Rec. IX, 28. Identical conclusion in the case 6–64 (*ENEL*) in regard to Arts. 53 and 37(2), Rec. X, 1167, and in the case 57–65 (second *Lütticke*) in regard to E.E.C., Art. 95(1), Rec. XII, 304.

recognized and available in law, and be enforced, allowed and followed accordingly."

1–11. The obligation of national courts to apply Community law is limited of course to those provisions which produce direct effects in the legal relations existing between the Member States and their citizens or between the citizens. This is the case of the so-called self-executing provisions; several Community provisions were directly enforceable from the moment the treaties became effective (*e.g.* E.E.C., Arts. 12 and 85) others after a certain time-limit had elapsed (*e.g.* Art. 93(1) became directly applicable from the beginning of the second phase of the transitional period in pursuance of Article 93(3), 1),[25] still others become applicable after the necessary implementing measures have been enacted by the Community institutions or by the authorities of the Member States or when the conditions provided for their applicability are fulfilled; this applies to both primary and secondary Community law.

1–12. In the past years persons and undertakings in the Community have in an ever increasing number of cases requested their national courts to apply Community law; the best proof of this is the many cases submitted to the Court of Justice under E.E.C., Art. 177 (Euratom, Art. 150) which provides that where a question regarding the interpretation or validity of the treaties and of the acts of the institutions of the Community is raised before a court or tribunal of a Member State, that court or tribunal may or must (the latter when there is no judicial remedy against its decisions) request the Court of Justice to give a ruling thereon. Out of forty-three judgments[26] pronounced in 1970, twenty-nine concerned rulings given at the request of national courts.

2. Precedence of Community law over national law

1–13. Since the national courts must uphold the Community provisions in cases brought before them and since Community law and national law constitute two independent legal orders, it is not unlikely that conflict will result from their simultaneous applicability. The European treaties contain no explicit provisions regarding the solution to be given to such conflicts and therefore the national

[25] Another example is Art. 37(1) which became directly applicable at the end of the transitional period.

[26] In this figure are not included the cases concerning European Civil Servants; normally those cases are handled by one of the Chambers of the Court.

judges would usually tend to solve such conflicts in accordance with the provisions of their national law.

1–14. Few national legal systems however provide for conflict-rules of this nature. The Dutch Constitution not only provides that the provisions of the European treaties have precedence over existing national laws and regulations, it also specifies that the same applies to the measures enacted by the institutions set up under these treaties and even adds that this precedence applies in cases of conflict between an existing Community rule and a subsequent national law. Article 66 of the Dutch Constitution provides that " legal provisions effective within the Realm will not be applied where this application might be incompatible with general binding rules of treaties which were concluded either before or after the enactment of these provisions " and according to the second paragraph of Article 67, Article 66 shall similarly apply to decisions of international organisations. Those provisions were incorporated in the Dutch Constitution in 1953. The Dutch Constitution is the only one within the Community to clearly specify the supremacy of Community law. The French Constitution provides in general terms that " treaties or agreements duly ratified or approved shall, from the moment of their publication, have an authority superior to that of laws, subject to their application by the other party " (French Constitution of 1958, Art. 55). The German refers to the precedence of " the general rules of public international law " (German Constitution, Art. 25); the Italian Constitution is even less precise, in so far as it only provides that " Italy's legal system conforms with the general principles recognized by international law " (Italian Constitution, Art. 10(1)).

These German and Italian texts and even the French Constitution are a rather meagre legal basis for the obligation that national courts should give precedence to Community law over national law in case of conflict between the two, to say nothing about those Member States: Belgium and Luxemburg whose Constitutions contain no provisions whatsoever referring to the relationship between international and municipal law. And even in the case of the Dutch Constitution which is so explicit about this precedence, if the sole justification for supremacy of Community law over national law were national law itself, this supremacy would be at the mercy of the next constitutional amendment.

1–15. But at the same time, the very existence of the common market requires that the Community regulations not only be applied everywhere within the Community, but also that this application takes place *de jure*, without any possible interference of the national authorities and in exactly the same manner. As will be seen the very essence of the Communities is the creation of one single area within which not only goods, persons, services, capital and payments can freely move, but where the enterprises enter the market under identical conditions at their own risk and on the basis of their own resources. Now, one essential condition for this equality of conditions under which enterprises should operate is the " equality before the law " and this in turn requires, as was just said, that they be all subject to the Community rules and all enjoy in like manner the rights provided under the European treaties. The Court of Justice clearly expressed this idea in several decisions; so for instance in the case 9–65, in its order of 22 June 1965, the Court rejected that " citizens could escape the integral and uniform application of the treaty and thus receive a treatment different from one of the other citizens of the Community."[27]

On what grounds did the Court base its conclusions? For the Court " it follows from the ratifications whereby the Member States bound themselves in an identical way, that all the Member States did adhere to the treaty under the same conditions definitively and without other reservation than those expressed in the protocols to the treaty and that therefore any pretension of a citizen of a Member State to question this adhesion would be contrary to the Community legal order; that in the present case such a pretension is the more inadmissible since a ruling deferring the decision would result in depriving the Community of its very substance, because it would accept the view that ratification either means only a partial acceptance or is a means to give it legal effects varying with the Member States, or an opportunity for the citizens to evade its rules."[28]

So also in the *ENEL* case in which the Court of Justice established that the Member States had restricted their sovereign rights and created a body of law applicable to both the Member States and their citizens, the Court concluded " that the integration into the law of each Member State of provisions of Community origin and more particularly the wording and the spirit of the treaty have as a corollary the impossibility for the Member States to give preference over a legal order they accepted on a reciprocity basis, to a subsequent

[27] Rec. XIII, 37–38.
[28] Rec. XIII, 37.

unilateral (national) measure; the latter cannot indeed be opposed to this legal order, since the binding force of Community law may not vary from one State to another because of subsequent national legislation without jeopardizing the implementation of the treaty objectives."[29]

1–16. The precedence of Community law over the national laws of the Member States, which was also recognised by several national courts,[30] is thus based not upon any national provision, constitutional or other, but on the very nature of the Communities themselves, whose very existence and functioning require identical applicability of the Community law in all the Member States. As Mr. Rippon stated it in the House of Commons " A common market depends on the elimination of trade barriers and of distortions of free and equal competition. This necessarily requires rules made centrally and operating in identical terms throughout the area of the market to secure fairness and consistency."[31]

1–17. It follows that what E.E.C., Art. 189 (Euratom, Art. 161) provides about Community regulations, *i.e.* that they " shall be binding in [their] entirety and directly applicable in all Member States " applies to all the provisions of Community law which confer upon the citizens rights which the national courts must uphold. It is worth quoting here a passage from Sir Derek Walker-Smith's speech in the House of Commons, concerning clause 2 of the European Communities Bill and Article 189 of the E.E.C.: " . . . it may perhaps be an odious Bill, but at any rate it is an honest Bill. Clause 2 is drafted and impeccably drafted, to give precise effect to Article 189 of the Treaty. The key words of the Article are that the regulations are to be directly applicable. If Britain were to seek membership of the Community and failed to ensure that the regulations were directly applicable in this country, we should be in breach of our Treaty obligations. The obligation goes with Membership."[32]

The precedence of Community law over national law is indeed recognised in the European Communities Bill: referring to clause 3 of the Bill, Mr. Rippon declared the following in the House of

[29] Rec. X, 1159.

[30] See Brinkhorst/Schermers, *op. cit.* 103. See also a recent judgment of the Belgian Cour de Cassation (27 May 1971) in the case *Fromagerie Franco-Suisse* " *Le Ski*," 86, *Journal des Tribunaux*, 460 (No. 4750, 3.7.1971): the Court held that the provision of Community law had precedence over conflicting national provisions, and that this followed from the very nature of the law created by the treaty.

[31] *Hansard*, 15 February 1972; Vol. 831, col. 271.

[32] *Ibid.*, col. 314.

Commons on 15 February 1972: " Clause 3 subsection (1) provides for the acceptance of the jurisprudence of the European Court. As the 1967 White Paper (Cmnd. 3301) recognizes, the directly applicable provisions of the Community are designed to take precedence over the domestic law of Member States, in the sense that they prevail in case of conflict. By accepting the directly applicable law in clause 2(1) and accepting the jurisprudence of the European Court in clause 3(1), the Bill provides the necessary precedence. In relation to statute law, this means that the directly applicable provisions ought to prevail over future Acts of Parliament in so far as they might be inconsistent with them. In practice, this means that – again quoting the Leader of the Opposition – " it would be implicit in our acceptance of the Treaties that the United Kingdom would, in future, refrain from enacting legislation inconsistent with Community law " – (*Hansard*, 8 May 1967; Vol. 746, col. 1089), Clause 2(4) accordingly provides that present and future enactments shall be construed and have effect subject to Clause 2."[33]

3. Co-operation between the Community and the national legal orders

1–18. In the preceding remarks there was only question of possible conflicts between the two legal orders; there are however several domains in which the two not only peacefully co-exist but interrelate and in which Community and national authorities closely co-operate.

1–19. When the national judge in a case pending before him considers that a decision on a question of interpretation of a European treaty, or of validity and interpretation of acts of the institutions of the Community, is necessary to enable him to give judgment, he may or must request the Court of Justice to give a ruling thereon (E.E.C., Art. 177).[34]

1–20. Another example is the enforcement of decisions of the European institutions which impose pecuniary obligations on persons or undertakings.[35] These decisions are taken by the institutions, independently of the authorities of the Member States, but it is the latter which are entrusted with the obligation to enforce them. E.E.C., Art. 192 provides indeed that " enforcement shall be

[33] *Hansard*, 15 February 1972; Vol. 831, col. 278.
[34] See Chapter 3, under Court of Justice.
[35] See Chapter 5, under Enforcement.

governed by the rules of civil procedure in force in the State in the territory of which it is carried out." And again in regard to the carrying out of the enforcement both the national and Community authorities, each have their specific tasks to fulfil; in accordance with the last paragraph of Article 192 of the E.E.C., enforcement may be suspended only by a decision of the Court of Justice, but the national courts shall have jurisdiction over complaints that enforcement is being carried out in an irregular manner.

1–21. Article 27 of the Statute of the Court of Justice[36] in conjunction with clause 11 of the European Communities Bill provides for the prosecution by the national authorities of persons who in sworn evidence before the European Court make any statement which they know to be false or do not believe to be true.

1–22. Co-operation is not limited to judiciary authorities. The administrations of the Member States also work in close liaison with the Community institutions to carry out the Community provisions; this is particularly so in the field of agriculture where the national offices collect levies and buy products at intervention prices set by the Community Council and also in the implementation of the competition rules for which a Consultative Committee on Cartels and Monopolies composed of officials designated by the Member States was set up and which must be consulted before important decisions regarding cartels and concentrations are taken by the Commission.[37]

1–23. Many more examples of this interpenetration of the two legal orders will be found in the following chapters but the few enumerated above will give an idea of the close link that exists between them. In this respect there is a " division of labour " between the national and Community authorities: the former do apply, besides their municipal law provisions, the Community regulations which are effective within the Member States, while the Court of Justice has exclusive competence to interpret the Community provisions and decide on their validity. This leaves one question unanswered, namely whether the European Court in turn, applies national law.

4. Application of national law by the Community Court

1–24. On several occasions the question of applicability of

[36] Protocol attached to the E.E.C. Treaty.
[37] For the Agricultural and Competition Policies, see Chapter 2.

national law by the Community institutions was raised before the European Court. In a judgment of 4 February 1959 (case 1–58) the Court held that " in pursuance of Article 8 of the E.C.S.C. Treaty the High Authority is only bound to apply Community law; that it lacks the competence to apply the internal law of the Member States; that in accordance with Article 31 of said Treaty the Court has similarly only the task to ensure that law is observed in the interpretation and application of the Treaty and of the rules laid down for the implementation thereof; that in general the Court must refrain from expressing an opinion concerning rules of municipal law and that consequently the Court could not examine the claim that by taking its decision the High Authority has violated principles of German constitutional law."[38] A similar statement can be found in the judgment of 15 July 1960, in the joint cases 36, 37, 38 and 40–59[39] and in a judgment of 21 January 1965, in the case 108–63.[40]

It was therefore surprising to find the Court, in the joint cases 17 and 20–61, judgment of 13 July 1962, interpreting German national law stating: " that reservation of property-right in regard to a non-qualitatively or quantitatively specified part of an item is not permitted under paragraph 93 B.G.B. which applies to questions of property of goods situated in the Federal Republic; that such a reservation is furthermore incompatible with the basic principles of the law concerning property which are applicable in all the Member States. . . ."[41]

1–25. Application of national law by the European Court does however take place when the European treaties refer explicitly or implicitly to national law concepts. So for instance E.E.C., Art. 58 refers to " companies and firms formed in accordance with the law of a Member State "; where the Court would be called upon to decide whether or not this article applies to an undertaking, it would have to apply national law. Of interest in this respect is the judgment of 20 March 1959 (case 18–57) where the plaintiff was a German undertaking which had gone into liquidation and the defendant raised the question whether this appeal was admissible; the Court held that " the Kommanditgesellschaft NOLD, incorporated and established in Germany, is in regard to its articles of incorporation,

[38] Rec. V, 63.
[39] Rec. VI, 890.
[40] Rec. XI, 13.
[41] Rec. VIII, 650–651.

its liquidation and its dissolution, governed by the national law provisions of the country where it is established; that under German law an undertaking in liquidation has the necessary capacity to appear in court and to vindicate its rights as far as needed for its liquidation; . . . that according to German law the sleeping partners of a limited partnership which is legally in liquidation for want of a partner, may commit an agent to accomplish certain legal acts required for the liquidation."[42]

1–26. Finally there are cases where the Court is called upon to apply general principles of law. As will be seen, violation of these principles can be a ground for annulment since E.E.C., Art. 173 (Euratom, Art. 146) refers to the jurisdiction of the Court of Justice in actions brought by a Member State, the Council or the Commission on grounds of infringement of this treaty or " of any rule of law relating to its application." In the joint cases 7–56 and 3 to 7–57, the Court found that the " possibility of revoking administrative acts is a problem of administrative law, well known in the case-law and in the doctrine of all the Member States; the treaty however does not contain rules in regard to this question. The Court must therefore – lest it become guilty of denial of Justice – solve this question on the basis of the rules which are accepted by the legislation, the doctrine and the case-law of the Member States."[43] According to the Court of Justice the precise meaning of general principles of law must be sought in the municipal law of the Member States. This applies not only to general principles, but to all concepts of law which are not further defined in the treaties; see for instance the interpretation given by the Court to " misuse of power " (*détournement de pouvoir*) (E.E.C., Art. 173) in its judgment of 11 February 1955 (case 3–54) which was based on a comparative study by the Advocate-General of this concept in the municipal law of the six Member States.[44] In regard to general principles which apply to the implementation of the European treaties reference can be made to the judgment of 6 April 1962 (*Bosch* case, 13–61) where the Court of Justice invoked the principle of legal certainty,[45] or the judgment of 15 July 1960 where the Court referred to the principle of good faith;[46] in each case

[42] Rec. V, 110–111. Another example can be found in Rec. XVI, 403, case 31–68.

[43] Rec. III, 114–115. Most concepts of Community law find their origin in the domestic laws of the Member States, particularly in their administrative law; much of the latter was modelled after French administrative law.

[44] Rec. I, 149.

[45] Rec. VIII, 104.

[46] Rec. VI, 956 (joint cases 43, 45, 48–59).

interpretation of the principle was done in accordance with the legislation, doctrine and case law of the Member States, even when this is not explicitly stated in the judgment.

5. Simultaneous application of Community law and national law

1–27. There are cases where both community and national law apply at the same time; the two legal orders then operate, so to speak, at different levels without necessarily interfering with each other. In the *Aniline* case (14–68) for instance, the Court of Justice found that " the same agreement between undertakings could, in principle, be the occasion for two parallel procedures, respectively initiated by the Community authorities in pursuance of Article 85, E.E.C. – and by the national authorities – in pursuance of national law."[47] In so-called " anti-trust " cases this could lead to a condemnation and the imposition of fines or penalties both under community and national law, and the fines paid under one legal order would not, as a matter of course, be deducted from the payments to be made under the other. Complications arise however when national authorities reach a conclusion different from that of the Community institutions, because then there exists a conflict or possible conflict between the two legal orders which can only be solved through the recognition, as said above, of the supremacy of Community law. This is what the Court repeated in the *Aniline* case: " Respect for the objectives of the Treaty implies however that such simultaneous application of national law can only be considered acceptable in so far as the uniform application within the whole Community of community law concerning agreements between undertakings and their implementing regulations is not put in jeopardy."[48]

The same principle applies in all fields where Community rules are applicable: agriculture, transport or regional policy. Since the Member States retain those powers which were not transferred to the Communities, they continue to exercise those powers as long as their application does not interfere with the uniform application of Community law.

6. Relations with international law

1–28. Does Community law take precedence over International

[47] Rec. XV, 14.
[48] Rec. XV, 14.

law? Obviously not, since the European treaties, *res inter alios acta*, cannot relieve the Member States of their commitments *vis-à-vis* third countries.[49] This principle is explicitly recognised by E.E.C., Art. 37(5): " the obligations on Member States shall be binding only in so far as they are compatible with existing international agreements "[50] and by E.E.C., Art. 234: " the rights and obligations arising from agreements concluded before the entry into force of this Treaty between one or more Member States on the one hand, and one or more third countries on the other, shall not be affected by the provisions of this Treaty "; however, this treaty provision goes on to say that " to the extent that such agreements are not compatible with this Treaty, the Member State or States concerned shall take all appropriate steps to eliminate the incompatibilities established. Member States shall, where necessary, assist each other to this end and shall, where appropriate, adopt a common attitude." In other words, although the principle of the precedence of international law over Community law is recognised, the Member States must endeavour to be relieved from their conflicting international obligations, taking all appropriate steps such as termination of the agreement when this possibility is provided for.

If it is not possible and the third country does not co-operate in arriving at a satisfactory solution from the Community's point of view, the other Member States must " join their efforts " which means to apply pressure to bring the third state to accepting modifications to the existing agreement. The kind of clause that would be incompatible with the treaty is the " most-favoured nation " clause, since it would in practice extend the customs union advantages to a third country without at the same time imposing on said country the obligations the Member States have accepted as a *quid pro quo* for the economic advantages. Furthermore, the E.E.C. treaty explains why third countries cannot expect to enjoy the same advantages as the Member States: " in applying the agreements referred to in the first paragraph, Member States shall take into account the fact that the advantages accorded under this Treaty by each Member State form an integral part of the establishment of the Community and are thereby inseparably linked with the creation of

[49] But a European treaty takes precedence over international agreements concluded between Member States; Rec. VIII, 22, case 10–61.

[50] See also Euratom, Arts. 16(5) and 17(4), the latter referring to the Paris Convention for the Protection of Industrial Property.

common institutions, the conferring of powers upon them and the granting of the same advantages by all the other Member States " (E.E.C., Art. 234, last paragraph).[51]

1–29. Another exception to the rules of international law is made by E.C.S.C., Art. 87 (see also E.E.C., Art. 219 and Euratom, Art. 193): " the High Contracting Parties undertake not to avail themselves of any treaties, conventions or declarations made between them for the purpose of submitting a dispute concerning the interpretation or application of this Treaty to any method of settlement other than those provided therein."

1–30. On the other hand, where the treaty explicitly refers to international law, the institutions, including the Court of Justice, will have to apply it, as with Euratom, Art. 16(5) and E.C.S.C., Art. 74(1). The Court of Justice has also applied rules of international law where the treaties do not make any specific reference: see for instance judgment of 29 November 1956 (case 8–55) where the Court referred to a rule of interpretation generally admitted both in international and in national law.[52]

1–31. As stated by various national courts, the very nature of the European Community implies the autonomy of Community law and its precedence over conflicting domestic law. The European Community and in particular the " common market " is, as will be seen in the following chapters, essentially an economic concept which must become a reality; this in turn demands an effective and uniform application of all the Community rules within the whole Community without exception. This approach, and not legal theory, is the only way to " make the thing work ". The question is, is legal theory going to stand in the way of political reality? If " effective and uniform application " of Community law must be translated into legal terms as " autonomy and paramountry of Community law," then domestic ways must be found to guarantee this independence and this precedence.

Many lawyers in the United Kingdom were prompt to point out that because of the classical principle of parliamentary sovereignty which ordains that no parliament can bind its successors, it is impossible to make Community law prevail over future Acts. Others

[51] See also Euratom, Arts. 105–106, and paragraph 20 of the Convention on the Transitional Provisions attached to the E.C.S.C. Treaty.

[52] Rec. II, 305.

have shown that classical principles have more than once been modified, and still others that various acts such as the Act of Settlement 1700, the Union with Ireland Act 1800 or the Acquisition of Land (Assessment of Compensation) Act 1919 did intend to bind succeeding parliaments.

To an outsider it appears that since accession has no sense or value without recognition of the fact that provisions of Community Law are by nature fundamental and override prior, as well as later, inconsistent domestic legislation, the United Kingdom, *i.e.* Parliament and the courts must accept that accession to the European Community implies constitutional changes. And there are cases where the validity of a statute has been examined. It may therefore very well be that, as in some Member States, the courts will be the means whereby these changes are spelled out.

Chapter 2

THE TREATIES ESTABLISHING THE EUROPEAN COMMUNITIES

I. Historical Background

2–1. Every institution is the product of a series of historical events and at the same time reflects the convictions, hopes and concerns of those who were instrumental in establishing it. The European Communities are no exception to this. For a full understanding and correct interpretation of the European treaties some knowledge as to the historical background seems therefore required.

2–2. Although the expression " United States of Europe " was already used by Victor Hugo in 1849[1] there is no need to go that far back! The end of World War II seems a fair starting point notwithstanding the existence before that time of a very active but not too influential Pan-European Movement inspired by Count Coudenhove-Kalergi.

2–3. The agreement reached at Yalta in 1945 by United Kingdom, the United States and the U.S.S.R. left Europe more divided than ever and the growing antagonism among the victorious " Allies " spelled only more tensions and catastrophes. It was then that on 19 September 1946, in a speech at Zurich University, Winston Churchill proposed a " sovereign remedy " *i.e.* to " recreate the European Family, or as much of it as we can, and provide it with a structure under which it can dwell in peace, in safety and in freedom. We must – said the British statesman – build a kind of United States of Europe." And he went on " to say something that will astonish you. The first step in the recreation of the European family must be a partnership between France and Germany." As will be seen, it was this (British) idea which also inspired the French Government in 1950 to propose the establishment of the European Coal and Steel Community. Towards the end of his Zurich speech, Churchill also proposed to start by setting up a regional structure and to form a Council of Europe.[2]

[1] See Henri Brugmans, *L'Idée Européenne*, 1920–1970, Bruges 1970.

[2] The Treaty establishing the Council of Europe was signed in London on 5 May 1949.

2–4. If Churchill's words were well received, the European states in those days lacked the necessary stamina to proceed with such far-reaching plans, preoccupied as they were by their daily fight for economic survival. Once again the United States came to the rescue. In another famous University speech, at Harvard this time, George Marshall, U.S. Secretary of State, announced on 5 June 1947, that the United States would do " whatever it is able to do to assist in the return of normal economic health in the world." But he added that " before the United States' Government can . . . help start the European world on its way to recovery, there must be some agreement among the countries of Europe. . . . The role of this country should consist of friendly aid in the drafting of a European programme and of later support of such a programme. . . . The programme should be a joint one, agreed to by a number of, if not all, European nations." This offer was accepted by sixteen European countries on 15 July 1947 and so the Marshall Plan was born, but more important for the future of European integration was the setting up, in 1948, in response to the American request for an agreement among Europeans, of the Organization for European Economic Co-operation (O.E.E.C.).[3]

2–5. Thus Europe's economic destiny became closely linked, for at least two decades, with that of the United States; this dependence was formally extended to the field of defence by the signature on 4 April 1949, in Washington, of the North Atlantic Treaty (N.A.T.O.).

2–6. In the meantime, Churchill's words about a partnership between France and Germany had not been forgotten and on 9 May 1950 Robert Schuman, French Foreign Minister, declared that a united Europe was essential for world peace and that a gathering of the European nations required the elimination of the century-old opposition between France and Germany. As a first practical step towards this end he proposed " to place the whole Franco-German coal and steel production under one joint High Authority, in an organization open to the participation of the other countries of Europe." He described this pooling of production as the " first stage of the European Federation." Germany, The Netherlands, Belgium, Luxemburg, and Italy accepted in principle and negotiations started at once. But, as Huizinga[4] writes, " what did Britain do ? Challenged

[3] In 1961, it became the Organization for Economic Co-operation and Development, O.E.C.D., with the participation of the United States and Canada.

[4] J. H. Huizinga, *Confessions of a European in England*, London 1958, p. 177.

to put her European cards on the table at last, she attempted to hide them by refusing to say yes or no. . . . And so we got the sorry spectacle . . . of British statesmen and diplomats, dutifully echoed by even the best organs of the British Press, endlessly and plaintively repeating that they were full of sympathy for Mr. Schuman's plan, but that they really had to have more details before they could decide, and that they should not be asked to ' take a leap in the dark ' or to ' sign on the dotted line ' or to ' commit themselves in advance to surrender certain fundamental rights '. As if anyone *had* asked them to do so; as if there *were* any details and as if there were any *plan* even, beyond the proposal to try and see whether those of us who accepted the federal principle could work out a first instalment of federal organization."

The negotiations progressed rapidly and were simplified by the fact that all the future partners had accepted the proposed principles; the work consisted mainly in giving them legal form. A sense of urgency was probably added to the existing good-will by the communist invasion of South Korea. The Treaty establishing the European Coal and Steel Community (E.C.S.C.) was signed in Paris, on 18 April 1951.

Ratification by the national parliaments met with little opposition and on 23 June 1952, the treaty entered into force. Although political considerations came first, the experience gained in the economic field from this first community was vital for future developments. It showed the workability of the system with its institutions and decision making process in organising international trade, but also the difficulties of limited economic integration.

2–7. The following two years were difficult indeed. It has been said that the easing of the international political situation – Stalin died on 5 March 1953 and 27 July 1953 marked the end of the Korean war – diminished the necessity for " closing the ranks." In any case two additional proposals for close co-operation among the " Six " – in the form of a European Defence Community and a European Political Community – failed miserably.

2–8. Undaunted by those setbacks, the Benelux countries proposed in 1955 to their partners in the Coal and Steel Community to take another step towards economic integration by setting up a Common Market and jointly developing transportation, classical and atomic energy. This led to the conference of Messina in the same year, at which Mr. Spaak was asked to report on the feasibility of those plans. At that time also an invitation was issued to the British Government to join the negotiations of the Six; alas, to no avail.[5]

The " Spaak Report " was ready in 1956 and was discussed in Venice, where the decision was taken to start negotiations for drafting treaties that would establish a " Common Market " and an Atomic Energy Community.

With incredible speed (June 1956 – February 1957) these two complex treaties were prepared for signature in Rome on 25 March 1957 and on 1 January 1958, the European Economic Community (E.E.C.) and the European Community for Atomic Energy (Euratom) became a reality.

2–9. This time the economic considerations were so much in the foreground that only one paragraph of the preamble to the E.E.C. treaty makes a vague reference to Europe's political future: " determined to establish the foundations of an ever closer union among the European peoples." The content of the treaty is described in more detail in section 4 of this chapter. Since each one of the three European treaties provided for similar institutions: a Council of Ministers, a Commission (or High Authority), a Court of Justice and an Assembly, there would in fact have existed twelve institutions! Fortunately, together with the E.E.C. and Euratom treaties, the Member States signed a Convention relating to certain institutions common to the European communities; this convention provided that there would be only one Court of Justice and one Assembly for all three Communities.

2–10. In 1961 the British Government decided to apply for negotiations to determine whether satisfactory arrangements could be made to meet the needs of the United Kingdom, of the Commonwealth and of E.F.T.A. The Government were " baulked in their objective, so that it was not possible to determine whether satisfactory conditions of entry could be obtained."[6]

2–11. On 8 April 1965, the institutional set-up was further simplified by the treaty establishing a Single Council and a Single Commission of the European Communities, commonly referred to as the " Merger Treaty." This treaty became effective on 1 July 1967; as frcm that date, there was therefore one Council (of Ministers), one European Commission, one European Court and one Assembly.

[5] See Hans Joachim Heiser, *British policy with regard to the unification efforts on the European continent*, Leyden, 1959, p. 96.

[6] Cmnd. 4715, 6.

2–12. A Customs Union was completed by the E.E.C. on 1 July 1968. It meant that tariff and quota restrictions between Member States had by then been completely abolished and that the replacement of the national external tariffs by the Common External Tariff had been completed. The Community was eighteen months ahead of the schedule laid down in the treaty (twelve years, see E.E.C., Art. 8 and Acceleration Decisions: J.O. 1217/60 and 1284/62).

2–13. After a debate in both Houses of Parliament at the end of which the Government's decision was approved in the Commons by a majority of 426, the British Government applied for membership of the Communities on 10 May 1967. By December of the same year it was clear however that the " Six " could not reach the unanimity necessary under the Community treaties to return a reply to Britain's application. Thus ended the second endeavour of Great Britain to enter " Europe." The British Government however decided to maintain their application for membership and it was discussed at many meetings of the Council of the Communities in the following two years.

2–14. Finally, at the meeting of heads of State and Governments on 1–2 December 1969 in The Hague, it was agreed to open negotiations between the Communities and the States which had applied for membership. Other important decisions taken at this " Summit " concerned the economic and monetary union and the Community's own resources, *i.e.* Community's direct income system.

2–15. Mention must also be made of the treaty of Luxemburg of 22 April 1970, entered into force on 1 January 1971, relating to the Community's budget and the replacement of the financial contribution of Member States by other resources of the Community itself, namely by revenue accruing from the common customs tariff, the agricultural levies and the added value tax.

2–16. The latest development was the signing of the treaty of Brussels relating to the accession of the United Kingdom, Ireland, Norway and Denmark, on 22 January 1972; this treaty is due to enter into force on 1 January 1973.

II. Treaty establishing the European Coal and Steel Community

2–17. In a White Paper presented to Parliament in July 1971 it is stated that the Coal and Steel Community " is designed to ensure an orderly supply of coal and steel to the Community, whilst at the same time taking account of the needs of third countries; to promote the orderly expansion and modernization of production; and to provide better conditions of living and employment for the workers in the industries." Even allowing for the brevity of this statement, it hardly does justice to the objectives pursued by the founders of this Community; it fails completely to mention that, as provided by Article 1 of the Paris Treaty, the Coal and Steel Community is " based on a common market, common objectives and common institutions."[7]

1. The common market

2–18. The establishment and functioning of this common market for coal and steel products[8] was of essential interest for the six countries, since it gave to their heavy industries a production and distribution basis comparable to that of the United States or the U.S.S.R.; by allowing the European enterprises to lower their production cost through economies of scale, they had a chance of becoming competitive on the world market. The powers attributed to the common institutions of the Community must be interpreted in relation to the necessities of setting up and maintaining this common market. The legal implications thereof are defined in Article 4; this provision specifies what existing measures in the field of trade, administration, finance or commerce are thereby abolished and prohibited within the Community.[9]

2–19. First, all import and export duties or taxes with equivalent effect[10] are abolished and as a result Member States have no longer the power to impose new ones: the same applies to quantitative restrictions on the movement of coal and steel.

2–20. Secondly, all measures or practices – whether public or private – which discriminate among producers, buyers or consumers – especially with regard to prices, delivery terms and trans-

[7] Cmnd. 4715, 37–38.

[8] The terms coal and steel are defined in Annex 1 to the Treaty; for instance steel tubes (seamless or welded), cold rolled strip less than 500 mm. in width are not included.

[9] See below, E.E.C. treaty, positive description of a " common market."

[10] In its judgment of 1.7.1969 (case 24–68), the Court of Justice stated that " a levy however small, unilaterally imposed, whatever its denomination or technique, and borne by national or foreign goods because of the fact that they cross the border, when it is not a customs duty proper, constitutes a charge with equivalent effect. . . ." Rec. XV, 201 (g).

port rates – are similarly considered to be " incompatible with the Common Market for coal and steel and are therefore abolished and prohibited." Consequently, the price-lists and conditions of sale applied by enterprises within the Common Market must be made public (Art. 60); the High Authority may, under certain circumstances, fix for one or more products maximum and minimum prices (Art. 61) and the High Authority is empowered to impose fines upon enterprises which violate those provisions (Art. 64). In regard to transport, the aim of the E.C.S.C. treaty is to ensure that the transport industry will not jeopardise the fulfilment of the treaty objectives; it therefore provides for two specific rules: the prohibition of " discriminatory prices, delivery terms and transport rates " (E.C.S.C., Art. 4(2)) and " the obligation to apply to the transport of coal and steel coming from and going to another country of the Community, the rates, prices and tariff provisions of all types applicable to internal transport of the same products over the same route " (E.C.S.C., Art. 70). The High Authority may however give a temporary or conditional agreement to the application of special domestic tariff measures in the interest of one or several enterprises.

Article 70 also provides that in order to ensure that comparable[11] price conditions are applied to consumers in comparable positions, the rates, prices and all other tariff rules applied to the carriage of coal and steel within each Member State and between the Member States shall be published or brought to the knowledge of the High Authority. In February 1959, the Commission issued Decision 18–59[12] concerning publication or notification of rates, prices and tariff provisions of all sorts for coal and steel road transport. This decision was annulled by the Court of Justice[13] which specified in its judgment what powers the High Authority possesses in regard to the implementation of E.C.S.C., Art. 70, since this provision is not directly applicable but requires implementation measures. The Court of Justice held that the Community does not have the power to enact binding measures with regard to transport conditions; it is

[11] The concept of comparability was clarified in several decisions of the Court of Justice; see for instance the judgment of 10.5.1960 in the joint cases 3 to 18 and 25, 26–58 (Rec. VI/I, 403): comparability in Article 70 must be appreciated solely " from a point of view of transport ". The Court also held that " discrimination " does not imply " direct injury " (*ibid.*); in other words, if there is injury, this might be considered proof for the existence of discrimination, but the absence of injury does not mean there is no discrimination.

[12] J.O. 287/59.

[13] Rec. VI/2, 669, case 20–59; see also case 25–59.

up to Member States to implement them. Consequently, the High Authority sent the Member States a recommendation (which is the equivalent of an E.E.C. Directive)[14] enjoining them to take all necessary measures to ensure that scales, rates and all other tariff rules of every kind applied to the carriage of coal and steel shall be published or brought to the knowledge of the High Authority. This recommendation concerns all means of transport; so far, it has not been implemented.

2–21. Thirdly, the common market entails the prohibition and abolition of subsidies or state assistance or special charges imposed by the State, in any form whatsoever. To ensure the implementation of this provision " any action by a Member State which might have appreciable repercussions on the conditions of competition . . . shall be brought to the attention of the High Authority by the interested Government " (Art. 67).[15]

2–22. Fourthly, the common market implies the maintenance and the observance of normal conditions of competition. This in practice means the absence of restrictive practices tending towards the division or improper exploitation of the market. This principle applies exclusively to enterprises and therefore all agreements among enterprises tending to distort the normal operation of competition are forbidden (Art. 65); concentrations of enterprises must be submitted to a prior authorisation of the High Authority (Art. 66).[16]

2–23. Finally it must be mentioned that within this common market workers of recognised qualifications have unrestricted access to employment in the coal and steel industries (Art. 69) and that the Community has at its disposal considerable funds which derive from levies on the coal and steel production of Community undertakings. As stated in the White Paper 1971, " these funds help the development of the industries, provide cheap loans for workers' houses and help finance new employment opportunities and retraining schemes

[14] J.O. 469/61.

[15] See Judgments of the Court of 23 February 1961, case 30–59, Rec. VII, 40; 10 May 1960, joint cases 27, 28 and 29–58, Rec. VI, 526 and 6 July 1971, case 59–70, Rec. XVII, 639.

[16] Several such authorisations have been given in recent years: see for instance: Ruhrkohle A.G., decision of 27.11.1969, third General Report, 68; Cockerill-Ougree-Providence and Esperance-Longdoz, 31.7.1969, Bulletin Nos. 9/10, 1969; Salzgitter and Peine, 5.7.70, Bulletin No. 8, 1970; Pompey, 30.10.70, Bulletin No. 12, 1970; Creuzot and Loire, 27.10.70, Bulletin No. 12, 1970; Arbed and Roechling, 11.6.71, Bulletin No. 8, 1971.

for any coal and steel employees who become redundant. They also provide grants for coal and steel research."[17]

2. Common objectives

2–24. The main objective of the Coal and Steel Community is to "establish conditions which will in themselves assure the most rational distribution of production at the highest possible level of production" (Art. 2). In concrete terms this means for instance the closing down of unproductive coal mines and the concentration of production in those basins which can compete with imported coal.

Other objectives are the expansion of the economy; the development of employment (not necessarily in the coal and steel industries), the improvement of the standard of living, the retraining of workers and the restructuring of the coal and steel industry.

2–25. In order to attain those objectives, the institutions of the Community must among others

(a) ensure that the common market is regularly supplied,
(b) assure to all consumers equal access to the sources of production,
(c) seek the establishment of the lowest possible prices while at the same time permitting necessary amortisation and normal returns on investments,
(d) maintain conditions which will encourage enterprises to expand and improve their ability to produce and
(e) promote the regular expansion and the modernisation of production (Art. 3).

Even the Court of Justice has implicitly recognised that some of those objectives are contradictory and may therefore conflict, when it stated that "it goes without saying that in practice it will be necessary to keep a balance between the various objectives of Article 3, since it is obviously impossible to implement them all together and each one of them to the full, since these objectives are general principles and that their realization and harmonization must be pursued as far as possible."[18]

3. Common institutions

2–26. The institutions of the Coal and Steel Community are:

– a High Authority, which was the equivalent of the E.E.C.

[17] Cmnd. 4715, 154.
[18] Judgment of 21.6.1958, Rec. IV, 242 (case 8–57).

Commission; it was merged with the latter, together with the Euratom Commission, as of 1 July 1967 under the so-called Merger Treaty;

- a Common Assembly; this institution was replaced by the Assembly provided for in the Rome treaties (E.E.C. and Euratom), on 1 January 1958, in conformity with Article 2 of the Convention relating to certain Institutions common to the European Communities, signed in Rome on 25 March 1957;
- a special Council, composed of Ministers; although this institution existed until it was merged in 1967, it ceased for all practical purposes to exist as an independent organ when the Council of Ministers for the Economic Community was set up on 1 January 1958;
- a Court of Justice which was replaced in 1958 by the single Court set up for the Economic Community and Euratom (Convention of Rome, Arts. 3 and 4).

The institutions will be discussed in more detail in Chapter 3.

4. Implementation of the E.C.S.C. Treaty in the United Kingdom

2–27. What is the implementation of the Coal and Steel treaty in the new Member States going to change in the United Kingdom?

In the first place, as was pointed out above, funds will be available from Community sources[19] for retraining redundant workers of the coal and steel industries and for loans to finance workers' houses. (In 1971, the Community spent 16.16 million units of account[20] – about £6.7 million – for readaptation).

2–28. Workers of the coal and steel industries with recognised qualifications[21] will be able to seek employment in the same industries all over the Community; however, for workers in the coal industry this is, at this point, pure theory owing to the general decline of that industry.

2–29. Consumers in the United Kingdom may find it easier to import certain coal and steel products and producers to export them

[19] The reserve funds of the E.C.S.C. now amount to about £90 million. The United Kingdom will make an investment in this fund of £24 million. According to the European Communities Bill it is expected that these funds will in general remain invested in the United Kingdom.

[20] A European Unit of Account was originally the equivalent of one U.S. dollar.

[21] See Decision of the Governments of the Member States of 8 December 1954, J.O. 367/57.

within the Community since all obstacles to the free movement of these goods will have disappeared by 1 January 1975.

2–30. Private persons will thus not be grossly affected by Britain joining this Community. For undertakings, the most concrete result will be the change in the pricing-system for steel: steel producers, instead of maintaining a single price over the whole country, now have to choose a number of " basing points " for establishing their prices (E.C.S.C., Art. 60(2) (*a*)) and publish their price-lists based on these points. Consequently steel consumers within the United Kingdom will pay prices equal to the listed price plus actual transport charges; this modifies for steel consuming industries the costs of their supplies, certain paying less, others paying more, according to their distance from the " points." For coal there will be no practical changes. Generally speaking the powers of the Government to give directions of a general character or on prices will need to be repealed.[22] In this respect mention must also be made of E.C.S.C., Art. 83 which provides that " the establishment of the Community shall in no way prejudice the system of ownership of the undertakings to which this Treaty applies." The control exercised by the British Steel Corporation over most of the steel industry in the United Kingdom will thus not be affected by accession. Neither will the fact that the British Government finances practically all capital investments except where such financing would amount to subsidising this industry.

2–31. Subsidisation, specific to the coal and steel industries, is indeed forbidden and will, if it exists in any form whatsoever, therefore have to be abolished. The only state-measures in favour of the coal and steel industries which are not per se prohibited under the Coal and Steel Treaty are those provided to all industries (E.C.S.C., Art. 67),[23] either in the form of general economic measures applicable across the country or of regional development incentives.[24]

[22] White Paper, Cmnd. 4715, 157.

[23] Act of accession, Art. 134 provides that the measures in force in the new Member States " which had they been introduced after accession would have fallen within the scope of Article 67 of the E.C.S.C. Treaty " and which " could, by comparison with the measures in force in the original Member States, give rise to serious distortions in conditions of competition " will be examined by the Commission. The latter may, after consulting the Council, propose to the Governments concerned any action which it considers appropriate to correct such measures or to offset their effects.

[24] This was clearly stated by the Commission in a letter to the French Government with regard to the Plan Professionnel for the French Steel Industry and by the Advocate-General in the case Dutch Government vs. Commission, case 59–70, Rec. XVII, 662. The White Paper of 1971 (Cmnd. 4715, 157) ambiguously mentions that " unfair subsidization " is prohibited.

2–32. With regard to transport, although after the enlargement of the Community maritime carriage will in theory also come under the provisions of E.C.S.C., Art. 70 it seems that not much will change since it has not been possible to implement this article within the Community of the Six. At the present time ways and means are being investigated to overcome the present lack of transparency of the transport market by the publication of freight prices by the producers themselves.

2–33. Furthermore, since agreements which restrict normal competition are prohibited, the coal and steel undertakings can only obtain authorisation from the Commission and then under very strict conditions to conclude agreements to specialise in the production of, or to engage in the joint buying or selling of specified products (Art. 65(2)). Consequently, agreements to fix prices, restrict production or allocate markets will, as a rule, be forbidden even if they were previously accepted by the Monopolies Commission. As regards concentrations, the treaty requires the prior authorisation of the Community (Art. 66). Companies will also be subject to inspection by Community inspectors and, if the Commission finds any company has violated a Community rule, it is liable to be fined. On the other hand enterprises have the right of appeal against individual decisions and recommendations affecting them.[25]

2–34. Finally, all custom duties on coal[26] as defined in Annex 1 to the E.C.S.C. treaty will be abolished as from the date of accession, between the United Kingdom and all other Member States (Act of accession, Art. 32(2)), while duties on steel will gradually disappear between 1 April 1973 and 1 July 1977 (Art. 32(1)). The same applies to charges having equivalent effect. Quota's will be abolished as from the date of accession and measures with equivalent effect on 1 January 1975 at the latest (Art. 34). In their relations with third countries coal and steel industries will have to take into account the unified E.C.S.C. tariff; here also the adaptation of existing duties will be gradual in order to be completed on 1 July 1977.

[25] For more details see Chapter 3, the Court of Justice.

[26] Duties on coal are practically non-existent: they concern only duties levelled in Germany on quantities exceeding a given quota and in Italy certain duties imposed on coke.

III. Treaty establishing the European Atomic Energy Community (EURATOM)[27]

1. Euratom's objective

2–35. The essential objective of Euratom is to create " conditions necessary for the speedy establishment and growth of nuclear industries " (Art. 1). After nearly fourteen years, the Community has not succeeded in achieving this aim. It might be useful briefly to explain at this point the reasons for this failure. In the first place, the expectations placed in nuclear energy in the fifties were much too high, also the expected need for this supplementary source of energy never materialised, partly because of the availability at reasonable prices of oil and of the seemingly unlimited discoveries of natural gas. On the other hand, the need for joint fundamental research disappeared as soon as the industrial applications appeared to promise rich commercial rewards, which seems to have been the case towards the mid-sixties. Finally, inside the Community itself the disparity between the partners was much too great to make fruitful co-operation possible: France was far ahead of the other countries at the start and (understandably) was suspicious of anything that could jeopardise its lead; it went its own way, trying to develop new techniques, whilst the others, particularly Germany, successfully adopted and adapted proven American or British technology. Consequently, France's advance rapidly disappeared creating bitterness and frustration and leaving Europe, in this field, more divided than ever.

2. Euratom's means

2–36. To achieve the above mentioned objective the Community (i) develops research and disseminates the results; this research is carried out either through research contracts[28] with individuals, laboratories, universities or industries or in the Community's Joint Nuclear Research Centre which was set up under Euratom, Art. 8. This research Centre at present has four branch establishments in the territories of the Member States: Ispra in Italy, Petten in The

[27] See P. Mathijsen, " Some Legal Aspects of Euratom," C.M.L.Rev. 1965–1966, 326.

[28] Between 1971 and 1975 the Community will be spending 45 million units of account for thermonuclear fusion and 18 million for radiobiology and health protection.

Netherlands, the Central Nuclear Measurement Bureau at Geel, Belgium, and the European Transuranium Institute at Karlsruhe, Germany. The implementation of the Community's research programme has thus imposed upon the European Commission a great variety of tasks ranging all the way from planning and building reactors and laboratories of the most elaborate kind, the acquisition of great quantities of scientific instrumentation and the training of personnel in the management of large research establishments to the actual operation of reactors. All these activities are carried out directly by the European Commission, unlike agencies elsewhere, which (like the United States Atomic Energy Commission) have entrusted most of this work, by contract, to private organisations.

According to Euratom, Art. 10 the Commission may " assign by contract the carrying out of certain parts of the Community's research programme." This has been done on a very large scale.

The technical and scientific information obtained through the implementation of the Community's research programme, is disseminated on a non-discriminatory basis. Articles 12 and 13 of the Euratom treaty provide that Member States, persons and enterprises have, under certain conditions, the right to receive all information acquired and to obtain a licence on all patents owned by the Community;[29]

2–37. (ii) has established by directive basic standards for the protection of the health of workers and of the general public from the dangers arising from ionising radiation.[30] Member States have enacted the legislative or administrative provisions required to ensure compliance;

2–38. (iii) has constituted the following Joint Enterprises in order to encourage the construction of basic facilities required for the development of nuclear energy: SENA, Kernkraftwerk Rheinisch-Westfälisches Elektrizitätswerk Bayernwerk G.m.b.H., Kernkraftwerk Lingen G.m.b.H. and Kernkraftwerk Obrigheim G.m.b.H.[31]; the Commission also expresses its views on all the investment pro-

[29] See Announcement of the Commission concerning the communication of information to persons and enterprises of the Community, J.O. 2569/63.

[30] J.O. 221/59 – modifications in J.O. 1633/62 and J.O. 3693/66.

[31] See for SENA, J.O. 1173/61; for K.R.B., J.O. 1745/63; for Lingen, J.O. 3642/64 and for Obrigheim, J.O. 2681/66.

jects in the nuclear field; all projects must therefore be communicated to the Commission (Euratom, Art. 41)[32];

2–39. (iv) has constituted a Supply Agency having a right of option on all ores, source materials and special fissile materials produced in the territories of Member States and having the exclusive right of concluding contracts relating to supply of ores, source materials and special fissile materials coming from inside or outside the Community (Euratom, Art. 52(2)(*b*)). The statutes of the Agency were laid down by the Council[33] and various regulations have specified the conditions under which nuclear materials can be required, sold and transferred.[34]

The Community also concluded various agreements with the United States[35] and Great Britain[36] to secure a regular supply of nuclear materials, especially enriched uranium;

2–40. (v) guarantees, by appropriate measures of control, that nuclear materials are not diverted for purposes other than those for which they are intended; Euratom in other words does not guarantee peaceful use unless materials have been intended for such purpose by their supplier or consumer. The control system which was set up under Euratom, Arts. 78, 79 provides mainly for declarations, inspections and production of operating records[37];

2–41. (vi) finally, Euratom has created a common market for specialised materials and equipment[38] and guarantees free movement of capital for nuclear investment (Euratom, Arts. 99, 100) and freedom of employment for specialists within the Community.[39]

2–42. This general survey of Euratom's means would not be complete without the mention of the vesting in the Community of property in all special fissionable materials (Euratom, Art. 86). This

[32] See Regulation of the Council determining the investment projects which must be communicated to the Commission, J.O. 417/58 and Regulation of the Commission, J.O. 511/58 and 571/59.

[33] See J.O. 534/58.

[34] See J.O. 777/60 (regulation of the Agency concerning the manner in which offers and demands are to be compared); J.O. 116/62 and 4057/66 (regulations of the Commission concerning the implementation of the supply provisions) and J.O. 1460/60 and 240/64 (Communications of the Agency).

[35] See J.O. 312/59; 57/61; 2038/62 and 2045/62.

[36] See J.O. 331/59.

[37] See Regs. of the Commission Nos. 7, 8 and 9, J.O. 298/59 and 651/59 and 482/60.

[38] The Member States concluded two agreements establishing a common customs tariff for the products mentioned in lists A_1 and A_2 of Annex IV to the Euratom treaty, J.O. 406/59.

[39] See Directive of the Council concerning freedom of access to qualified employment in the nuclear field, J.O. 1650/62.

ownership is limited to materials subject to Euratom's safety control; this control does not, according to Euratom, Art. 84 extend to " materials intended for the purposes of defence. . . ."

3. Euratom's institutions

2–43. Two of the institutions of the European Atomic Energy Community were from the beginning institutions common to the three Communities: the Assembly and the Court of Justice.

The Council, composed of Ministers was, for all practical purposes, the same as the Council of the Economic Community.

The Commission ceased to exist in 1957 and was replaced, under the Merger treaty, by the European Commission.

The four institutions will be examined in more detail in Chapter 3.

4. Implementation of the Euratom treaty in the United Kingdom

2–44. Here again the question should be asked in which way the application of the Euratom treaty in the United Kingdom is going to affect persons and enterprises.

With regard to research, individuals and enterprises will, under conditions identical to those which exist for inhabitants of the Six, have access to information resulting from the implementation of the common research programme. They will also be in the same position with respect to research contracts: because the United Kingdom is well advanced in nuclear techniques, some are certain to be placed in the United Kingdom.

2–45. All undertakings engaged in nuclear work will have to apply the basic standards for health protection, communicate to the Commission any investment project relating to new facilities, replacements or conversions, offer their production of materials, if any, to the Supply Agency, buy and sell all ores, source materials and special fissionable materials exclusively through the same Agency,[40] submit to Euratom's safety control and respect the Community's property rights over all special fissionable materials.

2–46. On the other hand, they might be able to enjoy some of the advantages which may be granted to Joint Enterprises if they choose

[40] Although the provisions concerning supply are at present under revision, they are still fully applicable as the Court recently stated in the case 7–71, *Commission* v. *French Government*, on 14 December 1971, Rec. XVII, 1003.

to become one, such as " exemption from all direct taxation to which their goods, assets and income would normally be liable."[41] They will also be in a position to claim a regular and equitable supply of ores and nuclear fuels which might be of some interest in times of scarcity.

2–47. Finally, it should be noted that import and export duties and charges having equivalent effect, between the Six and the new members and between the latter will be abolished on 1 January 1974 for " Euratom " products (see Act of accession, Arts. 32(2)(*b*), 36(2)(*b*) and 37). Quotas and equivalent measures will disappear on 1 January 1975. The balance of trade between the United Kingdom and the Six in nuclear items is already heavily in favour of the former; this favourable position will probably further improve after elimination of all obstacles to trade.

IV. Treaty establishing the European Economic Community (E.E.C.)

2–48. The E.E.C. treaty is by far the most important of the three European treaties, not only because of its scope – practically it touches upon all aspects of the economy – but mainly because its full implementation requires a common policy of all Member States in fields not directly mentioned in the treaty itself: such as a common policy for regional and industrial development, a monetary and economic union[42] and a foreign policy.[43]

1. E.E.C.'s objectives

2–49. The preamble to the E.E.C. treaty lists the basic objectives of the Community; these include the establishment of " the foundations of an ever closer union among the European peoples," the furtherance of " economic and social progress by common action in eliminating the barriers which divide Europe," improvement of " living and working conditions," concerted action to guarantee " steady expansion, balanced trade and fair competition," reduction

[41] See Euratom, Art. 48, together with Annex III to the Treaty.

[42] See Werner Report, Supplement to the Bulletin No. 11, 1970 and Communication and Proposals of the Commission to the Council, Bulletin No. 11, 1970, Pt. I, Chap. II.

[43] See Report of the Ministers of Foreign Affairs to the Member States concerning the question of political unification, Bulletin No. 11, 1970, Pt. I, Chap. I.

of " the differences existing between various regions," abolition of " restrictions on international trade " and development of the prosperity of associated overseas countries. These very broadly formulated objectives can hardly be considered as practical guidelines for action; more specific aims are assigned to the Community by the Articles 2 and 3.

2–50. Article 2 summarises in a few lines the whole E.E.C. treaty: it formulates a series of tasks and indicates the means by which these tasks are to be performed. It is the task of the Community to promote

- a harmonious development of economic activities throughout the Community; here it is clearly indicated that all the regions should participate in the economic development of the Community and this calls for a deliberate regional policy;
- a continuous and balanced expansion, *i.e.* avoidance of too-accentuated cyclical ups and downs;
- increased stability; this undoubtedly is a reference to the monetary questions and
- an accelerated raising of the standard of living: this should cover not only the welfare but also the well-being of individuals.

2–51. The E.E.C. treaty provides two means to fulfil these tasks:

(1) the establishment of a common market and

(2) the approximation of the economic policies of the Member States.

These two means or instruments are indeed very different in nature, but essentially complementary: the first is of a rather technical character, it is based on a set of rules which can be more or less specified a priori and apply to industrial and agricultural products and to transport: these rules are intended to establish and guarantee the basic freedoms of movement of goods, persons, services, capital and connected payments, the right of establishment and the rules governing competition. It is mainly in these domains that the Community institutions exercise their law-making powers.

The second means provided in Article 2 under the name of " approximation of economic policies " is much less defined: it is a question of policy rather than law making, it is essentially dynamic and varies with economic and political circumstances: this policy is referred to in the E.E.C. treaty as "policy relating to Economic Trends, Balance of Payments, Commercial Policy, Social Policy, etc.," but, as pointed out above, it will not be fully effective without an Economic and Monetary Union and close political co-operation.

2. E.E.C.'s activities

2–52. A summary of the Community's activities is given in E.E.C., Art. 3, and to each activity correspond several provisions in Parts Two, Three and Four of the treaty which define in more detail their content and also the procedure to be followed for enacting the required implementing legislation. The activities, the corresponding treaty provisions and the most important related legislation will be examined hereunder.

(a) *Elimination of customs duties and quotas*

2–53. " the elimination, as between Member States, of customs duties and of quantitative restrictions in regard to the importation and exportation of goods, as well as all other measures with equivalent effect " (E.E.C., Art. 3(*a*)).

An essential element of the common market is the series of freedoms which constitute the " bases of the Community " (Part Two). Of these freedoms, the most important certainly is the free movement of goods which is provided for in the Articles 9 to 37.[44] This free movement requires the prohibition (and therefore elimination) of customs duties on imports and exports and of all charges with equivalent effect (Art. 9(1)) of quantitative restrictions and of measures with equivalent effect (Art. 30). This freedom applies to products originating in Member States and also to products from third countries for which the necessary import formalities have been complied with, for which the customs duties and charges having equivalent effect have been levied and which have not benefited from a total or partial repayment of such duties or charges (Arts. 9(2) and 10(1)). Within the Community of the Six, those duties, charges,

[44] See Judgment of 14 December 1962, joint cases 2 and 3–62, Rec. VIII, 826: " The fundamental importance of the prohibitory provisions of Arts. 9 and 12 is apparent from their being placed at the beginning of that part of the treaty which is devoted to the 'Foundations of the Community.' . . . These provisions are of such great importance. . . ."

restrictions and measures were gradually abolished over a period of ten and a half years (1 January 1958 – 1 July 1968), although the treaty provided for a time-limit of a minimum of twelve and a maximum of fifteen years. Indeed the Member States decided twice to accelerate the pace.[45] An analogous elimination will take place under the Brussels treaty of 22 January 1972 between the original Member States and the new Member States and between the latter, over a period extending from 1 April 1973 to 1 July 1977.[46] For these new Member States the rule of E.E.C., Art. 12 also applies namely that from the date they become members of the Community they shall refrain from introducing new duties or charges or increasing the existing ones. This last rule was declared by the Court of Justice to be self-executing.[47]

The implementation in the United Kingdom of E.E.C., Art. 12, onwards will bring about important changes for manufacturing industries as will be seen in connection with a complementary activity – the establishment of the common customs tariff.

(b) *Common customs tariff and commercial policy*

2–54. " the establishment of a common customs tariff and a common commercial policy towards third countries " (E.E.C., Art. 3(*b*)).

The elimination of customs duties and charges with equivalent effect is nothing new for the United Kingdom, Denmark and Norway, since Article 3 of the Convention establishing the European Free Trade Association (E.F.T.A.) provides for the same measures. There is however an essential difference: in the E.E.C. the elimination applies to *all* goods and this is possible since the Community is " based upon a customs union covering all trade in goods and which (includes) the prohibition as between Member States of customs duties on imports and exports and all charges having equivalent effect and the adoption of common customs tariff as against third countries " (E.E.C., Art. 9), while within E.F.T.A. the elimination only applies to goods " which are eligible for Area Tariff treatment " (E.F.T.A., Art. 3); roughly speaking, these are goods " produced

[45] See First Acceleration Decision of 12 May 1960, J.O. 1217/60 and Second Acceleration Decision of 15 May 1960, J.O. 1284/62.
[46] See Act of accession, Art. 32.
[47] Judgment of 5 February 1963, case 26–62, *Van Gend en Loos*, Rec. IX, 5.

within the Area of Association " (E.F.T.A., Art. 4). The fact that the Community as a whole is surrounded by a single common tariff barrier *vis-à-vis* third countries is conducive of increasing dependency of the various Member States upon each other, of specialisation and therefore division of labour: in terms of trade such a customs union invariably results in shifts in the previously existing trade patterns since goods became less expensive for Community consumers when imported from other Member States than when imported from outside the Community: consequently internal Community trade tends to increase while trade with third countries is reduced.[48] So the intra-Community trade multiplied four times between 1958 and 1968, from £2,800 million to nearly £11,000 million, while the share of E.E.C. imports obtained by third countries fell, during the same period, from 70.3 per cent. to 54.2.

2–55. The Common Customs Tariff (E.E.C., Arts. 18–29) was gradually introduced over a period of ten and a half years. It was adopted in its final form as Council Regulation 950/68 on 28 June 1968[49] and as such replaced the customs tariffs of the Benelux countries, Germany, France and Italy. As to the level at which the common external tariffs were established, E.E.C., Art. 19 provides that with certain exceptions[50] it is equal to the arithmetical average of the duties applied on 1 January 1957 in the four customs territories comprised in the Community. Individual Member States can no longer impose duties on goods entering the Community from third countries other than those of the common tariff, nor can they modify them, for E.E.C., Art. 28 provides that " any independent modification or suspension of duties in the common customs tariff shall be unanimously decided by the Council."

Having stated that " on 1 July 1968 . . . the customs union was completed . . . (and) was given concrete form by two essential measures: the abolition of customs duties between Member States and full application by all these Member States of the common

[48] See White Paper, February 1970, Cmnd. 4289, 29.

[49] J.O. L 172, 1968. See the Customs Tariff of the European Communities, published by the Commission in the four Community languages; it lists the customs duties applicable on 1 January 1972. This work is kept up to date with all the amendments or suspensions occurring in the course of the year. For latest modifications, see Regulation 1/72, J.O. L 1, 1972.

[50] The main exceptions are the products of the lists B, C, D and E, for which the Treaty provides a maximum and those of List F for which the duties are provided therein.

customs tariff,"[51] the second General Report on the activities of the Communities (1968) states that " Tariff union is, however, only a stage on the road to a real customs union. The latter calls for uniform interpretation of the common customs tariff, its continuing administration and Community legislation to replace national legislation in this field."[52] Consequently, the Council has on several occasions adopted regulations among which it is worth mentioning the one concerning the nomenclature of the tariff needed to ensure uniform interpretation of the common customs tariff[53] leading to the levying of one and the same duty on a given item everywhere in the Community.[54] As the Member States no longer have the power to take binding measures in these fields they turn increasingly to the Commission for the solution of the problems facing them and so have trade circles in connection with their problems: the administration of the customs union is a continuing process often requiring adaptation of existing rules and procedures.

2–56. Having briefly examined the principal features of the Community's Customs Union, the question arises as to the effects it will have for the United Kingdom after it has become an E.E.C. Member.

As stated in the White Paper of July 1971, there are two main processes involved here. First, all tariffs and charges having equivalent effect on trade between the United Kingdom and the original and new Member States have to be eliminated. This is to be done in five equal stages, starting three months after accession (Act of accession, Arts. 32–38). Secondly, subject to some special tariff arrangements,[55] the United Kingdom has to apply the Common Customs Tariff to all countries outside the enlarged Community, unless they enjoy special arrangements with the Community.[56]

[51] General Report, 1968, p. 21.

[52] *Ibid.*, p. 22.

[53] Regulation 97/69, J.O. L 14, 1969.

[54] For more details, consult General Reports: 1969, p. 44, 1970, p. 2 and 1971, p. 75.

[55] See Annex B to July 1971, White Paper (Cmnd. 4715) and Protocols 8 to 15 annexed to the Act of accession.

[56] Special arrangements exist with the countries associated under the Yaounde Convention (see J.O. L 282, 1970), Kenya, Uganda and Tanzania under the Arusha Agreement (signed on 24 September 1969 along the same lines as the Yaounde Convention. See J.O. L 282, 1970), the dependent territories of the Six (see J.O. L 282, 1970), Greece (see J.O. 294/63) Turkey (see J.O. 3687/64), Tunisia (see J.O. L 198, 1969), Morocco (see J.O. L 197, 1969), Israel (see J.O. L 183, 1970), Spain (see J.O. L 182, 1970) and Malta (see J.O. L 61, 1971). The agreement with Nigeria was not ratified. Agreements with those members of E.F.TA. which have not joined the Community were signed at Brussels on 22 July 1972.

Under these arrangements developing countries enjoy preferential or duty-free access to the common market, usually in return for preference which they grant on exports from the Community to their markets. Gaining preferential access to these countries (as well as to Greece, Turkey, Tunisia, Morocco, Israel and Spain, with a total population of just under 100 million), should be of substantial benefit to British exporters.[57] With regard to third countries not enjoying such arrangements the application of the Community tariffs will involve minor adjustments to the duties presently applied to their goods: in general, the Community tariff is rather lower than the present British one. However, for those countries which currently enjoy free entry to the British market, it will mean the gradual application of those tariffs to their products.

2–57. In the new Member States, the C.C.T. will indeed be applied gradually in four stages, starting a year after accession (Act of accession, Art. 39). The new tariff will be fully applicable as of 1 July 1977, the same date which was set for the total abolition of internal Community tariffs. This latter abolition will start on 1 April 1973 and will be carried out in five stages of a 20 per cent. reduction (1 April 1973, 1 January 1974 – 1975 – 1976 and 1 July 1977).

According to the British Government, these arrangements have two substantial advantages. . . . In the first place, they will ensure that within three years of entry (when tariffs between the United Kingdom and the other members will have been cut by 80 per cent.) British exporters will have virtually duty-free access to the large and rapidly growing market of the Six. The opportunities will therefore be considerable, because, even if – as was pointed out earlier – the external community tariffs are not, on average, very high, in several sectors of importance to British industry the barriers are substantial: 22 per cent. on commercial vehicles, up to 18 per cent. on organic chemicals, 16–18 per cent. on plastics, 18 per cent. on tractors and 14 per cent. on diesel engines. In the second place, the delay of one year before the first move towards the Community's external tariff should usefully lengthen the period of adjustment for the Commonwealth countries.[58]

2–58. Since the implementation of the European Customs Union will affect commerce and industry rather than the ordinary citizen, the possible consequences for British manufacturers should be briefly

[57] White Paper, July 1971, Cmnd. 4715, 36.
[58] Cmnd. 4715, 21.

examined. However, before going into more concrete considerations, one should always bear in mind that whatever the subject under discussion, the fundamental change, not always explicitly stated, will be that from the date of accession, preference is to be given to products of the Community. This " Community preference " is the underlying principle of a great number of Treaty provisions and is therefore essential for their understanding and interpretation. It applies for instance to the freedoms and very much to the Agricultural Policy.

2–59. Very generally stated " the main consequences of United Kingdom membership of an enlarged Community would be that (Britain) then forms part of a customs union of up to 300 million people, stretching from Scotland to Sicily and from the Irish Republic to the borders of Eastern Europe. Within this vast area, industrial products would move freely – without tariff or quota restrictions – as soon as any transitional period had been completed."[59] The consequences of this enlargement for the individual firm is therefore on the one hand a duty-free access to the European and associated markets, but on the other, strong competition at home from other Community products; the conditions of competition will most probably be modified, although, generally speaking, trade patterns do not change abruptly. And it should be clear also that not only will British manufacturers no longer enjoy tariff or quota protection against competition from the Six, but whatever the problems of British undertakings, no British Government will any longer be in a position to impose duties or quotas on imports to help them out: " Member States shall refrain from introducing, as between themselves, any new customs duties on imports or exports or any charges having equivalent effect . . ." (E.E.C., Art. 12)[60]; the Court of Justice confirmed that this provision is " self-executing " which means that it must be upheld in the national courts even against conflicting national legislation.[61] But, on the other hand, Article 136 of the Act of accession provides that " if, before 31 December 1977, the Commission, on application by a Member State or by any other interested party, finds that dumping is being practised between the Community as originally constituted and the new Member States, or between the new Member States themselves, it shall address

[59] Cmnd. 4715, 21.

[60] The levying of a charge such as the 15 per cent. tax the British Government imposed on most imports in 1964 will no longer be permitted.

[61] Case 26–62, Rec. IX, 5.

recommendations to the person or persons with whom such practices originate for the purpose of putting an end to them. Should the practices continue, the Commission shall authorize the injured Member State or States to take protective measures, the conditions and details of which the Commission shall determine." Such protective measures against dumping could of course be drawn up in the form of customs duties or quotas.

2–60. Together with the Common External Tariff, the E.E.C. treaty in its Article 3(*b*) mentions " the establishment of a common commercial policy towards third countries." In the foregoing remarks the Common External Tariff was viewed in connection with the elimination of internal tariffs and quotas since the emphasis was put on the Customs Union. However, external tariffs are also part of the various measures of commercial policy and should therefore also be examined as such. Indeed, the duties of the external tariffs are not fixed once and for all, but can be manipulated as an instrument of commercial policy; they can be raised or lowered according to the needs of this policy. There are in principle two procedures for such modification: first under Article 28, the so-called " autonomous " modification, and secondly, under Articles 111 and 113 through agreements with non-member countries. In addition, under Article 25, the Council acting on a proposal of the Commission, may grant a Member State tariff quotas at a reduced rate of duty or duty-free in case the production within the Community is insufficient to supply the demands of one of the Member States and such supply traditionally depends to a considerable extent on imports from third countries; also under Article 25, the Commission may authorise suspension of duties; in fact under Article 25 a considerable number of dispensations have been granted.[62]

As for Article 113, its first paragraph provides that " after the expiry of the transitional period [*i.e.* 1 July 1968] the common commercial policy shall be based on uniformly established principles, particularly in regard to tariff amendments, to the conclusion of tariff and trade agreements, to the establishing of uniform practice as regards measures of liberalization, to export policy and to commercial protective measures. . . ." The third and fourth paragraphs establish the procedure to be followed when the putting into effect

[62] See for instance the judgment of the Court of Justice in the case 24–62 (Rec. IX, 141) and in the case 34–62 (Rec. IX, 296).

of this common commercial policy requires that agreements be concluded with third countries (see para 2-176).

AUTONOMOUS COMMERCIAL POLICY

2–61. Although various measures were taken by the Community institutions, disparities still exist between the import arrangements of the various Member States. As the Commission pointed out in its Third General Report, this is " all the more regrettable as the field of commercial policy is more sensitive than others to relatively slight disparities which can force up costs and distort conditions of competition in the common market . . . they are very damaging to internal trade. As long as they subsist, all the relevant products originating in non-member countries must be examined and, as appropriate, barred from free circulation, and all the products of the same kind, *i.e.* including those originating in the Community, must be checked at the frontiers to ensure that products declared as Community products do not originate in the non-member countries in question and do not contain parts manufactured in those countries."[63]

2–62. In 1970 three important regulations on *import* policy came into force: two establish the common systems applicable to imports, the first from State-trading countries[64] and the second from members of G.A.T.T. and countries on the same footing.[65] The third regulation institutes a common procedure for administering quantitative quotas.[66] These new arrangements confirm the basically liberal common commercial policy of the European Communities and establish a flexible procedure based on close co-operation between the Commission and the national authorities of the Member States. They also provide for a considerable widening of the geographical scope of the system. The regulations on the import systems establish freedom of import for a very wide range of products, the list of which is annexed to the regulations; they also allow for the introduction of safeguard measures in the event of serious danger. They allow for some supervision in order to guarantee that the import of particular products will not prejudice the interests of Community producers. The application of escape clauses is in principle the

[63] Third General Report, 1969, p. 374.
[64] Regulation 109/70, J.O. L 19, 1970.
[65] Regulation 1025/70, J.O. L 124, 1970.
[66] Regulation 1023/70, J.O. L 124, 1970.

prerogative of the Council, but the Commission is empowered to act in an emergency and so are the Member States, though their action is limited in time.

As for the administration of quantitative quotas fixed autonomously by the Community or established by formal agreement with a non-member country, the amount is determined by the Council and administration is in the hands of the Commission in " liaison " with a Community Committee. However, the issuing of licences and the carrying out of other formalities continue to be the business of Member States, but will be standardised.[67]

Through successive liberalisation measures[68] the Member States no longer apply any quantitative restrictions for most of the free-market-economy countries. In 1968, the Council adopted the first anti-dumping regulation[69] which gives the Commission authority to open anti-dumping procedures; a certain number of cases have already been dealt with: nitrate fertilisers from Greece,[70] sisal packing string from Cuba,[71] explosives[72] and certain fertilisers from Yugoslavia.[73] It is worthwhile noting that for one other product: uranium, the Commission has initiated Community control of certain imports.

2–63. As for *exports*, in a regulation of 1969,[74] the Council established the principle of freedom of export for almost all the headings of the Common External Tariff and fixed the criteria for the introduction of restrictions where serious crises, such as supply difficulties, occur; this freedom does not apply, at Community level, to 52 tariff headings (1 January 1972); the Commission has formulated proposals to unify the present system whereby a certain number of other headings are subject to export restrictions only in one of the Member States.

Another important item of commercial policy is the export credit system with or without insurance or guarantees. In October 1970, the Council adopted two directives based on E.E.C., Art. 113 concern-

[67] See also regulation 1471/70, J.O. L 164, 1970.

[68] See list in Fifth General Report, Chap. V, § 6, s. 498, fn. 3.

[69] Reg. 459/1968 on measures against dumping, premiums and subsidies practised by non-member states, J.O. L 93, 1968.

[70] See notices of opening and closing of the investigation procedure, J.O. C 52, 1970 and C 123, 1970.

[71] J.O. C 133, 1970.

[72] J.O. C 8, 1971.

[73] J.O. C 103, 1971.

[74] Regulation 2603/69 of the Council establishing a common régime for exports, J.O. L 324, 1969.

ing the introduction by Member States of common insurance policies for medium- and long-term transactions, based on suppliers' credit and intended for public and private buyers.[75]

At the same time the Council adopted a work programme[76] under which the Commission submitted proposals in the following fields:

(i) a common system of premiums applicable to medium- and long-term transactions with both public and private buyers;
(ii) introduction of a common insurance policy for financial credits and of the relevant system of premiums;
(iii) adoption of a certain number of basic principles with the aim of setting up a common system of guarantees for cost increases in trade relations with non-member countries;
(iv) fixing of general principles for granting of exchange guarantees for exports to non-member countries.[77]

COMMERCIAL POLICY THROUGH AGREEMENTS

2–64. Under the terms of Title I of the Council decision of 16 December 1969,[78] bilateral treaties, agreements and arrangements between Member States and non-member countries may be extended, if, during the envisaged extension period, they do not constitute an obstacle to the implementation of the common commercial policy. The Council has since authorised certain Member States to extend or renew a number of treaties.[79] The Member States have declared that the extension of these agreements was not likely to prevent the opening of any negotiation or the conclusion, under the terms of E.E.C., Art. 113, of Community trade agreements which would supersede the bilateral agreements already in force with the non-member countries concerned. The Commission has also made proposals to the Council for a decision establishing measures for the progressive standardisation of all such agreements. Such an agreement was concluded with the United Kingdom in 1963,[80] and

[75] J.O. L 254, 1970.
[76] See Annex D to Council Decision 70/509, J.O. L 254, 1970.
[77] See Fifth General Report, 1971, § 500.
[78] J.O. L 326, 1969.
[79] For details, see General Reports 1970, § 446 and 1971, § 501.
[80] Decision of the Council of 30 July 1963, J.O. 2735/63.

renewed in 1967,[81] concerning the suspension of duties on tea, maté and tropical wood. Agreements were also concluded with Iran,[82] Israel[83] and Lebanon.[84]

2–65. How will the Community's commercial policy affect the United Kingdom? Article 108 of the Act of accession provides that the agreements concluded with Greece, Turkey, Tunisia, Morocco, Israel, Spain and Malta will be implemented by the new Member States immediately after accession and that these agreements will be modified accordingly. It was pointed out above that British exporters would thereby gain preferential access to new markets with a population of just under 100 million.[85] On the other hand existing trade arrangements, most likely beneficial to British manufacturers, might have to be modified or replaced by Community agreements. It is of course impossible to assess what the consequences will be for existing trade relations; it can however be assumed that owing to the liberal nature of the Community's common commercial policy, no new obstacles (except those resulting from the application of the common external tariff) will be introduced. Also British manufacturers will be subjected to Community regulations with regard to exports and imports from state-trading countries and areas; *e.g.* the restrictions on imports of pig iron and steel from state trading countries.[86]

Before examining the other activities of the E.E.C. Community, it should be noted that there exist a number of escape clauses which make it possible to prohibit or restrict imports and exports, under certain conditions, even within the Community. These clauses, *e.g.* Articles 36, 103 and 108(3), will be examined with those relating to other activities, at the end of the following paragraph (c).

(c) *Free movement of persons, services and capital and right of establishment*

2–66. " the abolition, as between Member States, of obstacles to

[81] Decision of the Council of 7 December 1966, J.O. 136/67.
[82] See J.O. 2554/63 and 3742/66.
[83] See J.O. 1517/64.
[84] See J.O. L 146, 1968.
[85] White Paper, July 1971, Cmnd. 4715, 36.
[86] More details on arrangements with third countries will be found in the General Reports 1970, § 447 and § 460, and 1971, § 501. See Act of accession, Art. 134(3): " if Decision No. 1/64 of the High Authority of 15 January 1964 prohibiting alignment on quotations for steel products and pig iron from state-trading countries or territories is extended after accession, that prohibition shall not apply until 31 December 1975 to products for the Danish and Norwegian markets."

the free movement of persons, services and capital" (E.E.C., Art. 3(*c*)).

Part II of the E.E.C. treaty concerns the "Foundations of the Community," which consists of the so-called "freedoms"; authors differ as to their exact number, which of course depends on whether or not one gives the name "freedom" to certain specific rights guaranteed by the treaty. Since Title I refers to "Free movement of goods" and Title III only to "Free movement of persons, services and capital," certain writers speak of the four fundamental freedoms; others consider the "right of establishment" which is also mentioned under Title III as another "freedom" and still others add to that series the right conferred by E.E.C., Art. 106, namely the "freedom" of payments connected with the exchange of goods, services or capital and of transfer of capital and wages. That this "sixth" freedom is essential does not need to be demonstrated: what would, indeed, be the use of the freedom to transfer goods or services from one's country to another, if the payments received in exchange could not be brought back or could only be brought back under disadvantageous exchange control terms?

i. FREE MOVEMENT OF PERSONS (E.E.C., Arts. 48–51 and 52–58)

2–67. The E.E.C. treaty distinguishes between labour (wage-earner) and non-wage earning activities; the former come under Chapter one (E.E.C., Arts. 48–51) while rules for liberation of the latter are to be found in Chapter two "the right of establishment" (E.E.C., Arts. 52–58); in so far as these provisions concern professional activities (*i.e.* non-wage-earning activities) they will be examined under "free movement of persons"; the right of establishment will be viewed hereafter as pertaining to the setting up and management of undertakings (E.E.C., Art. 52(2)). It will be noticed that since 1965 in the General Reports of the Commission the "free movement of workers" is classified as part of "social policy" under the heading Establishment of the Economic Union, while freedom of establishment is reviewed under Establishment and Functioning of the Common Market. It should be clear however that the objective of free movement of workers is mainly economic and closely linked with free movement of goods,[87] rather than social, although that aspect must not be under-estimated.

[87] See preambles of Reg. 1612/68 on the free movement of workers, J.O. L 257, 1968.

2–68. *Free movement of labour* does not mean that every worker is absolutely free to claim any job anywhere within the Community; it means that " any discrimination based on nationality between workers of the Member States as regards employment, remuneration and other labour conditions " must be abolished (Art. 48(2)). More concretely it entails, according to paragraph 3 of the same article, the right " subject to limitations justified on the grounds of public policy, public security and public health[88]:

(a) to accept offers of employment actually made;
(b) to move freely within the territory of Member States for this purpose;
(c) to stay in a Member State for the purpose of employment in accordance with the provisions governing the employment of nationals of that State laid down by law, regulation or administrative action;
(d) to remain in the territory of a Member State after having been employed in that State, subject to conditions which shall be embodied in implementing regulations to be drawn up by the Commission."[89]

These provisions which, by the way, do not apply[90] to employment in public service, were worked out in detail in Regulation 1612/68, which among other matters regulates access to employment (Art. 49(*b*)), non-discrimination in employment conditions (Art. 49(*c*)) and the functioning of the system for checking against one another the offers and requests for employment (vacancy clearance) (Art. 49(*d*)).

2–69. According to E.E.C., Art. 48(1) the free movement of labour must be secured within the Community, not later than by the end of the transitional period; as will be remembered this period ended on 30 June 1968. This deadline was practically met when the

[88] On 6 June 1971 the Commission submitted to the Council, for adoption, a proposal for a directive extending the scope of a directive of 25 February 1964 (J.O. 850/64) co-ordinating special restrictions on travel and residence for foreigners if justified on grounds of " *ordre public*," public safety and public health and which applies to all nationals of Member States whatever their occupation.

[89] After consulting the European Assembly and the Economic and Social Committee, the Commission adopted in 1970, Regulation 1251/70 (J.O. L 142, 1970) on the right of workers to stay in the country after having been employed there; the arrangement is that the residence permit he held when in paid employment is automatically renewed; relatives living with him are also entitled to stay on, even after the worker has died.

[90] Reg. 1612/68 on the free movement of workers within the Community, entered into force on 8 November 1968, J.O. L 257, 1968.

Council adopted on 29 July 1968 a regulation and a directive[91] completing freedom of movement for workers. Indeed this freedom was not yet " complete " since Member States maintained during the first stage (till 31 December 1961) a priority for national workers; during the second stage (till 31 December 1965) this priority became equal treatment with escape clauses. Under the 1968 regulation the latter was replaced by a possibility for the Commission acting at the request of a Member State to determine that a dangerous situation exists on the labour market in a given area or branch of industry and consequently to suspend the activities of the Community system for vacancy clearance.

2–70. Free movement of labour would be illusory if by moving from one country to another the worker would lose the rights he has acquired under *social security* regulations; this applies particularly to pension rights. Article 51 therefore empowers the Council acting unanimously on a proposal of the Commission, to adopt in the field of social security, the measures necessary to ensure the free movement of labour, in particular a system which will ensure to migrant workers and their dependants that

(a) all qualifying periods for benefits under domestic legislation shall be added together for the calculation of benefits and

(b) these benefits will be paid to persons resident in the territories of Member States.[92]

According to various judgments of the Court of Justice, this provision, in connection with E.E.C., Arts. 48, 49 and 50, means that any measure which places migrant workers in regard to social security benefits in a less favourable position than nationals or which results in the migrant worker losing advantages acquired in another Member State, is to be abolished.[93]

The basic implementing provisions[94] of E.E.C., Art. 51 are to be found in Regulations Nos. 3 and 4 of 1958.[95] The former was

[91] Directive 68/360 on the abolition of restrictions on movement and residence within the Community of workers of the Member States and their families, J.O. L 257, 1968.

[92] See E.E.C., Art. 227.

[93] See Rec. X, 557 and 1105; see also Rec. XV, 363 (case 15–69).

[94] Yearly about 2 million people (workers, pensioners and dependants) come under the implementation of these provisions, resulting in transfers estimated at 140 million units of account (1970).

[95] J.O. 561 and 597/58.

replaced in 1971 by a completely revised Regulation 1408/71.[96] The main provisions are: a broad definition of the concept " workers,"[97] payments under health insurance to workers and pensioners, calculations of pensions, unemployment indemnities and the creation of a Consultative Committee composed of representatives of the workers, the employers and the governments. As a result of the replacement of Regulation No. 3, the same became necessary for Regulation No. 4 containing implementing provisions of an administrative and financial nature. The new Regulation 1408/71 will not become applicable before Regulation No. 4 has been amended. Once the new regulations have become community law it is to be hoped that the many difficulties of interpretation which led to several Court judgments[98] will have been solved.

As was mentioned earlier, the E.E.C. treaty provides for a series of escape clauses which make it possible under certain conditions, to suspend temporarily the basic freedoms. The various escape clauses will be examined globally at the end of this Section (c).

2–71. *Free movement of non-wage earners* (E.E.C., Arts. 52–58) presents more problems than free movement of workers. Formally provided for under the heading " The right of establishment " (Chap. 2 of Title III) it confers on nationals of the Member States the right to " engage in and carry on non-wage earning activities . . . under the conditions laid down for its own nationals by the law of the country where such establishment is effected." The treaty therefore does not confer a real " freedom " to establish oneself everywhere in the Community, but as is the case for workers, only the right not to be discriminated against as compared to the nationals of a country. This right could then be considered a corollary of E.E.C., Art. 7 according to which " within the scope of application of this Treaty, and without prejudice to any special provisions contained therein, any discrimination on grounds of nationality shall be prohibited." This discrimination is not limited to legal provisions, but also applies to their implementation (administrative) provisions.

[96] J.O. L 149, 1971.

[97] Under Reg. No. 3 the benefit was limited in accordance with Art. 4(1), to citizens of the Member States, stateless persons and refugees residing in a Member State. Under Reg. 1408/71 a " political " status is no longer required: the criterion is the fact of being insured, either compulsory or voluntarily within the framework of a social security system of a Member State organised for the benefit of salaried employees.

[98] See for instance cases 68–69, 3–70, 32–70, 35–70, 23–71, 26–71, 27–71 and 28–71 to name only a few recent ones.

2–72. The right to establish oneself in another country shows great similarities with the free movement of services: whether for instance a doctor living close to a border sets up office on the other side or comes across to take care of patients is economically similar: the only difference is that setting up office is of a more permanent nature; this is the reason why E.E.C., Art. 60, refers to " temporarily " practising an activity. Most commentators of the E.E.C. treaty however make no differentiation between the supply of services and the right to establish oneself in another country whether to carry out professional or commercial activities and whether this right pertains to individuals or to companies (E.E.C., Art. 58). Although both Articles 54(1) and 63(1) require the Council, acting unanimously on a proposal of the Commission and after consultation with the Economic and Social Committee and the Assembly, to draw up a general programme for the abolition of existing restrictions (and although two programmes were indeed established[99]), it seems that a global analysis of the two freedoms (establishment and services) will permit a more systematic and logic approach. Furthermore, some implementing provisions, *e.g.* directives provided for under E.E.C., Arts. 57 and 66 pertain to both freedoms.

ii. RIGHT OF ESTABLISHMENT, FREEDOM TO SUPPLY SERVICES AND APPROXIMATION OF LEGISLATION ON PROFESSIONS, TRADES AND CRAFTS AND ON COMPANY LAW (Arts. 52–58 and 59–66)[1]

2–73. In its General Report published in 1972, the Commission underlines the interdependence which exists between the right to set up business and supply services in all the Member States and other aspects of European integration, such as industrial policy, energy policy, regional policy and competition policy, and also between these rights and the establishment of the economic and monetary union.[2] And indeed what the common market with its basic freedoms of movement of goods, labour and capital aims to achieve is the optimum allocation of production factors; only when freedom of establishment and of supply of services is achieved will this aim become realisable.

All three, free movement of workers, freedom of establishment

[99] J.O. 36/62 and 32/62.
[1] See also General Report 1971, ss. 155–165.
[2] See *ibid.*

and freedom of supply of services, do in fact mean one and the same thing, namely prohibition of discrimination on the grounds of nationality. The general programmes setting out the conditions and the stages of achievement of these freedoms have already been mentioned. E.E.C., Arts. 54(2) and 63(2) provide that in order to initiate these general programmes the Council, acting once again on a Commission proposal and after consulting the Economic and Social Committee and the Assembly, shall, acting by a qualified majority, issue directives. Various directives have been issued, as will be seen, others have been proposed to the Council and still others have to be drafted.

2–74. *Liberal professions* present a particular problem in respect to establishment and services, because in certain cases diplomas are required. In case the mere removal of restrictions based on nationality does not in practice ensure effective freedom of establishment and of supply of services because of special national regulations governing the access to certain activities and their exercise, E.E.C., Art. 57 provides that the Council shall issue directives " for the mutual recognition of diplomas, certificates and other evidence of qualification " and also " for the co-ordination of the provisions laid down by law, regulation and administrative action in Member States concerning the taking up and pursuit of activities as self-employed persons." These provisions are of particular importance for the liberal professions.

Since 1963, 39 directives concerning freedom of establishment and freedom to supply services were adopted by the Council. Two of them concern the conditions of entry and residence by nationals of Member States in as far as they affect freedom of establishment and freedom to supply services.[3] The majority of the adopted directives concern industry, trade and handicraft; freedom of establishment in those sectors has been almost completely achieved.[4]

Not yet liberalised are namely the professions, banking, insurance (except re-insurance) and transport. However, for most of these activities, the Commission has submitted drafts of directives to the Council; others are in preparation.

A list of the measures for removal of restrictions on freedom of

[3] J.O. 845/64.

[4] See for instance: the transitional measures in the field of wholesale trade and intermediaries (J.O. 857/64), freedom of establishment and freedom to supply services in the wholesale trade (J.O. 863/64), for intermediaries in trade industry and handicrafts (J.O. 869/64) and for re-insurance (J.O. 878/64).

establishment and freedom to supply services for the nationals of other Member States was first published in the First General Report on the Activities of the Communities 1967, p. 80 and additions to this list are to be found in the Second, Third and Fourth General Reports. In 1972 the Commission will publish a complete list of all the Community measures regarding freedom of establishment in a supplement to the Bulletin of the European Communities.[5]

2–75. In regard to *companies*, a first directive based on E.E.C., Art. 54 was adopted by the Council on 9 March 1968[6]; it co-ordinates the general guarantees required of joint stock companies; they concern publication of particulars, validity of commitments undertaken on behalf of the company and causes of nullity of such companies.

On 29 February 1968 a Convention on the mutual recognition of companies and bodies corporate was signed by the Member States (E.E.C., Art. 220); the object of the Convention is to enable companies and other legal persons to avail themselves fully of the Community freedom.[7]

iii. E.E.C. ESCAPE CLAUSES

2–76. The measures examined above, *i.e.* elimination of customs tariff and quotas, establishment of the common customs tariff and of a commercial policy and the abolition of obstacles to freedom of movement for persons, services and capital do apply within the Community subject to various escape clauses.

Article 36 provides that notwithstanding the obligation imposed by Articles 30 to 34 to eliminate quantitative restrictions and all measures having equivalent effect, the Member States may prohibit or restrict imports, exports or transit of goods when this can be justified on grounds of public morality, public policy or public security[8]; the protection of health, of national treasures or of industrial or commercial property.[9] Such prohibitions or restrictions may not, however, " constitute a means of arbitrary discrimination

[5] Most of these directives are amended by the Treaty of accession: see Cmnd. 4862–II, 50.
[6] J.O. L 65, 1968.
[7] For more details see Second General Report, 1968, 85.
[8] A reference to public security can be found in the Commission's recommendation made pursuant to E.E.C., Art. 37(6) regarding the adjustment of the French powder and explosives state monopoly; see J.O. L 31, 1970, 26.
[9] See below subparagraph (f): competition policy.

or a disguised restriction on trade between Member States." This article will be applicable to the new Member States from the date of accession.

Article 48(3): freedom of movement of workers is also subject to limitations justified on grounds of public policy, public security or public health.[10]

Article 56(1) provides that in regard to the right of establishment, " the provision of Chapter 2 and the measures taken in pursuance thereof shall not prejudice the applicability of provisions laid down by law, regulation or administrative action providing for special treatment for foreign nationals on grounds of public policy, public security or public health."

Article 91(1), which was only applicable during the transitional period contains provisions regarding dumping: it provided that if the Commission finds that dumping is being practised, it shall address recommendations to the person with whom such practices originate. If the recommendation has no success the Commission shall authorise the injured Member State to take protective measures, the conditions of which the Commission determines. According to Article 136(1) of the Act of accession the same provisions will apply until 31 December 1977, if the Commission finds that " dumping is being practised between the Community as originally constituted and the new Member States or between the new Member States themselves."

Article 226: this provision is no longer in effect, since it applied only during the transitional period.[11] Its provisions have however been embodied in Article 135 of the Act of accession for application between the new Member States before 31 December 1977. In pursuance of this provision new Member States may if " difficulties arise which are serious and liable to persist in any sector of the economy or which could bring about serious deterioration in the economic situation in a given area," apply for " authorization to take protective measures in order to rectify the situation and adjust the sector concerned to the economy of the common market." The Commission determines the protective measures.

Under Article 135(4) of the Act of accession original Member

[10] See J.O. 850/64.

[11] The Commission's decisions authorising Member States to take safeguard measures are mentioned in the yearly General Reports on the activities of the E.E.C. and those concerning the activities of the Communities. See for instance: First General Report, 1967, 45.

States may, in the same circumstances and according to the same procedure, apply for authorisation to take protective measures in regard to one or more new Member States.

It should be noted that Article 137 of the Act authorises Ireland " until 31 December 1977 [to] take the necessary measures in cases of extreme urgency "; these measures must be notified forthwith to the Commission, which may decide to abolish or modify them.

Denmark, on the other hand, may retain until 30 June 1974 the special excise duties on table wines imported in bottles or other similar containers notwithstanding the second paragraph of Article 95 of the E.E.C. treaty.

(d) *The agricultural policy*

" the adoption of a common policy in the sphere of agriculture "
(E.E.C., Art. 3(*d*))

2–77. One could have imagined a common market without agriculture for several reasons. There is conflict of interests between certain Member States: France needs to export her overproduction, but Germany and The Netherlands which need to import would probably prefer to import from somewhere else at lower prices. Including agriculture also made it more difficult for the United Kingdom to envisage joining the common market; it was also suggested that since " agriculture " had always been a problem for the solution of which each country had over the years conceived elaborate measures, it should be left to the Member States each to remedy its own particular difficulties. As it turned out, the agriculture policy became somehow the " corner stone " of the Community.

However, as stated by E.E.C., Art. 39(2)(*c*), " in the Member States, agriculture constitutes a sector closely linked with the economy as a whole," and it would indeed have been difficult to establish a common market if prices for agricultural products were to vary widely from one region to another thereby creating within the Community differences in the costs of living and consequently in the levels of prices and salaries: under such conditions competition would have been distorted in the industrial sectors also. Furthermore, it was hoped that the economic growth which one expected to result from the development of the common market would automatically involve rapid progress in agriculture.

2–78. It is none the less obvious that agriculture presents some very particular problems: in the first place, it is very much dependent upon climatological conditions and production therefore is somewhat problematical; secondly, production cannot be reduced or increased at will to correspond to a change in demand (although demand for agricultural products is not submitted to variation due to changes in fashion as are some industrial products); thirdly, production cannot be increased at will, since the main factor of production, land, cannot be increased at will; fourth, demand for agricultural products is practically inelastic (the consumption of basic agricultural products will, in developed countries, not change greatly with variation in prices); neither can production be drastically reduced lest one is confronted with a social problem for which there is no short-term remedy (at least not in a system of small farms which is mostly the case in Europe). Finally, where most of the farming is done in family-enterprises with an average of 30 acres, there never existed a real " market " for agricultural products, owing to the existence in each country, as said before, of complicated regulations. There could therefore be no question of abolishing the existing measures, including quotas and duties, without replacing them by others. Here again the treaty draftsmen showed realism, when they wrote that " the operation and development of the common market for agricultural products must be accompanied by the establishment of a common agricultural policy among the Member States " (E.E.C., Art. 38(4)) and " the need to effect the appropriate adjustments by degree " (E.E.C., Art. 39(2)(*b*)).

2–79. In other words, the necessity of including " agriculture " in the Community on the one hand and the necessity of " taking into account the particular nature of agriculture "[12] on the other, resulted in an inclusion but under special terms. The " inclusion " principle is to be found in the first paragraph of E.E.C., Art. 38: " The common market shall extend to agriculture and trade in agricultural products "[13] and the special treatment in paragraph 2: the rules laid down for the establishment of the common market apply to

[12] See E.E.C., Art. 39(2)(*a*) which states that this particular nature " results from agriculture's social structure and from structural and natural disparities between the various agricultural regions."

[13] The term "Agricultural products" means " the products of the soil, of stock-farming and of fisheries and products of first stage processing directly related to these products " (Art. 38(1)). They are listed in Annex II to the E.E.C. treaty. This list was completed on 18 December 1958 in accordance with Art. 38(3): Reg. 7 *bis*, J.O. 71/61.

agricultural products, " save as otherwise provided in Articles 39 to 46." Such provisions are already mentioned in Article 38(4) which provides that there can be no common market for agricultural products without a common agricultural policy among the Member States; this policy must include " the replacement of the national organizations by one of the forms of common organization provided for in Article 40(2)," and the implementation of " the measures specified in this Title" (E.E.C., Art. 43(2)). The common organisations will be examined below.

2–80. A second provision excluding the application of treaty provisions on agricultural products is Article 42 according to which " the provisions of the Chapter relating to rules on competition shall apply to production of and trade in agricultural products only to the extent determined by the Council." In 1962 together with the first regulation concerning the financing of the Common Agricultural Policy (Regulation 25),[14] the Council issued Regulation 26 concerning the application of the rules of competition[15] in agriculture. This regulation provides that Articles 85[16] (prohibition of agreements between undertakings which are liable to affect trade between Member States and which are designed to affect competition or have this effect) and 86 (prohibition of improper exploitation of a dominant position by one or more undertakings) are not applicable to most agricultural agreements, namely agreements which form an essential part of a market-organisation or concern the production and sale of agricultural products (Reg. 26, Art. 2). More important is the non-applicability of Articles 92 (state aids are in principle incompatible with the common market) and 93(2) (procedure against Member States in case the Commission finds that an aid is not compatible with the common market), because the only obligation left for Member States with regard to agricultural aids is to help the Commission in its constant review of all systems of aid existing in the Member States (E.E.C., Art. 93(1)) and to inform the Commission previously to their implementation of any plans to grant or modify grants of aid (E.E.C., Art. 93(3), first sentence). However, it should be noted that each market organisation for agricultural products provides for normal implementation of the rules in regard to State aids: so for instance Article 22 of Regulation 120/67 concerning

[14] J.O. 991/62.
[15] J.O. 993/62.
[16] Arts. 85 and 86 are analysed in subparagraph (f) hereafter.

a common market-organisation for the cereals sector[17]: " except where otherwise indicated in this Regulation, Articles 92 to 94 of the treaty are applicable to the production of and trade in the products enumerated in Article 1."

THE COMMON ORGANISATION FOR AGRICULTURAL MARKETS

2–81. Practically all the products enumerated in Annex II to the treaty are presently submitted to a " Common Organisation "; no more than ten products or groups of products still have to be " organised."

2–82. The market organisations have been established by the Council in accordance with E.E.C., Art. 43: " The Council shall, on a proposal from the Commission and after consulting the Assembly, acting unanimously during the first two stages and by a qualified majority thereafter, make regulations, issue directives, or take decisions, without prejudice to any recommendations it may also make." The Commission's proposals were to be based upon the work of a conference to be convened immediately after the entering into force of the treaty. This conference was held in Stresa in July 1958 and defined the broad lines of the Common Agricultural Policy.[18] On 30 June 1960, the Commission, after consulting the Social and Economic Committee submitted its proposals to the Council: they covered four main areas: structural, market, commercial and social policy.[19] Those proposals were discussed by the " Special Committee for Agriculture " created by the Council in 1960 and which still exists.

2–83. The Council adopted a certain number of " basic principles " which were to determine the future orientation of the common agricultural policy: free movement of agricultural products within the Community, establishment of a commercial policy jointly with the agricultural policy and a common price level for all agricultural products in the whole Community. The result of the common market policy should be an economic balance between supply and demand (including imports and exports) and fair earnings for those employed in agriculture. It was also accepted that a system

[17] J.O. 2269/67.

[18] See First General Report, 1958, ss. 97–101, including text of resolution of the conference.

[19] For a general analysis see Third General Report, 1960, s. 230 and Fourth General Report, 1961, s. 103.

of levies would remain in existence on trade between Member States during a preparation stage, and would progressively decrease until they disappeared; this system would imply the elimination of all other protective measures, in particular minimum prices and quantitative restrictions. In regard to third countries, a uniform system of levies would be established. Finally, the national measures for structural reform would be co-ordinated.

2–84. The first proposals for market organisation in the form of regulations were submitted to the Council by the Commission in 1961. On 14 January 1962 the Council adopted the first market organisation: that concerning cereals.[20] This first regulation of 1962[21] which applied to the transitional period (during which the existing national market organisations remained in force in the various Member States and were progressively replaced by the " common " organisation of the Community) was later replaced by another definitive one. Indeed, in 1967 the final form of market organisation was established for most products. Not all organisations are identical and several classifications have been tried either according to the kind of guarantees they afford or according to the degree of liberty left to the producers in regard to prices; the Commission itself in its Fourth General Report refers to three groups:

- wheat, coarse grains, sugar and dairy products: characterised by a system of target and intervention prices, intervention purchases to be made under certain conditions on the internal market and external protection in the form of variable levies;
- beef and veal, pigmeat, poultry and eggs: support is afforded mainly through appropriate external protection. For beef this is customs duties, for pigs, poultry and eggs it is a reduced customs duty and a variable levy designed solely to compensate differences in animal feeding costs;
- fruit, vegetables and wine where the determinant factor is quality control: only the standardised or graded products will be allowed on the market; in addition, measures to reduce production and a customs duty are applicable.

[20] This regulation applies to the following products: (a) wheat, rye, barley, oats, maize, buckwheat, millet, etc., (b) hard wheat, (c) meal and groats of wheat, rye, etc. and (d) processed products.

[21] Reg. No. 19, J.O. 933/62.

For a proper understanding of the functioning of these market organisations, the one applying to cereals will be examined in some detail.

THE MARKET ORGANISATION FOR CEREAL, REGULATION 120/67[22]

2–85. If the previous Regulation (19/62) was based on the existence of six different national markets, the basic principle of Regulation 120/67 is the establishment of one single market, equal protection at the borders of the Community and a common internal price system consisting of a target price, an intervention price, and import prices (threshold price).

2–86. *The target price*, which is established once a year before the first of August by the Council, in accordance with the procedure provided for in E.E.C., Art. 43(2),[23] is definitely not a fixed price; it is the price at which it is expected the product can be sold on the market during the next marketing period beginning the following calendar year (1 August – 31 July); it is intended to help the farmers plan their production accordingly. For 1971–1972 this price was, for durum wheat, established at 127,50 units of account per metric ton (Reg. 120, Art. 2).

2–87. *The intervention price*, which is also established yearly by the Council, before the first of August in accordance with the procedure of Article 43(2), is the price at which the designated national authorities must buy the cereals offered to them. The intervention price lies, of course, below the target price (for 1971–1972 it was established at 119,85); it constitutes for the farmers the guarantee that their products, in case they cannot sell them on the market, will be bought anyway at a given price.

While the target price is the same within the whole Community, the intervention price varies from region to region in accordance with the normal differences in market-prices resulting from natural circumstances: in regions with an abundant production, prices naturally tend to be lower than in regions where demand is larger than supply. The intervention price fixed by the Council therefore is a basic-intervention price which applies in Duisburg (Germany), the region with the lowest production. In addition the Council designates other

[22] J.O. 2269/67.
[23] This means " acting on a proposal of the Commission and after consulting the Assembly."

marketing-centres and the derived intervention prices for these centres (about forty main centres) (Reg. 120, Art. 4).

Intervention of the authorities on the market requires strict control of the quality of the products which can be offered to the intervention organs; they are established by regulation (Reg. 120, Art. 7).

A particularity of the market organisation for cereals is the fixing of a minimum price to producers (wholesale) for durum wheat (1971–1972: 147,90).

2–88. *The threshold price* (Reg. 120, Art. 5) is the price fixed for cereal products imported from third countries; it is established in such a way that cereals imported through Rotterdam (Reg. 120, Art. 5(4)) will sell in Duisburg (Reg. 120, Art. 5(1)) at a price which is at the level of the target price. In other words, the threshold price is equivalent to the target-price minus the transport costs Rotterdam-Duisburg.

The threshold-price is established by the Council, acting on a proposal of the Commission (no consultation of the Assembly), every year before 15 March. The threshold-price is arrived at through a system of levies imposed on imported products which are equal to the difference between the threshold-price and the c.i.f.-price Rotterdam, the latter being practically always lower than the Community prices. The levies are fixed daily by the Commission (Reg. 120, Art. 13(5)).

It should be quite clear that this system of levies on imports of agricultural products from third countries was set up to protect Community agricultural products, and thereby their producers, against (unfair) competition from non Member States. This is the practical expression of a fundamental principle of the European Communities – " Community preference."

2–89. Finally the market organisation provides for *refunds* granted to exporters of Community products to third countries (Reg. 120, Art. 16). These subsidies are the same for the whole Community and vary according to their destination. The subsidies are periodically established in accordance with a particular procedure provided for in Article 26 of Regulation 120/67. They are equal to the difference between the world prices for a product and the Community's prices (Reg. 120, Art. 16); such subsidies are necessary to permit export to third countries of surpluses produced within the Community, since as already mentioned, world prices are generally speaking much lower than Community prices.

2–90. For all exports from and imports into the Community, import or export certificates are required (Reg. 120, Art. 12(1)).

2–91. Under Article 25 of this Regulation a *Management Committee* was set up composed of representatives of the Member States and chaired by a representative of the Commission. The Chairman submits proposals to the Committee which expresses an opinion within the time-limit set by the chairman, by a majority vote of forty-three[24] (before accession twelve). The Commission implements the proposals by a decision which becomes immediately applicable. If the Committee's opinion is unfavourable, the Commission must inform the Council without delay; the Council can within a time-limit of one month decide on a different measure.

Target prices, intervention prices and threshold prices are increased monthly, namely to take into account the costs of stockpiling and the payment of interest (Reg. 120, Art. 6); these increases are fixed by the Council every year before 15 March.

STRUCTURAL REFORM IN AGRICULTURE

2–92. The above mentioned measures aim solely at a market equilibrium through price-systems within the market and protection against imports; they are at the most a palliative but do not contribute towards a solution of the fundamental problems of agriculture within the Community. Therefore, the Commission submitted to the Council on 18 December 1968 a " Memorandum on the Reform of Agriculture in the European Economic Community " (Agriculture 1980).[25] Two and a half years later the Council adopted, on the basis of the proposals contained in the Memorandum, a resolution concerning the general lines of a social-structural policy for agriculture.[26] Starting from the social-economic situation in the Community's agriculture, the Memorandum sets out the aims of an agricultural policy; the concrete measures to be taken and an estimate of the costs.

2–93. In regard to the *social-economic situation of agriculture*, the Memorandum points out three particularities:

[24] See Cmnd. 4862–II, 21. See Chap. 3, Council, 3. Voting procedure.
[25] An analysis of this document is given in the Second General Report of the European Communities, 1968, 135. The present section is based upon this report.
[26] J.O. C 52, 1971.

(1) the agricultural *population*, *i.e.* the number of persons employed in agriculture, dropped from 20 million in 1950 to 10 million in 1970. Consequently, labour productivity rose yearly by 7 per cent. (more rapidly than in industry). As against this the annual growth rate of expenditure on foodstuffs has slackened and the annual growth rate of expenditure on agricultural products in total expenditure on foodstuffs has dropped from 2.5 per cent. (1965) to 1.9 per cent. (1970).

Fewer people are producing more goods and the growth rate of production is higher than that of demand. The Community has become more than self-sufficient in some commodities, this in turn, creates heavy financial burdens: in 1971 market support cost 1,800 million units of account.[27] Furthermore, the age pyramid is quite disturbing: 50 per cent. of all farmers are over fifty-seven years of age;

(2) *the farms*: the average farm within the Community is far too small. Only 170,000 farms, a mere 3 per cent. of all farms in the Community, have an area of 125 acres or more. The national efforts in this " field " have had little or no effect. This now is a crucial problem because of rapid advances in mechanisation;

(3) the *marketing* problems: with outdated production structures, farmers are forced into highly intensive production methods to ensure a minimum of income; unable to adapt to the market, they go on producing to maintain this minimum: the result is that the price and market machinery cannot function properly and farmers' incomes are, generally speaking, lower than these of the rest of the Community and the income gap has continued to widen.

Because of this situation and the imbalance between supply and demand, price measures alone will not be enough to improve incomes.

2–94. *As for the population*, three types of help were proposed for the 5 million people who are expected to leave the land:

(1) general help measures to those who leave the land (structural reform grants and scholarships);

[27] Fifth General Report, 1971, 216, table 16.

(2) measures to help farmers of fifty-five or over who are willing to give up farming (annual income equalisation fund) and

(3) measures to help those who want to take up another occupation (readaptation, training, job creation).

2–95. The *size of farms* should be drastically increased; examples are given in the Memorandum for various types of production: for grain and root crops minimum 200 to 300 acres; for milk, 40 to 60 cows; for beef, 150 to 200 cattle; for chickens, 100,000 a year; for eggs, 10,000 laying hens; for pigs, 450 to 600 animals. It is proposed that modern agricultural enterprises be set up with special aids such as start-up grants, investment aid and guaranteed credits. Due to the fact that many people will give up farming, land will become available for increasing the size of farms and land will be withdrawn from agriculture: twelve and a half million acres it is hoped.

2–96. Measures are also proposed in regard to *marketing* problems: establishment of European product councils to perform market intelligence, information on sales prospects, etc.

It was estimated that during a period of 10 years the structural measures would cost 2,500 million units of account a year (to be shared by the Community and the Member States), 2,000 million for job creation and 480 million for vocational retraining.

2–97. On the basis of this Memorandum, the Commission submitted a proposal to the Council on 29 April 1970[28]; after the European Assembly and the Economic and Social Committee had expressed their opinion, the Council, by resolution of 25 May 1971, fixed new trends for the common agricultural policy. These trends concern the basic principles for common action in the social-economic field, the agricultural prices for 1971–1972 and competition policy in agriculture.

The Community is to provide 25 per cent. of the money needed (65 per cent. in those areas where no measures for encouraging people to leave the land have yet been taken); the measures would benefit those who wish to cease farming, those who wish to pursue an agricultural activity, professional training of farmers and measures in favour of improving the marketing of agricultural products.

2–98. On the basis of this Resolution, the Commission submitted to the Council modified proposals for the reform of agriculture[29];

[28] J.O. C 70, 1970.
[29] J.O. C 75, 1971.

these proposals are: a directive concerning modernisation of farms, a directive concerning encouragements to leave farming and to affect farming land to improving agricultural structures, a directive concerning professional qualifications in agriculture and a regulation concerning farmers' unions.

In regard to State aids, it is admitted that they must all be eliminated when in conflict with the common measures; the Council furthermore took good note in its Resolution of the decision of the Commission to re-examine all the subsidies granted in agriculture, on the basis of the Articles 92 to 93 and of the principle that only these aids producing lasting restructuring can be considered as compatible with the common market; this implies the elimination of all other aids which have an influence on production costs.

In the above mentioned Resolution the Council considered that success in the agricultural field can only be achieved if progress is made in other domains, such as the economic and monetary union, the regional policy and the social policy.

2–99. Nothing has been said yet of the financing of the common agricultural policy. The definitive financing system was established together with the decision concerning the Community's own resources and will be examined in Chapter 4: Financial Provisions. The principle of financing as embodied in the first regulation concerning the Community's agricultural policy was that, since there exists a common price system and a common policy, the financial consequences should be borne by the Community. From the beginning therefore the refunds and interventions on the market have been paid out of a Fund set up under E.E.C., Art. 40(4): the European Agricultural Guidance and Guarantee Fund.[30] It is not however a Fund proper since it is part of the Community's budget.

2–100. The common market organisations have to be made to function through administrative machinery. The basic decisions are taken by the Council acting in accordance with either the procedure of E.E.C., Art. 43(2) (*i.e.* on a Commission proposal and consultation of the Assembly) or the voting procedure of said provision (*i.e.* on a Commission proposal); other measures are taken by the Commission either acting autonomously (*e.g.* levies on imports, Reg. 120, Art. 13) or after consulting a Management Committee

[30] Reg. 25, Art. 1, J.O. 991/62, replaced by Reg. 130, J.O. 2965/66, in turn replaced by the Decision of 21 April 1970. See Act of accession, Art. 127.

(*ibid.*). The implementation of the decisions of the Council on the other hand is the task of the existing bodies of the national governments: the import or export certificates required under Article 12(1) of Regulation 120/67 are delivered by the Member States, the levies are collected by them and the refunds are paid by them also. More important, the purchase of agricultural products at the intervention price set by the Council is the responsibility of the national intervention offices. In conflicts concerning the implementation of these measures it is not the Community, but the Member States which are considered liable. In several cases the Court of Justice has, in preliminary rulings, interpreted provisions of the agricultural regulations[31]; from this it follows that farmers or importers/exporters of agricultural products should not attempt to seek redress in the Court of Justice directly against the Community, arguing that for instance the intervention offices act as agents of the Community. Instead those regulations impose obligations on the Member States and, their provisions being self-executing, they can ask the national judge to uphold them.

2–101. How is this Common Agricultural Policy going to affect the United Kingdom after accession? From the first year of membership the support system will be applied, although with somewhat different target, threshold and intervention prices. These prices will be raised (or lowered) gradually in such a way that the common prices will be applied by 1 January 1978 at the latest.[32] As long as there is a difference between British and Community prices, the United Kingdom may retain production subsidies (Act of accession, Art. 54). The Community market and that of each of the new Member States will remain separated by levies and grants to account for the differences in price levels; compensatory amounts granted will be financed by the Community from the Guarantee Section of the European Agricultural Guidance and Guarantee Fund (Act of accession, Art. 57). As prices are increased, British farmers will increasingly get their returns from the Community and deficiency payments will be phased out.[33]

Since it is the purpose of the common agricultural policy to create one single market for agricultural products, existing customs duties will have to be abolished between the original Community

[31] *E.g.* case 76–70, Rec. XVII, 393.
[32] Act of accession, Art. 52(2) and (4).
[33] Cmnd. 4715, 1971, s. 82.

and the new Member States and between the new Member States themselves (Act of accession, Arts. 59–63).

According to the White Paper of July 1971, it is estimated that accession will affect food prices gradually over a period of about six years with an increase of about 2½ per cent. each year in retail prices although a recent British Government estimate now puts the increase at 2 per cent. As food accounts for about a quarter of total consumer expenditure, the effect on the cost of living would be about ½ per cent. each year.

(e) *Common transport policy*

"the adoption of a common policy in the sphere of transport" (E.E.C., Art. 3(*e*))

2–102. Transport is covered in a special Title of the E.E.C. treaty (Title IV of Part Two); together with free movement of goods, of persons, of services and of capital and with the common agricultural policy, common transport policy provided for under E.E.C., Art. 74, constitutes the "Foundations of the Community." The situation of "transport" is somewhat comparable to that of "agriculture": because of specific and particular problems, special provisions apply; but, whilst production and commercialisation of agricultural products are subjected to the "rules laid down for the establishment of the common market" (E.E.C., Art. 38(2)), in regard to transport, the treaty only provides that the "objectives of this Treaty shall apply" (E.E.C., Art. 74) in both cases however the treaty calls for a "common policy" (E.E.C., Arts. 38(4) and 74).

2–103. What makes transport such a special case?[34] Demand for transport varies widely in time reaching a maximum during short periods and falling, sometimes to practically zero, at others; the supply on the other hand must be available at full capacity all the time and consequently very heavy investments remain very often idle and unproductive. This applies to all kinds of transport. But in regard to investments there exists an enormous discrepancy between the various means of transport: compare a railway with a bus which uses public infrastructure. Connected with this first aspect is the obligation imposed by public authorities on certain carriers (mainly railways) to maintain in operation, for social reasons, services which

[34] E.E.C., Art. 75(1) refers to "distinctive features of transport."

economically speaking should be abolished. There is the problem of public safety, since this service affects, more than any other industrial enterprise, the lives of the citizens; there are also the social aspects; it often is at the cost of normal working conditions that the carriers are able to sustain heavy competition: since labour is such an important production-cost factor, it pays to make drivers work long hours. All this requires control.

2–104. Under the E.E.C. treaty, Member States were required to develop a Common Transport Policy; specifically this meant that the Council acting on a proposal of the Commission, and after consulting the Economic and Social Committee and the Assembly, was to lay down

(a) common rules applicable to international transport and

(b) the conditions under which non-resident carriers might operate transport services within a Member State;

these provisions were to be laid down during the transitional period (before 1 January 1970); as if it were an afterthought E.E.C., Art. 75 adds under (c) and " any other appropriate measure." Since the first two categories of measures are rather limited in scope, the common transport policy as such is included under this last subparagraph for which, unfortunately, no time-limit was set!

2–105. The Commission at first suggested to the Council the adoption of general principles covering all aspects of a common transport policy. In a " Memorandum concerning the orientations of a common transport policy "[35] the Commission proposed the institution of a system of competition in the transport field and three objectives: the elimination of obstacles to the implementation of the common market which may result from transport, integration of transport at Community level and general organisation of transport within the Community. These three objectives are closely interlinked and would have to be put into practice through measures based on the following principles: equality of treatment, financial autonomy of carriers, freedom of action of these enterprises, free choice of customers and co-ordination of investments.

This Memorandum was not formally accepted by the Council but can be considered as having received general agreement. The Commission submitted to the Council on the basis of the principles

[35] Not published.

contained therein a whole series of proposals.[36] It soon appeared however that such a global approach was not politically possible and that the only way to obtain at least some results would be to proceed little by little by presenting small packages to the Council which would permit it to reach compromises by limited mutual concessions.

2–106. Some of the more significant measures enacted by the Council as a result are mentioned hereafter.

Regulation 11[37] *of* 27.6.1960 implementing E.E.C., Art. 79(3): abolition of discrimination by carriers in transport rates and conditions for the carriage of the same goods over the same transport links must be abolished.

Directive of 23.7.62[38]: first directive on the establishment of common rules for international transport (carriage of goods by road for third parties).

Regulation 141[39] *of* 26.11.1962 exempting transport from the application of Council Regulation No. 17 (implementation of E.E.C., Arts. 85 and 86).

Decision of 13.5.1965[40] concerning harmonisation of certain provisions affecting competition in transport by rail, road and inland waterways.

Directive of 19.7.1968[41] on the standardisation of provisions regarding the duty-free admission of fuel contained in the fuel tanks of commercial vehicles.

Regulation 1017[42] *of* 23.7.1968: application of E.E.C., Arts. 85 and 86 to transport by rail, road and waterways.

Regulation 1018[43] *of* 23.7.1968 establishing Community quotas for road transport between the Member States.

Regulation 1174[44] *of* 6.8.1968 establishing a system of rate-fixing for goods carriage between Member States.

Regulation 543[45] *of* 25.3.1969, on harmonisation of certain social legislation relating to road transport.

[36] Those proposals referred to the following fields of activity: (a) competition, (b) access to the market, (c) rates and conditions, (d) investments, (e) infrastructure.
[37] J.O. 1121/60.
[38] J.O. 2005/62.
[39] J.O. 2751/62.
[40] J.O. 1473/65.
[41] J.O. L 175, 1968.
[42] J.O. L 175, 1968.
[43] J.O. L 175, 1968.
[44] J.O. L 194, 1968.
[45] J.O. L 77, 1969.

Regulation 1191[46] *of* 26.6.1969, on action by Member States concerning the obligations inherent in the concept of public service in transport by rail, road and inland waterways.

Regulation 1192,[47] establishing common rules for the normalisation of the accounts of railway undertakings.

Regulation 1107[48] *of* 4.6.1970 on the granting of aids for transport by rail, road and inland waterways (E.E.C., Art. 77).

Regulation 1463[49] *of* 20.7.1970 on the introduction of recording equipment (tachygraphs) in road transport.

Resolution of 7.12.1970[50] inviting the railway companies to co-ordinate the Community network.

The measures enumerated above do not represent an harmonious common transport policy globally conceived and implemented. They are a patchwork of various measures taken by the Council whenever politically possible. Most of these measures concern the organisation of road transport.

2–107. An irritating problem not yet solved within the Community concerns preferential rates and conditions for transport towards seaports (E.E.C., Art. 80): they are applied in Germany and in France on transport operations to national ports thereby discriminating against similar operations to other (non-national) harbours. Without these special rates traffic might choose another means of transport such as waterways and in that case the exception of Article 80(3) could be invoked for these rates: " the prohibition provided for in paragraph 1 shall not apply to tariffs fixed to meet competition (*i.e.* of other transport means) "; but these rates also prevent the free choice among various railway-routes, *i.e.* other railways which might carry the goods at better conditions, but to other (*i.e.* Benelux) ports. The Commission submitted proposals for a regulation concerning the elimination of discrimination in rates and transport conditions based on E.E.C., Art. 79(2): this draft regulation which provided for the prohibition of different rates on grounds of origin or destination of the goods was not accepted by the Council.

2–108. Progress in the field of transport will become possible

[46] J.O. L 156, 1969.
[47] J.O. L 156, 1969.
[48] J.O. L 130, 1970.
[49] J.O. L 164, 1970.
[50] J.O. C 5, 1971.

when agreement can be reached on conditions of access to the market and rates and conditions of carriage, both being closely linked. In regard to the latter, the Commission proposed free determination of prices, subject to the treaty provisions regarding discrimination and competition. This in turn would require frank publication of prices to provide information for users and control by the Commission.

The Council in the meantime agreed upon a work programme for 1972, including the adoption of certain harmonisation measures and of a new market organisation. During the negotiations for accession, the United Kingdom pleaded for a system of free competition in a harmonised transport market.

(f) *Competition policy*

" the institution of a system ensuring that competition in the common market is not distorted " (E.E.C., Art. 3(*f*))

2–109. In its first report concerning the Community's competition policy,[51] the Commission described as follows the role of competition in the common market: " Competition is the best incentive for economic activity since it guarantees to its participants the widest possible freedom of action. An active competition policy based upon the treaty provisions facilitates the continual adaptation of the demand and supply structures to technical evolution; thanks to the implementation of a system of decentralized decision-making, a constantly improved efficiency can be obtained from undertakings; this is the basic condition for a continuous raising of the standards of living and employment opportunities within the Member States of the Community. When so understood, competition policy is an essential instrument to ensure a high degree of satisfaction of private and collective requirements."

It is indeed important to state right from the beginning not only that competition is an essential instrument for economic development but that its ultimate goal (as indeed that of all the Community activities) is the well-being and the welfare of the peoples of the Member States. Competition is not an end in itself; it is, however, essentially an instrument which must be adaptable to attain the objectives desired. The European treaties do not define the concept

[51] First report on competition policy, annexed to the Fifth General Report on the activity of the Communities, April 1972.

" competition "; they refer to a certain number of measures which interfere with competition and are therefore prohibited subject to exemptions granted by the Commission. Neither has the Court of Justice defined what " competition " is, nor is it therefore, actually possible to specify " how much " competition is required under the E.E.C. treaty: " fair " competition is what it is called in the Preamble. The safest approach is the one used by the Court of Justice: the required measure of competition is that which is needed to achieve the treaty objectives, particularly free movement of goods[52] or, as the Commission puts it in the above mentioned report, the competition policy must, in the first place, prevent measures by private undertakings from replacing the state restrictions and obstacles to free trade abolished by the treaty. In other words, any action by a private undertaking or by a public authority (acting directly or by way of a public undertaking[53]) which jeopardises the unity of the common market violates the principle of free competition. As the various prohibitions provided for under the treaty are successively examined hereafter, the practicality of this approach will become more apparent. However, before examining the actions of private undertakings on the one hand and those of public authorities on the other, which interfere with competition, certain recurring terms should be briefly examined to avoid confusion. Indeed, the treaty refers to " discrimination,"[54] " competition[55]" and " distortions."[56]

2–110. *Discrimination* exists when a different treatment is applied to legal or natural persons who are in the same position or when the same treatment is applied to persons in different position,[57] by an individual (producer, carrier, consumer, etc.) or by a public or private legal person (public administration, nationalised industries, undertakings, etc.). In the economic field, the scope of the principle of non-discrimination is narrower in the case of measures of intervention than in the case of normal trade relations within a liberal framework. This can be easily explained since the object of intervention is to modify the normal trade relations in view of certain objectives: it is therefore, only in regard to these objectives that the

[52] *Grundig-Consten* case (56, 58–64), Rec. XII, 430.
[53] See E.E.C., Art. 90.
[54] See for instance E.E.C., Arts. 7, 37, 44, 67, 79.
[55] See for instance E.E.C., Arts. 85, 92.
[56] See Art. 101.
[57] See Rec. IX, 360, case 13–63.

principle must be respected: violation will only occur when one treats differently persons who are in a similar position in regard to these ends.[58] Essential, also, is the fact that the difference of treatment must result from the behaviour of a single person or institution: measures imposed by a single government can be discriminatory, measures imposed by two different governments cannot have a discriminatory effect; they can however cause *distortions*. Not every discrimination affects competition in the sense of the European treaties, but every discrimination between nationals of the Member States " on grounds of nationality " disrupts competition and " shall be prohibited " (E.E.C., Art. 7). It disrupts competition because the persons concerned, although operating within a single common market, are arbitrarily placed in different positions.

As was just mentioned, differences resulting from dissimilarities between the laws of various countries do not constitute a discrimination. The Court of Justice confirmed this in a judgment of 13 February 1969: " Article 7 does not refer to possible disparities in treatment and to distortions which may result for the persons and enterprises subject to the administrative jurisdiction of the Community from divergences existing between the legislations of various Member States, as long as these apply to all persons under their jurisdiction, in accordance with objective criteria and without regard to their nationality."[59] The Court in this judgment used the term " distortion " which is commonly used to designate differences in treatment resulting either from general measures or from discriminatory measures: the former being referred to as " general distortions," the latter as " specific distortions." A definition of general distortions is given in the above quoted passage of the Court's judgment; an example of it is to be found in Article 101 of the E.E.C. treaty: " Where the Commission finds that a difference between the provisions laid down by law, regulation or administrative action in Member States is distorting the conditions of competition in the Common Market and that the resulting distortion needs to be eliminated, it shall consult the Member States concerned, etc." (Article 101 comes under Chapter 3 " approximation of laws," which therefore indicates that the solution to " general distortions " is to be found in such approximation.) Specific distortions on the other hand, *i.e.* the ones that do not apply to all persons, but to a

[58] See Rec. IV, 247, case 8–57.
[59] Rec. XV, 16(13), case 14–68.

certain number, are considered to be incompatible with the common market; examples are: state monopolies (E.E.C., Art. 37), certain agreements between enterprises (E.E.C., Art. 85) and State aids (E.E.C., Art. 92). The Community competition policy is concerned solely with specific distortions caused either by actions of undertakings or by measures of the Member States.

COMPETITION RULES APPLICABLE TO UNDERTAKINGS

2–111. The rules of competition applicable to undertakings aim at preventing them from introducing new divisions within the common market, *e.g.* through a clause granting absolute territorial protection.[60] Most of the treaty provisions mentioned earlier in this chapter can indeed be considered as creating the conditions necessary for the existence and functioning of competition between undertakings at Community level; competition can indeed very well exist within Member States while " interstate trade " remains subject to conditions which distort competition. The treaty therefore contains two sets of rules: the first concern exclusively the Member States and are destined to establish a single market within which all undertakings of the Community can offer their products and services to all consumers unhampered by any kind of restriction. Thus E.E.C., Arts. 12 to 17 abolished customs duties and E.E.C., Arts. 30 to 37 quantitative restrictions on exports and imports between Member States while at the same time a common external tariff was established (E.E.C., Arts. 18–29), *i.e.* the creation of a customs union[61]; furthermore the treaty provides for free movement of workers (E.E.C., Arts. 48–51), the right of establishment (E.E.C., Arts. 52–58), the free supply of services (E.E.C., Arts. 59–66), the free movement of capital (E.E.C., Arts. 67–73) and free movement of payments (E.E.C., Art. 106) and finally by prohibiting discriminatory taxation (E.E.C., Arts. 95–99) and by approximating legislative and administrative provisions (E.E.C., Arts. 100–102) the treaty provides for the creation of a real free trading area where all measures which might prevent or distort competition should no longer exist. This economic " climate " called " Common Market " so created is further completed and preserved by the provisions concerning co-

[60] Rec. XII, 495, case 56, 58–64.

[61] See in this Chap. 2, sect. IV: the Treaty establishing the E.E.C., paragraph 2, E.E.C.'s activities.

ordination of " conjunctural " policies, *i.e.* policies relating to economic trends (E.E.C., Art. 103) and these relating to the balance of payments (E.E.C., Arts. 104–109), due account being taken of the fact that totally free trade will only become possible with the establishment of an Economic and Monetary Union.[62] It is within this economic framework that undertakings should operate each according to its own capabilities and at its own risk. Any measure or act which artificially upsets the economic conditions of this common market is in principle prohibited. When referring to undertakings such prohibited measures can consist either in agreements (E.E.C., Art. 85) or in the abuse of a dominant position (E.E.C., Art. 86).

2–112. As will be seen this does not mean however that the Communities competition policy is essentially negative and opposed to any form of co-operation between undertakings; the Commission has declared that it intends to reinforce the competitive position of enterprises not only within the Community, but on the world market by excluding from the treaty's prohibition (the Commission has the power to do so under E.E.C., Art. 85(3)) agreements for co-operation which have a positive effect for the development of competition: this is the case for instance for small and medium-size undertakings which otherwise could not compete with larger ones; in the same way the Commission does not consider incompatible with free competition these restrictions which do not have a noticeable effect.

Article 85

2–113. " The structure of Article 85 of the E.E.C. treaty is characterized by the formulation of a prohibition (para. 1) and the consequences attached thereto (para. 2) subject to the power (of the Commission) to grant exemptions (para. 3)."[63] By summarising the lengthy provisions of Article 85 this way, the Court of Justice intended to emphasise the fact that the various paragraphs are interrelated in such a way that the interpretation of each one depends upon the meaning of the others. The main problem in regard to

[62] See the Resolution of the Council and of the Representatives of the Government of the Member States of 22 March 1971 concerning the establishment in phases of the economic and monetary union in the Community, point I (1); the measures provided for are destined to ensure that at the end of the process the Community " constitutes an area within which free movement of persons, goods, services and capital takes place without distortion of competition . . . ," J.O. C 28, 1971.

[63] Rec. XV, 316 (*g*).

Article 85 concerned the second paragraph: " any agreements or decisions prohibited pursuant to this Article shall be automatically void." If taken at face value, this would have meant that if the prohibition of the first paragraph were self-executing from the date of entry into force of the Treaty (1 January 1958) all agreements covered by the prohibition would have been void as of that date. This question was raised in a Dutch Court in 1960 and referred to the Court of Justice under E.E.C., Art. 177[64]; in its judgment of 6 April 1962 (*Bosch* case), the Court held " that the Court of The Hague raises the question whether or not Article 85 was applicable from the date of entry into force of the Treaty; that the answer to this question is, in principle, affirmative; that this is implied by Articles 88 and 89 which empower the national authorities and the Commission to apply Article 85; that however Articles 88 and 89 do not ensure a complete and integral implementation of Article 85, such as to allow the conclusion that the complete applicability of Article 85 follows from the mere existence of those articles. In particular, one may not conclude that the automatic nullity provided for in Article 85(2) is effective in all those cases which fall within the description of Article 85(1) and for which a declaration such as provided for under Article 85(3) has not yet been given."[65]

2–114. In clear this means that agreements which prevent, restrict or distort competition, although prohibited under Article 85(1), are *not* " automatically void " in accordance with Article 85(2), as long as there exists a possibility of obtaining an exemption under Article 85(3). The question therefore is when does this possibility exist. Since the answer is not to be found in the treaty provisions, one must look for the " appropriate regulations or directives (adopted by the Council) to give effect to the principles set out in Articles 85 and 86 " (E.E.C., Art. 87). The first such regulation was adopted in 1962 and became effective as Regulation No. 17 on 13 March 1962.[66] According to Article 4 of this regulation no decision under Article 85(3) may be given[67] as long as the Commission has not been notified of the agreement, subject to certain

[64] See Chap. 3, the Court of Justice.
[65] Rec. VIII, 103.
[66] J.O. 204/62.
[67] As will be seen hereafter, before Reg. No. 17 became applicable the authorities of the Member States had the power to grant exemptions under Art. 85(3), see E.E.C., Art. 88. Since Reg. No. 17 the Commission has sole competence to apply Art. 85(3), see Art. 9(1) of Reg. No. 17.

categories of agreements being exempted from such notification (Reg. No. 17, Art. 4(2)). In other words, once an agreement has been notified, there exists this possibility of obtaining an exemption under Article 85(3).

Consequently, as the Court held in the *Bosch* case,[68] as long as the Commission has not decided on the request for exemption under Article 85(3), the agreements which are prohibited by Article 85(1) must be considered " valid " when they are exempted from notification, and " provisionally valid " when they have been notified to the Commission. In case notification is required for the granting of the exemption, the validity is only provisional since the exemption, if granted, will not necessarily cover the whole period between the notification and the Commission's decision (Reg. No. 17, Art. 6(1)) and therefore the presumed validity might after all be (partly) abolished by the Commission's decision.

2–115. So much for the general structure of E.E.C., Art. 85; many problems still remain, they will be examined hereafter but this first broad approach is a prerequisite for a fuller comprehension of the provisions of Article 85 and of Regulation No. 17.

Article 85(1) prohibits as " incompatible with the Common Market: all agreements between undertakings, decisions by associations of undertakings and concerted practices which may affect trade between Member States and which have as their object or effect the prevention, restriction or distortion of competition within the Common Market." Several terms and expressions used in this provision require further examination: " undertaking," " agreement," " concerted practice," " to affect trade between Member States " and " distortion of competition."

2–116. " *Undertaking* " can be understood in a legal or in an economic sense. Is legal personality required for a business entity to be subject to the prohibition of Article 85? In this respect reference must be made to other treaty provisions. Article 52 (right of establishment) provides that " Freedom of establishment shall include the right . . . to set up undertakings, in particular companies and firms within the meaning of the second paragraph of Article 58." It follows that the category " undertaking " includes " companies and firms " which in turn are described in Article 58: " companies or firms " means " companies or firms constituted under civil or com-

[68] Rec. VIII, 105.

mercial law, including co-operative societies, and other legal persons governed by public or private law, save for those which are non-profit making." The expression " and other legal persons " seems to indicate that where the treaty requires legal personality the terms " companies or firms " or the expression " legal persons " are used as in E.E.C., Arts. 173, 175. The conclusion therefore is that on the basis of textual interpretation alone the word " undertaking " in E.E.C., Art. 85(1) is not limited to legal persons. On the other hand however, the " undertakings " of E.E.C., Art. 85 must be able to legally bind themselves by agreements, to bring actions in the Court of Justice,[69] to pay fines and to own property against which a possible Commission's decision could be enforced.

Therefore legal autonomy is needed[70] but not necessarily legal personality[71]; this is the case for instance of the Dutch " Vennootschap onder Firma " and the German " Offene Gesellschaft "; consequently, the question whether or not a business entity possesses the required legal autonomy, must be decided according to the applicable national law.

2–117. The best definition probably for " undertaking " is a business or collection of endeavours under common ownership and direction.[72] Besides " legal autonomy " " economic autonomy " is also required; in several decisions of the Commission this was clearly stated. So for instance in the Commission's decision of 18 June 1969,[73] regarding a request of Christiani and Nielsen for a negative clearance,[74] the Commission found that the agreement in question existed between a Danish firm and its wholly owned Dutch subsidiary and that although both firms enjoyed legal personality (were legally autonomous), " the subsidiary cannot, in the present case, be considered as an economic entity which can compete with its mother-company " and that therefore " the sharing of markets provided for in the agreement is nothing else but a distribution of tasks within a single economic unit." In other words, where there is no

[69] See E.E.C., Art. 173, para. 2: " Any natural or legal person may . . . institute proceedings."

[70] See Judgment of 13 July 1962, case 19–61, Rec. VIII, 681.

[71] It is true that the Court of Justice in the *SNUPAT* case held that " the concept undertaking under the Treaty is identical to the concept natural or legal person," Rec. VII, 151 and also in the case 36–62, Rec. IX, 601, but there the Court added " as long as this (interpretation) is not in opposition with the context."

[72] Stein and Hay, *op. cit.*, 575; Rec. VIII, 681, case 19–61.

[73] See J.O. C 37, 1968.

[74] See hereunder, Art. 2 of Reg. No. 17.

economic autonomy there can be no competition and therefore no restriction of competition.

2–118. A similar case is the decision of 30 June 1970 in the *Kodak* case,[75] where the Commission held that " when, as in the present case, the subsidiaries are in exclusive and total dependence upon the (American) mother company and the latter exercises its powers of control by giving the former precise instructions, these subsidiaries are not in a position to behave independently " and that therefore the instructions given by the mother-company to the subsidiaries to apply identical sales conditions, do not result from an " agreement or a concerted practice " between the mother company and the subsidiaries or between the various subsidiaries. But the Commission added that although these instructions do not constitute an agreement between Kodak and its subsidiaries, they do constitute an " agreement between undertakings " since they must in turn be embodied in the agreements concluded by the subsidiaries and their wholesalers. What the Commission implied was that the agreement concluded between Kodak and its subsidiaries could not, because of the lack of economic autonomy of the latter, restrict competition between the parties to the agreement, but could cause competition to be limited between one of the parties and third parties.

2–119. This aspect also played a role in the *Grundig* case concerning the relationship between a producer, and his sole agent. The Italian Government which intervened[76] in this Court case maintained that exclusive sales contracts do not constitute " agreements between undertakings" as provided for in Article 85(1), since the parties are not on an equal footing and that in regard to those agreements, competition can only be preserved on the basis of E.E.C., Art. 86 (dominant position). The Court of Justice rejected this thesis, pointing out that Article 85 which refers generally to all agreements which distort competition within the common market, does not distinguish between agreements according to whether they are concluded between operators competing on the same level (horizontal agreement) or between non-competing operators situated at different

[75] J.O. L 147, 1970. This *Kodak* case is also interesting in as far as it shows that notification extends to agreements concluded between " European " and foreign-based undertakings.

[76] Art. 37, Protocol on the Statute of the Court of Justice, attached to the E.E.C. treaty.

levels (vertical agreements),[77] since competition can be distorted in the sense of Article 85(1) not only by agreements which limit competition between the parties, but also by agreements which limit competition between one of the parties and third parties.[78] And the Court added that a comparison cannot be made between, on the one hand, a situation (which falls under the jurisdiction of Article 85) of a producer bound by an exclusive agreement to the distributors of his products and, on the other hand, the situation of a producer who integrates the distribution of his products into his undertaking by any means whatsoever (commercial representation for instance) and which does not come under Article 85. This distinction based upon the legal and economic autonomy of the parties to the agreement is clearly underlined also in the Commission's Communication concerning contracts for exclusive representation concluded with commercial agents.[79]

2–120. The second term in E.E.C., Art. 85(1) which needs closer examination is " *agreement* " in connection with the expression " *concerted practice.*"

" Agreements " are legally enforceable contracts. Although some authors have pleaded for a " less legalistic interpretation "[80] in the sense that the term would comprehend any agreement whatsoever, whether legally enforceable or not, it appears to be the only logical one in regard to the system of Article 85 but also the one that corresponds most closely to existing terminology and interpretation in the Member States, particularly in The Netherlands and in Germany. And indeed Article 85(1) refers to both " agreements " and " practices," whilst Article 85(2) only mentions " agreements," which seems logical since a practice cannot be void. However, a " practice " *i.e.* a way of behaving is only prohibited by Article 85(1) when it is " concerted," *i.e.* when an informal agreement is at its origin. Parallel price increases, for instance, are not prohibited when they are purely coincidental or result from a particular market situation known as oligopoly with price leadership; they are how-

[77] Concerning vertical and horizontal agreements, see also the *ULM* case (56–65), Rec. XII, 358 and the case 32–65, *Italian Government* v. *Council and Commission,* Rec. XII, 592.

[78] *Grundig* case, Rec. XII, 492-3 (case 56, 58–64).

[79] J.O. 2921/62: ". . . the Commission considers that the decisive criterion for distinguishing a commercial representative from an independent merchant is the commitment which may be tacit or expressed, relating to the assumption of the financial risks connected with the sale or the implementation of the contract."

[80] Stein and Hay, *op. cit.*, 573.

ever prohibited when they are the consequence of a gentlemen's agreement. It is wrong therefore to say that concerted practices are informal agreements between enterprises; they exist when undertakings behave in a certain way and this behaviour is " dictated " by an informal agreement. Therefore, if these " informal agreements " were also included under the term " agreements " in the sense of Article 85(1) and (2), there would be no need to refer to " concerted practices " as a separate category of acts prohibited by Article 85(1).[81] The distinction however is important with regard to proof of the existence of such an act.[82] In the case of an " agreement " the question whether or not competition was actually distorted is irrelevant since according to the treaty it suffices that " the acts have as their object " distortion of competition; as the Court held in the *ULM* case " it is only in case the clauses of the agreement do not reveal this intention that one must investigate what the effects of the agreement were on the market."[83] Normally speaking there must therefore exist a legal document permitting the scrutiny of its clauses. On the other hand, in regard to " practices," the situation is quite different: " one must establish at the same time a factual behaviour of the parties concerned and on the other hand the existence of a link between this behaviour and a pre-established plan."[84] This pre-established plan can be anything: a gentlemen's agreement, meetings, other forms of combination etc. A typical example is the *Aniline* case, where the Commission concluded that the various price-increases applied by several firms, including Imperial Chemical Industries Ltd., were the result of a " concertation "[85] and imposed heavy fines for violation of E.E.C., Art. 85.

2–121. Article 85 forbids only those agreements and practices " which may affect trade between Member States and which have as their object or effect the prevention, restriction or distortion of competition." The term " and " indicates that these criteria are cumulative and that for instance agreements which may affect trade

[81] Unless, of course, one considers as a " practice " not the actual market behaviour, but the behaviour which precedes it: a gentlemen's agreement or any other informal expression of the will of the parties would thus be considered as a " practice " forbidden by Art. 85; this would mean that any expression of the intent to disrupt competition could be penalised even if this informal intention were not implemented.

[82] See Submissions of the Advocate-General in the case 41–69 (*Chemiefarma*), Rec. XVI, 718.

[83] Rec. XII, 359, case 56–65 (*ULM*).

[84] Submissions in the *Chemiefarma* case, 41–69, Rec. XVI, 718.

[85] Decision of the Commission of 24 July 1969, J.O. L 195, 1969.

without distorting competition on the common market are not prohibited under Article 85. Since it seems difficult, on the other hand, to imagine agreements which would distort inter-state competition without at the same time affecting inter-state trade, some authors propose to examine first the condition regarding competition, since, once that one is fulfilled, the other one (trade) is also. The Commission in its decisions first examines whether the agreements have as their object or effect to disrupt competition and once the answer is affirmative, usually goes on to examine the second criterion (although it did not, for instance, in the *Grundig* case[86]). This can of course be explained by the Commission's wish to mention all relevant arguments in case one or more of them should not be accepted by the Court of Justice. The latter, in all its judgments respects the sequence of the treaty provision.[87] The two conditions will therefore be examined here in that order.

2–122. Agreements or practices "*which may affect trade between Member States.*" The Court of Justice has defined this concept, first in the *ULM* case[88] and later in the *Grundig* case.[89] In the *ULM* case, the Court of Justice pointed out that this criterion serves in the first place to demarcate the category of cases coming under the jurisdiction of community law, that is, those which affect inter-state trade. An agreement fulfils this condition " when on the basis of a body of factual or legal existing elements, one can foresee with a sufficient degree of probability that it could directly or indirectly, potentially or actually, influence the trade relations between the Member States." In the case of an exclusive sales right this meant that an agreement is prohibited when it might partition the market for certain products and thereby render more difficult the economic interpenetration provided for by the Treaty.

The judgment in the *Grundig* case is more elaborate on this point since the Court rejected the views expressed by the German Government (which intervened in pursuance of Article 39 of the Statute of the Court of Justice) and those of the Commission. The former submitted that trade between Member States is only affected when it is demonstrated that without the agreement this trade would have been more intense; the Court of Justice held that an increase in

[86] J.O. 2545/64 and Rec. XII, 496, case 56, 58–64.
[87] *ULM, Grundig-Consten, Washing Machines* (case 5–69, Rec. XV, 295), *Chemiefarma.*
[88] Case 56–65, Rec. XII, 359.
[89] Case 56 and 58–64, Rec. XII, 495.

trade, even when considerable, does not exclude the possibility that the agreement might " affect " inter-state trade. The Commission maintained that the first condition of Article 85 is fulfilled when trade develops under conditions other than those which would have existed in the absence of the restrictions resulting from the agreement. The Court held that " what matters is the question whether the agreement is liable to jeopardize, either directly or indirectly, actually or potentially, the freedom of trade between Member States in a way which might prejudice the realization of the objectives of a single market between the States."[90] Of utmost importance is the fact that the Court of Justice refers to the objectives of the common market which are, as pointed out above, the fundamental freedoms of movement of goods, workers, capital, services, payments and freedom of establishment. This teleological interpretation appears as the only acceptable one; practically speaking it means that any agreement which limits (or could limit) in any way whatsoever the freedom, for instance, of movement of goods, is prohibited by E.E.C., Art. 85(1).

2–123. The second condition in Article 85 deals with " agreements or practices which have as their object or effect *the prevention, restriction or distortion of competition within the common market.*" As was pointed out above, in its judgment in the *ULM* case (56–65), the Court held that the term " or " indicates that this condition provides for an alternative, but adds that one " must " examine in the first place whether or not the clauses of the agreement have as their object the limitation of competition; only when this cannot be established, should one examine the effects of the agreement.[91] And, the agreement will only then be prohibited, when it is established that the limitation of competition is " noticeable." It is clear that the Court, in concurring here with the views expressed by the Commission, wanted to limit the prohibition of Article 85 to those agreements which really matter: *de minimis non curat lex.* In order to establish whether an agreement does noticeably limit competition, for instance in the case of an exclusive sales right, one must take into account, according to the Court of Justice, various aspects: the nature of the products and the question whether or not their quantity is limited, the position and the importance of the producer and of the agent on the market for the products concerned, the fact that

[90] Rec. XII, 495, case 56, 58–64.
[91] Rec. XII, 359, case 56–65.

the agreement in question is an isolated one or, if not, its position in a series of agreements, the severity of the clauses aiming at protecting the exclusive right or, on the contrary, the possibility left to other trading in the same products such as re-exportation and parallel import.

In the *Grundig* case, the German Government advocated the " rule of reason " and expressed the opinion that the Commission should not have limited its investigations to the effects of the agreement upon competition between products carrying the same trade-mark, but should have examined whether or not competition between similar products bearing others' trade-marks had not increased because of the agreement. The Court of Justice held that by granting its agent an absolute territorial protection, Grundig had limited competition between distributors of Grundig products, had thus isolated the French market and thereby falsified competition within the common market.

As it appears, the *Grundig-Consten* agreement was a typical example of one of the cases mentioned in Article 85(1).

2–124. It may be assumed that any agreement whose object corresponds to one of those described in Article 85(1) is prohibited and can only be declared inapplicable under certain limited conditions. *The declaration of inapplicability of the prohibition* provided for in Article 85(3), can be given either for particular agreements or for categories of agreements. In regard to the latter, such declarations can only be given in the form of regulations or directives in accordance with Article 87 by the Council acting on a proposal of the Commission and after consulting the Assembly. Such a regulation was adopted by the Council in 1965[92]; however, it did not specify categories of agreements which would be exempted from the prohibition of Article 85(1), but it empowered the Commission[93] to exclude by regulation from that prohibition certain agreements concluded between only two undertakings. Acting in pursuance of the Council's regulation, the Commission issued Regulation 67/67 in March 1967, the only one of its kind. Regulation 67/67 concerns the application of Article 87(3) to groups of exclusive sales agreements.[94] By this regulation, Article 85(1) (prohibition) is declared inapplicable

[92] Regulation 19/65, J.O. 533/65.
[93] See E.E.C., Art. 155.
[94] J.O. 849/67.

to three groups of agreements between no more than two undertakings:

(a) those in which one undertakes to supply the other exclusively with certain products for the purpose of resale in certain geographical areas, or
(b) those in which one undertakes to buy only from the other for the purpose of resale or
(c) those in which both have undertaken the agreements provided under (a) and (b).

Other obligations may be imposed which are defined in Article 2 of that Regulation.

2–125. On 24 December 1962, the Commission published an Official Communication concerning contracts for exclusive agency concluded with commercial agents,[95] wherein the Commission declared its opinion that contracts concluded with commercial agents in which such agents undertake with respect to a particular part of the common market to negotiate business transactions for the account of an undertaking or to do so in the name and for the account of the latter or to do so in their own name and for the account of the latter are not prohibited by E.E.C., Art. 85(1).

2–126. On the same date was published a " Communication " of the Commission concerning *patent licensing agreements* wherein the Commission expressed the opinion that certain provisions (set out in the " Communication ") in patent licence contracts do not fall under the prohibition of Article 85(1). In respect to licensing reference must be made to the judgment of the Court of Justice in the case *Parke, Davis* (24–67)[96] where the Court of Justice held:

1. the rights granted by a Member State to the holder of a patent are not affected in their existence by the prohibitions of E.E.C., Arts. 85(1), 86;
2. the exercise of these rights could not in itself fall under Article 85(1) in the absence of any agreement, decision or practice referred to in that provision, nor under Article 86, in the absence of any abuse of a dominant position and
3. the higher selling-price of the patented product above that of the non-patented product from another Member State does not necessarily constitute an abuse.

[95] J.O. 2921/62.
[96] Rec. XIV, 82. Judgment of 29 February 1968.

On the other hand, it will be recalled that in the *Grundig* case, the Court of Justice held that Community law could very well influence the exercise of national industrial property rights and that the Community's competition régime does not allow the abusive use of the rights resulting from the national trade-mark laws to evade the Community's cartel legislation.[97] In a recent judgment, *Sirena* (case 40–70),[98] the Court of Justice held that Article 85 is applicable when the holder of a licence prevents imports from other Member States of products bearing the same trade-mark as a result of agreements concluded either among the licence holders or with third parties. Shortly after, the Court reached an identical conclusion in a copyright case (*DGG/Metro*).[99]

2–127. Thirdly, there is the Commission's Communication relating to agreements, decisions and concerted practices concerning *co-operation between undertakings.*[1] Once again the Commission expresses as its opinion that the agreements mentioned therein do not limit competition and therefore do not fall under the prohibition of Article 85(1). Although this official publication is addressed to all undertakings, it particularly concerns small and medium-size ones. Indeed, the Commission indicates that it encourages co-operation between small and medium-size undertakings in so far as it puts them in a position to work more rationally and to increase their productivity and competitiveness on an enlarged market. The Commission adds however that co-operation between large undertakings can also be desirable from an economic point of view without raising objection under the competition policy.

From this publication and also from a number of decisions by which the Commission granted dispensation[2] follows clearly enough the Commission's policy to put in a certain way " efficiency " before " competition ": although, strictly speaking the agreements referred to in the publication of 1968 fall under the prohibition of Article 85(1), the Commission finds it " desirable " from an economic point of view (not a strict competition point of view) to express approval of such agreements.

[97] Rec. XII, 499, joint cases 56 and 58–64.
[98] Rec. XVII, 85.
[99] (78–70) Rec. XVII, 487.
[1] J.O. C 75, 1968.
[2] See for instance the decision *ACEC/Berliet*, J.O. L 201, 1968; European Exhibitions of machine-tools, J.O. L 69, 1969.

2–128. Finally, there is also the Commission's Communication of 27 May 1970, concerning agreements of *minor importance* which do not fall under E.E.C., Art. 85(1).[3] This is for instance the case when the product covered by the agreement does not represent more than 5 per cent. of the volume of the trade in identical or similar products in that area of the common market where the agreement applies and when the total annual turnover of the undertakings participating in the agreement is not higher than 15 million units of account or 20 million for commercial undertakings, *i.e.* undertakings which do not produce.

Article 86

" Any abuse by one or more undertakings of a dominant position within the Common Market or in a substantial part of it shall be prohibited as incompatible with the Common Market in so far as it may affect trade between Member States "; this text is followed by a few examples of such abuses.

2–129. Until recently there were no cases falling under this Treaty provision which, owing to the size of business undertakings on the continent is not surprising. As was seen above, in the *Grundig* case, the Italian Government unsuccessfully proposed to consider that agreements granting exclusive sales rights create an economic unit composed of the producer and the reseller and that such a business entity can only be prohibited under Article 86. The Court of Justice rejected this thesis on the ground that the applicability of Articles 85 or 86 does not depend on the economic level at which the parties to an agreement operate.[4] The same arguments were put forward by the Italian Government in the case 32–65 and with the same results.[5] In its judgment of 18 December 1971, the Court of Justice defined as follows a " dominant position ": " it is not sufficient that the undertaking is in a position to prevent third parties from selling within the territory of a Member State products bearing the same trade-mark; that since Article 86 requires that this position extends at least to a substantial part of the common market, it is necessary furthermore that the undertaking has the possibility to prevent effective competition within an important part of the

[3] J.O. C 64, 1970.
[4] Rec. XII, 492, case 56, 58–64.
[5] Rec. XII, 591.

relevant market, taking into account inter alia the possible existence, and the position, of producers and distributors of similar or substitute products."[6] The same reasoning is to be found in the judgment of 8 June 1971, in the *DGG/Metro* case.[7]

In its Report 1972 on the Community's Competition Policy, the Commission stated that it intends to apply E.E.C., Art. 86 also to concentrations carried out by undertakings enjoying a dominant position when this causes prejudice to consumers.

Recently the Commission took its first two decisions under Article 86: in the cases *Gema*[8] and *Continental Can Cy.*,[9] the first concerned an abuse of a dominant position, the second a concentration by which an undertaking with a dominant position virtually excluded competition in a substantial part of the common market. A description of both cases will be found in the First Report on competition policy attached to the Fifth General Report.

Regulation No. 17

2–130. This Regulation was adopted by the Council, in pursuance of E.E.C., Art. 87 on 6 February 1962 and published on 21 February 1962[10]; since the date of entering into force was not specified therein, it became effective " on the twentieth day following (its) publication," *i.e.* 13 March 1962 (E.E.C., Art. 191).[11] Regulation No. 17 was modified by Regulations Nos. 59[12], 118[13] and 2822[13a].

2–131. This first Regulation " to give effect to the principles set out in Articles 85 and 86 " *grosso modo* provides for the procedures to be followed when the Commission decides to give a " negative clearance " (Art. 2), or to " oblige the undertakings . . . concerned to put an end to . . . infringement (of Arts. 85 or 86) " (Art. 3), or to issue a declaration under Article 85(3) granting an exemption from the prohibition (Art. 6), or to fix the period of applicability of the

[6] Rec. XVII, 84(16), case 40–70.
[7] Rec. XVII, 487, case 78–70.
[8] J.O. L 134, 1971, see also case 45–71, Rec. XVII, 791.
[9] J.O. L 7, 1972.
[10] J.O. 204/62.
[11] In accordance with Annex I referred to in Art. 29 of the Act of accession, the date of accession shall be substituted for that date as regards agreements to which Art. 85 applies by virtue of accession (Cmnd. 4862 II, 74).
[12] J.O. 1655/62.
[13] J.O. 2696/63.
[13a] J.O. L 285, 1971.

prohibition of Article 85(1) to undertakings which existed before 13 March 1962 (Art. 7), or revoke an exemption (Art. 8), or to impose fines (Art. 15) or penalties (Art. 16); in all these cases the Commission must, before taking a decision, make known to the undertakings concerned the points to which it objects and which it has taken into consideration, and give the undertakings an opportunity to express their views thereon (Reg. No. 17, Art. 19(1)). If the Commission or the competent authorities of the Member States (with whom the Commission works in close and constant liaison, see Reg. No. 17, Art. 10), consider it necessary, they may also hear other natural or legal persons; they must do so if natural or legal persons who show they have a sufficient interest so request[14] (Reg. No. 17, Art. 19(2)). And finally, in all those cases the Commission shall or may[15] publish its decision (Reg. No. 17, Art. 21). Besides these general procedural rules, Regulation No. 17 provides for other special proceedings:

2–132. (a) *The negative clearance* (Art. 2): is issued at the request of undertakings which want to make certain their agreements are not prohibited by E.E.C., Art. 85(1); such a request should be accompanied by a request for exemption under Article 85(3) in case the Commission finds that Article 85(1) does apply; both these requests should be sent to the Commission either within the time-limit set for existing agreements (for British undertakings within six months from the date of accession) or at the date on which these agreements become effective since the date from which the decision granting exemption shall take effect may not be prior to the date of notification (Reg. No. 17, Art. 6). Before granting a negative clearance, the Commission must besides the above mentioned procedure, publish the essential content of the application and invite interested third parties to submit their observations (Reg. No. 17, Art. 19). Examples of decisions granting a negative clearance are:

[14] See judgment of 13 July 1971 in the *Deutscher Komponistenverband* case (8–71), Rec. XVII, 705, where plaintiff reproached the Commission for having refused to grant it a hearing in the *Gema* case.

[15] Publication is not obligatory for decisions imposing fines or penalties; but the Commission has, in the past, published those also; the Court of Justice upheld this right in the *Chemiefarma* case (41–69) adding that " the publicity given to the decision may even contribute to ensure the observance of the competition rules," Rec. XVI, 695 (104).

Eurogypsum,[16] *Cogemas*,[17] *Cobelaz*,[18] *Rieckermann*,[19] *Christiani and Nielsen*[20] and *Kodak*.[21]

2–133. (b) *Finding of infringements* (Art. 3): when the Commission on request from a Member State or a natural or legal person showing a justified interest or *ex officio* finds that an enterprise is infringing Article 85 or Article 86, it can by means of a decision oblige the undertaking to put an end to such infringements. Before taking such a decision, the Commission must besides applying the procedural rules examined above, consult the Consultative Committee on Cartels and Monopolies (Reg. No. 17, Art. 10), after having sent, if need be, a request for information to the Governments and competent authorities of the Member States or to the undertaking concerned (Reg. No. 17, Art. 11), or after having either requested an investigation by authorities of the Member States (Reg. No. 17, Art. 13) or carried out an investigation itself (Reg. No. 17, Art. 14). Before taking a decision as provided for under Article 3 of Regulation No. 17, the Commission must also publish the essential contents of the notification inviting all interested third parties to submit their observations (Reg. No. 17, Art. 19(3)). Examples of decisions finding infringements are *Grundig-Consten*,[22] *International Quinine-Cartel*,[23] *Aniline* case,[24] *Julien/Van Katwijk*[25] and *Continental Can Cy.*[26]

Before taking a decision, the Commission may also address a recommendation to the enterprise concerned (Reg. No. 17, Art. 3(3)); see *Convention Fayence* case.[27]

2–134. (c) *Granting an exemption* (E.E.C., Art. 85(3), together with Reg. No. 17, Art. 6). Exemptions may be granted for agreements which are prohibited under Article 85(1), but which fulfil the conditions of E.E.C., Art. 85(3). Before Regulation No. 17 became effective, only the authorities in Member States could grant such an exemption (E.E.C., Art. 88. See also Reg. No. 17, Art. 23). With the

[16] J.O. L 57, 1968.
[17] J.O. L 201, 1968.
[18] J.O. L 276, 1968.
[19] J.O. L 276, 1968.
[20] J.O. L 165, 1969, see para. 2-117 above.
[21] J.O. L 147, 1970, see para. 2-118 above.
[22] J.O. 2545/64.
[23] J.O. L 192, 1969.
[24] J.O. L 195, 1969.
[25] J.O. L 242, 1970.
[26] J.O. L 7, 1972.
[27] See E.E.C. Bulletin, 1964, 43–44.

entry into force of the said Regulation this exclusive right passed to the Commission (Reg. No. 17, Art. 9(1)). A decision to issue a declaration under E.E.C., Art. 85(3) can only be taken once the Commission has been notified of the agreement concerned. Regulation No. 17 therefore provides for the notification of agreements, distinguishing between agreements which existed when the Regulation entered into force (13 March 1962) – for the new Member States this date will be six months after the date of accession – and new agreements which should, as was pointed out above, be notified on the date they become effective, since the exemption will not enter into force before the date of the notification (Reg. No. 17, Art. 6(1)). Consequently, if a new agreement becomes effective for instance on 1 January 1974 and the Commission is notified on 1 July 1974, a decision granting dispensation cannot become effective before this last date, which means that the agreement is to be considered void (E.E.C., Art. 85(2)) between 1 January 1974 and 1 July 1974.

Once an agreement has been notified in accordance with Articles 4 or 5 of Regulation No. 17, it is " provisionally valid," while agreements which are exempted from notification in pursuance of Arts. 4(2) or 5(2) of the said Regulation are " valid " (see above " Article 85 "). For the latter, even if the exemption of Article 85(3) were refused, Article 85(2) would only become applicable as from the date of the decision[28]; for the former, if exemption is refused they will be void for as long as they existed but at the earliest from 13 March 1962 onwards[29]; if exemption is granted the Commission indicates the date from which the exemption shall take effect (Reg. No. 17, Art. 6(1)).

Exemptions must be limited in time and may have certain conditions and stipulations attached[30] (Reg. No. 17, Art. 8). They may be renewed but also revoked.

[28] See *Bilger* case, judgment of 18 March 1970, case 43–69, Rec. XVI, 127.

[29] Since Reg. No. 17 only became effective on 13 March 1962, the Commission cannot find that an agreement is void before that date, since it is only from that date on that the Commission can apply Art. 85(3); however, Member States are still free to declare an agreement void before that date in pursuance of E.E.C., Art. 88 (see however Reg. No. 17, Art. 9(3)).

[30] See the following decisions: *Transocean* (J.O. 163/67) imposing notification of all further agreements and of reports on the activities; *EEMO* (J.O. L 69, 1969), *Omega* (J.O. L 242, 1970) and *Cematex* (J.O. L 227, 1971) requiring the notification of all cases in which accession is refused or *Henkel-Colgate* (J.O. L 14, 1972) requiring the undertakings to keep the Commission informed as to their licensing policy.

Examples of decisions granting exemptions are: *ACEC/Berliet*,[31] *Machine-Tools Exhibition*,[32] *Jaz-Peter*[33] and *Omega*.[34]

2–135. (d) *Fines and penalties* (Reg. No. 17, Arts. 15, 16): in two cases fines have been imposed for infringement of Article 85(1)[35] and in one case for submitting " in incomplete form . . . the books or other business documents required."[36]

RELATIONSHIP BETWEEN COMMUNITY AND NATIONAL COMPETITION RULES

2–136. Article 9(3) of Regulation No. 17 provides that as long as the Commission has not initiated any procedure pursuant to Articles 2 (negative clearance), 3 (infringement) or 6 (exemption), the authorities of the Member States remain competent to apply Articles 85(1) and 86 in accordance with E.E.C., Art. 88. Neither the E.E.C. treaty nor Regulation No. 17 say anything however about the application by the national authorities of their own national anti-trust legislation.

2–137. In its judgment of 13 February 1969,[37] the Court of Justice had to answer the question whether or not both Community and national law could be applied simultaneously to the same agreement. The Court held that in principle this is possible, but that respect for the object of the Treaty implies that such a simultaneous application of national regulations can only be accepted in so far as the uniform implementation of the Community provisions is not thereby put into jeopardy, since Community law has precedence above national law. With this " golden rule " it should be possible to solve all questions regarding the possibility of applying national law to agreements to which Articles 85 or 86 also apply. So for instance, once the Commission has made it known (Reg. No. 17, Art. 19) that it intends to grant an exemption under E.E.C., Art. 85(3) or once it has effectively granted such an exemption, national authorities

[31] J.O. L 201, 1968.
[32] J.O. L 69, 1969.
[33] J.O. L 195, 1969.
[34] J.O. L 242, 1970.
[35] *Chemiefarma*, J.O. L 192, 1969 and *Aniline*, J.O. L 195, 1969. In the first case, fines ranged from 10,000 to 210,000 units of account (= approx. one U.S. $); in the second case from 40 to 50,000.
[36] See Special Report on Competition, 1972, § 99; the fine amounted to 4,000 units of account. See also Bulletin 11–1971.
[37] Rec. XV, 1, case 14/68.

may no longer prohibit or declare void the agreement concerned on the basis of their national law, otherwise this agreement would be void in one Member State and valid in all the others. In the same way the national authorities may not declare valid an agreement which was found by the Commission to be prohibited by E.E.C., Art. 85(1). However, when applying national law, national authorities are under no obligation to take into account possible infringement of Community law, as long as the Commission has not opened proceedings, and nothing prevents those authorities from prohibiting under national law agreements which are void under E.E.C., Art. 85(2) nor from imposing fines upon the concerned undertakings, even if fines were already imposed by the Commission. It is, on the other hand, generally admitted that as soon as the Commission starts proceedings, the national authorities must suspend all national procedures.

COMPETITION RULES APPLICABLE TO MEMBER STATES

2–138. Three sets of provisions contain rules regarding measures of organs of Member States which may affect competition and interstate trade: Article 37 (State monopolies), Article 90 (public undertakings) and Articles 92 to 94 (State aids).

STATE MONOPOLIES OF A COMMERCIAL CHARACTER (Art. 37)

2–139. E.E.C., Article 37 provides that " Member States shall progressively adjust any State monopolies of a commercial character so as to ensure that when the transitional period has ended no discrimination regarding the conditions under which goods are procured and marketed exists between nationals of Member States "; the second subparagraph describes what is meant by monopolies of a commercial character, namely " any body through which a Member State, in law or in fact, either directly or indirectly supervises, determines or appreciably influences imports or exports between Member States." And indeed, as the Commission points out in its First Report on competition policy " whatever the ultimate goal of the monopoly the effect on imports from other Member States is, in most cases, essentially the same. The object of the exclusive import and sales rights on the national market is to allow the monopoly to decide what quantities of foreign products will be admitted and under what conditions. It is thanks to these exclusive rights that monopolies have been able for instance to prevent all imports, or to limit them either directly or indirectly by imposing more onerous trading conditions on imported products as compared to national ones. The same applies to the exclusive export rights: the monopolies have either prevented exports or imposed different conditions according to their destination; in both cases they thus discriminated against consumers situated in other Member States."

The question has never been solved whether in order to abolish the existing discrimination and to make future discriminations impossible (the French text of Art. 37(1) uses the expression " ensure the exclusion of any discrimination "; the English text[38] " ensure that no discrimination exists " seems more restrictive) the exclusive import, export and trading rights[39] must be abolished. Some have argued that since the treaty refers to " adjust " and since abolition of the exclusive rights would in fact be equivalent to the abolition of the monopoly itself, the answer should be negative. Others have maintained that Article 37 cannot be properly implemented when the exclusive rights remain. The Commission, in the recommendations which it has addressed to the Member States[40] in pursuance of Article 37(6) has expressed the opinion that the abolition of the exclusive rights would be the most effective and therefore the best way to comply with the obligations imposed upon them by Article 37. In several cases, Member States have indeed decided to simply abolish the existing monopolies: with regard to manufactured tobacco the French and Italian Governments have agreed to abolish their monopolies by 31 December 1975; the French Government has also announced the abolition of the matches monopoly and the gunpowder and explosives monopoly; the Italian Government has already abolished the lighter monopoly and informed the Commission that the abolition of the flint, salt and cigarette-paper monopolies will be effective in April 1972. This however still leaves practically unchanged the spirits monopolies in France and Germany (but since Article 37(4) requires equivalent safeguards for the employment and standard of living of the producers concerned, adjustment of these monopolies will have to wait for the establish-

[38] Cmnd. 4864, January 1972.

[39] Since Art. 37(1) only refers to procurement and marketing, production monopolies are not included.

[40] J.O. L 6 and L 31, 1970.

ment of a Common Market Organisation for Spirits), the potash and basic-slag monopolies in France and the matches monopoly in Italy. The matches monopoly in Germany is temporarily protected by E.E.C., Art. 37(5).

Although the time-limit provided for in Article 37(1) is since long passed and all the required adjustments have not yet taken place, the abolition of a certain number of monopolies constitutes in itself an important step towards trade liberalisation.[40a]

PUBLIC UNDERTAKINGS (Art. 90)

2–140. E.E.C., Art. 90(1) provides that in the case of public undertakings and undertakings to which Member States grant special or exclusive rights, Member States shall neither enact nor maintain in force any measure contrary to the rules of the treaty, in particular the rules concerning competition. Much has been written regarding the precise meaning of " public undertakings " and their special role within the Community, but as far as paragraph 1 of Article 90 is concerned one meaning or another does not make any difference. Indeed, Article 90 only provides on the one hand that with regard to obligations imposed upon the Member States, the latter may not through undertakings they control, take measures which would be prohibited had they taken them themselves and, on the other hand, that when such undertakings behave in a way which results in measures which would be prohibited had the Member States themselves taken them, the State is responsible for abolishing those measures. For instance, discrimination in regard to employment in industry on the basis of nationality is prohibited (E.E.C., Art. 48(2)); now, if a nationalised industry were to apply such discrimination either it is the State which has imposed this behaviour on this state-controlled undertaking and thereby violates Articles 48(2) and 90(1) or the undertaking acted on its own initiative and in that case the Member State concerned has failed to impose upon this state-controlled undertaking the obligation to abide by the treaty rules, in that it has maintained in force a measure (or failed to remedy a default) contrary to the rules contained in the treaty (E.E.C., Art. 90(7)).

This rule applies in all cases where a Member State exercises some amount of control over an undertaking either through financial participation in its capital or by granting it special and exclusive

[40a] See Act of accession, Art. 44, concerning new Member States.

rights, such as railways, electricity producers, telecommunications, etc. In case difficulties arise in the implementation of the provisions of Article 90(1), the Commission may address appropriate directives or decisions to Member States (E.E.C., Art. 90(3)).

2–141. Paragraph 2 of Article 90 on the other hand provides an exemption from the application of the treaty obligations in case of undertakings entrusted with the operation of services of general economic interest.[41] This is the case for instance of a national railway company enjoying the exclusive right of rail-transport and thereby preventing other rail-transport undertakings, including those from other Member States from establishing themselves in a given country; normally, this situation would be contrary to E.E.C., Art. 52, but here the application of such rule would "obstruct the performance of the particular task assigned to [it]." However, it is the task of the Commission to ensure that the development of trade is not " affected to such an extent as would be contrary to the interests of the Community," this is of particular importance with regard to the rules on competition.

AIDS GRANTED BY STATES (Arts. 92–94)

2–142. As pointed out at the beginning of this section, competition constitutes an essential instrument of economic development and implies in principle that the undertakings enter upon the market entirely on their own, with their own resources only and at their own risk. These resources can be artificially (*i.e.* through means other than the normal market procedures) increased and this risk artificially reduced not only by agreements between undertakings which for instance allocate market areas, fix prices or guarantee a minimum return (Arts. 85 and 86) but also and probably much more by state aids which reduce either investment or production costs or both, in the form of building grants or fiscal measures or guarantees for loans, for export credits, for exchange rates, etc. Aids therefore, whatever their form or their amount, always modify the conditions of competition, since they place an undertaking in a more favourable position in relation to its competitors; aids consequently also necessarily affect trade between Member States. It is important to note that Article 92 refers to measures favouring " certain " undertakings

[41] See the *GEMA* case where this provision was invoked but the plea rejected by the Commission, J.O. L 134, 1971.

or the production of " certain " goods and that consequently economic measures which apply for instance to all investors in a given country (not area) wherever they invest, do not constitute aids under E.E.C., Art. 92 since they benefit indiscriminately all investors and not " certain " investors. The same applies to infrastructure, whether economic, commercial, social or cultural; since they profit everybody they do not constitute " specific distortions." The inequalities resulting from such nationwide economic measures can only be abolished through approximation of legislation, not through competition policy.

2–143. If state aids proper affect competition and interstate trade, they also constitute an instrument of structural development policy when certain legitimate objectives of economic growth cannot be attained by the sole interplay of the market forces (or not within an acceptable time-limit) or would cause unacceptable social frictions.

E.E.C., Art. 92 therefore establishes the principle of incompatibility of state aids with the common market (para. 1), but furthermore provides for certain categories of aids (rather loosely defined) which either are or may be considered by the Commission to be compatible with the common market.[42]

Article 93(3) consequently provides that " the Commission shall be informed, in sufficient time to enable it to submit its comments on any plan to grant or alter aid." The Commission can then decide whether or not the intended measures are compatible with the common market. If it considers this is not so " it shall without delay initiate the procedure provided for in paragraph 2." This procedure consists in " giving notice to the parties concerned[43] to submit their comments " and afterwards in a determination by the Commission, in case these comments do not modify its opinion, that the aid must be altered. When the Commission initiates such a procedure, the Member State concerned may not put its proposed measures into effect until this procedure has resulted in a final decision, unless the Council, on the application of this Member State, acting unani-

[42] Any aid therefore not falling into one of these categories is automatically prohibited, see for instance J.O. L 10, 1972.

[43] The parties concerned are not only the Member States but any third party which might find its competitiveness on the common market put in jeopardy by aids granted to competitors. Therefore the Commission has in certain cases published a notice concerning proposed aids in the Official Journal. See for instance: J.O. C 32, 1971.

mously, decides that " the aid which that State intends to grant shall be considered to be compatible with the common market " (Art. 93(2), third sub-para.).

2–144. A first series of aids which are automatically compatible with the common market are defined in Article 90(2), they are aids having a social character, aids to make good the damage caused by natural disaster and aids granted in Germany to areas affected by the division of the country. Although the treaty provides that these aids are " compatible," it is the Commission's task to verify whether the conditions required for granting such aids are indeed fulfilled. Of much greater importance, is the power granted to the Commission by Article 92(3) to declare compatible with the common market regional development aids, aids destined to promote projects of European interest or to remedy serious disturbances in the economy and sectoral aids, *i.e.* aids destined to develop a given economic activity.

In regard to " regional development aids " the treaty distinguishes between the development of underdeveloped or backward areas (E.E.C., Art. 92(3)(*a*)) and other areas where aids for development are needed (E.E.C., Art. 92(3)(*c*)). Legally speaking the difference resides in the fact that where the latter are concerned aids may " not adversely affect trading conditions to an extent contrary to the common interest," whereas no such condition is provided for the backward areas.

2–145. The *regional development aids* have presented the Commission with considerable problems: the granting of aids has remained a national responsibility and the absence of a Community regional policy has rendered the co-ordination of national policies more difficult. This absence of co-ordination resulted in many cases in conflicting policies whereby Member States seeking to attract new industries into their depressed areas initiated development programmes which not only sought to offer more and better incentives, thereby initiating stiff competition between the Member States or even their regions, but did not take into account the possible repercussions of the proposed measures on their neighbours. The Commission therefore developed, in close liaison with the Member States, co-ordination measures in the form of principles which would apply to regional aids. These principles were embodied in a Notice which the Commission addressed to the Council[44] and which were adopted

[44] See J.O. C 111, 1971.

in the form of a Resolution by the representatives of the Governments of the Member States on 20 October 1971.[45]

In brief, these principles are based on the following elements:

- they apply for the time being only to the so-called central regions, *i.e.* the most industrialised ones of the Community[46];
- aids are not to exceed 20 per cent. of the investment (after taxes);
- the existing aids must be adjusted in order to permit their evaluation (for instance fiscal privileges cannot be evaluated *a priori*);
- the 20 per cent. is a maximum and the Commission will ensure that within this maximum aids will be granted in accordance with the needs of the areas;
- a method will be devised to check the sectoral effects of regional aids;
- finally, in order to allow the Commission to control the implementation of these principles, it must be informed of the most significant cases in which aids were granted.

Applications of these principles are to be found in the *Kohlengesetz* case[47] and the Belgian Law concerning economic development.[48]

2–146. In regard to *aids to certain industries* the Commission's task is generally speaking easier since their scope is much more limited and their measures more clearly defined. In several cases the Commission has sought to establish certain principles which should guide the Member States when setting up aid-systems: this was done for aids to the textile industry (see First Report on competition policy), and for the shipbuilding industry in which case the Commission proposed to the Council the adoption of a Directive establishing inter alia at 10 per cent. the ceiling of aids which the Member States may grant.[49]

[45] See J.O. C 111, 1971.

[46] Presently, these areas cover the entire Community with the exception of the Mezzogiorno, the West and South-West of France and Berlin and the Zonenrandgebiet. Article 154 of the Act of accession provides that the text of the Notice and the Resolution " will be supplemented to take account of the new situation of the Community after accession. . . ."

[47] J.O. L 57, 1971.

[48] J.O. L 105, 1972.

[49] J.O. L 206, 1969.

Finally, the Commission recently considered as compatible with the common market in pursuance of Article 92(3)(*b*) aids given by the Italian Government to remedy the structural consequence of the recent economic depression.[50]

Since the E.E.C. Treaty provides for a limited number of exceptions to the principle of non-compatibility of State aids with the common market, any aid which does not fall in one of those exceptions or which does not fulfil the conditions provided for the application of these exceptions, are prohibited. This is the case for instance with state aids to exports within the common market[51] and with aids financed by a parafiscal tax levied not only on national products but also on imported goods from the Member States.[52]

2–147. In regard to State aids the Commission's activity thus appears not so much as a negative one aimed at implementing a treaty prohibition, but rather as an " incentive " to the co-ordination of the national policies which, generally speaking, fail to take into account the Community's point of view. Therefore, when the Commission submits its comments in pursuance of Article 93(3) or takes a decision provided for in Article 93(2), it is always careful to examine the proposed measure in relation with the objectives the Member State hopes to achieve, whether regional or industrial. It is obvious that it is not always easy to reconcile those national objectives with the requirements of the normal functioning of the common market, especially since the Memorandum the Commission submitted to the Council regarding Regional Policy[53] and Industrial Policy has not resulted yet in establishing a Community policy in those fields.

(g) *Regional policy*

2–148. In regard to regional policy the Commission submitted to the Council on 15 October 1969 a draft decision under E.E.C., Art. 235 to provide the Community with additional instruments to promote regional development. Measures in this field are needed to meet the requirements and consequences of establishing the common market and gradually approximating the Member States' economic policies. It was proposed that the Commission should regularly

[50] Not published.
[51] See cases 6 and 11–69, Rec. XV, 523.
[52] See case 47–69, Rec. XVI, 487.
[53] See Third General Report, 1969, 277.

examine with each Member State, the situation of the regions for which development plans should be drawn up and implemented without delay. The Commission also proposed the setting up of a Standing Regional Development Committee which would examine the regional policy forecasts and general programmes prepared by the Member States and the regional problems in general. To facilitate implementation of the plans submitted to the Standing Committee and approved by the Commission, Community aid might be granted in the form of interest rate rebates or guarantees for loans made by the European Investment Bank; a Regional Development Rebate Fund would be set up. Funds could also be made available by the Guidance Section of the Agricultural Fund, by the Social Fund or under E.C.S.C., Arts. 54, 56.

On 28 May 1971 the Commission submitted to the Council two draft regulations[54] concerning Community activities for regional development. The first one was adopted in March 1972, while the Council expressed a positive reaction in regard to the second. A first step towards a Community Regional Policy was thus made at last.

(h) *Industrial policy*

2–149. Since the objective of State Aids, when not aimed at regional development, is to develop certain economic activities (E.E.C., Art. 92(3)(*c*)) mention should be made here of the Commission's *Memorandum on Industrial Policy*[55] submitted to the Council on 18 March 1970 and proposing principles and guidelines which should govern the Community industrial policy. The five basic lines of policy are the following:

(a) it should enable all undertakings to take full advantage of the existence of a large market;

(b) the work on approximation and standardisation of the legal, fiscal and financial framework within which firms have to operate must be speeded up;

(c) the Memorandum recommends a higher degree of concentration in certain branches of industry;

(d) the fourth basic theme concerns employment and management; and

[54] J.O. C 90, 1971.
[55] See Fourth General Report, 167.

(e) extension of the Community's solidarity to cover external economic relations.

(j) *Tax provision* (Arts. 95–99)

2–150. The objective of the E.E.C. tax provision is to ensure that free movement of goods is not hampered by discriminatory indirect taxation.

E.E.C., Art. 95(1) prohibits the imposition on products imported from other Member States of internal taxes of any kind in excess of those imposed upon similar domestic products; this principle is emphasised in Article 95(2) which prohibits internal taxation of such a nature as to afford protection to national goods. The question of taxation of imported products arises since, in conformity with the provision of the General Agreement for Tariffs and Trade (GATT), indirect taxes are levied by the importing country while the exporting country grants remissions or repayments in respect of exports. In regard to the latter, Article 96 provides that "any repayment of internal taxation shall not exceed the internal taxation imposed on (exported products) whether directly or indirectly." And indeed any repayment in excess of the taxes actually levied would constitute an unfair advantage for the exporter concerned and distort competition while at the same time affecting trade between Member States.

2–151. The repayment of indirect domestic taxes by the exporting country or imposition of countervailing charges by the importing country might run into unsolvable problems in case of a "turnover tax calculated on a cumulative tax system." Article 97 therefore allows, for those cases, the establishment of "average rates for products or groups of products." The second paragraph of this article empowers the Commission to address directives or decisions to Member States when it is of the opinion that the established average rates do not conform to the principles laid down in Articles 95 and 96.[56]

In its judgment of 16 June 1966,[57] the Court of Justice held that E.E.C., Art. 95 constitutes in the field of taxation the indispensable

[56] One such directive was addressed to the Italian Government concerning the indirect taxes on oil, see J.O. L 52, 1969; another concerned agricultural products taxed in Luxemburg, see J.O. L 10, 1969.

[57] Rec. XII, 294 *et seq.*, case 57–65. Important for the interpretation of Art. 95(1) is the judgment of 3 April 1968, case 28–67, Rec. XIV, 212 *et seq.*

foundation of the common market; that Article 95 contains a general rule accompanied by a simple suspensive clause concerning the national provisions in existence at the time it became effective and that it follows that at the end of the set time limit the provisions of Article 95 are applicable without reservation. In regard to Article 95(3), which imposes upon Member States the obligation to repeal or amend not later than at the beginning of the second stage, *i.e.* 1 January 1962 existing provisions which conflict with the rules of Article 95(1) and (2), the Court held that it does not leave the Member States a discretionary power as to the date at which this repeal or amendment must take place and that, past this date, the national judge must enforce the principles of Article 95(1), irrespective of whether or not the Member States have fulfilled their obligation. The Court of Justice concluded that after 1 January 1962 citizens within the Community can ask the national courts to enforce Article 95(1); in other terms, after that date E.E.C., Art. 95(1) was directly applicable.

In regard to E.E.C., Art. 97 the Court of Justice held that it is not directly applicable.[58]

The implementation of Article 95 proved important for certain specific excise duties: the Commission initiated several procedures against Member States (E.E.C., Art. 169) and some of them led to actions before the Court of Justice; see for instance judgments of 14 December 1962, joint cases 2 and 3–62[59] and of 8 July 1965, case 10–65.[60]

2–152. Article 98 refers to charges " other than turnover taxes, excise duties and other forms of indirect taxation ": remission or repayment in case of exports may not be granted and countervailing charges in case of imports may not be imposed, unless previously approved by the Council. Experience has shown that this provision has no practical importance.

2–153. Finally, Article 99 provides for approximation of legislation concerning turnover taxes, excise duties and other forms of indirect taxation; the Commission must submit proposals to the Council which decides unanimously. The Council has issued several directives to implement Article 99; noteworthy are the two directives concerning the establishment of a common added-value tax system

[58] Judgment of 3 April 1968, case 28–67, Rec. XIV, 230–231.
[59] Rec. VIII, 828 *et seq.*
[60] Rec. XI, 607–608.

in the Member States[61] and the directive concerning indirect taxation of capital gathering.[62]

2–154. The E.E.C. treaty does not contain specific provisions in regard to harmonisation of direct taxation, but Article 100 provides the necessary powers; in 1969 the Commission submitted two draft directives to the Council, one concerning the common taxation system applicable to fusions, splits and contribution of assets between companies of different Member States and the other concerning the common taxation system applicable to mother companies and subsidiaries in different Member States.[63]

(k) *Monetary and economic policy*

" the application of procedures by which the economic policies of Member States can be co-ordinated and disequilibria in their balances of payments remedied " (E.E.C., Art. 3 (*g*)).

2–155. The provisions of E.E.C., Arts. 103, 104–109 which are part of Title II " Economic Policy " have been overshadowed by plans for the Community's Economic and Monetary Union which will be analysed later. Mention should be made of the only case in which these treaty provisions were applied: following the French crisis of May and June 1968, the Commission addressed to the French Government, on 5 July 1968, a recommendation based on E.E.C., Art. 108. Finding furthermore that the difficulties facing the French economy proved to be particularly serious, the Commission proposed to the Council that France should be granted the mutual assistance provided for by Article 108; on 20 July 1968 the Council adopted a directive to this effect[64] and in its decisions of 6 and 23 July 1968 the Commission authorised France to adopt exceptional and temporary measures,[65] *inter alia* to re-introduce exchange control for certain capital transactions, impose quota restrictions on imports of certain items and grant temporary aids to exports.[66]

THE PLANS FOR ECONOMIC AND MONETARY UNION[67]

2–156. On 1 and 2 December 1969, the Heads of State or

[61] J.O. 1301/67.
[62] J.O. L 249, 1969.
[63] J.O. C 39, 1969.
[64] J.O. L 189, 1968.
[65] See Second General Report, 1968, 110.
[66] See Judgment in the cases 6 and 11–69, Rec. XV, 523.
[67] See Fourth General Report, 65 and Fifth General Report, section 184.

Government meeting in The Hague instructed the Community Institutions to draw up in 1970, on the basis of the Commission's Memorandum of 12 February 1969, a plan for establishing by stages an economic and monetary union.

On 6 March 1970, the Council invited a Committee, under the chairmanship of Mr. Pierre Werner, the Luxemburg Prime Minister and Minister of Finance to draw up a report that would enable the fundamental choices to be made. An interim report was submitted to the Council which endorsed the joint conclusions on 8 and 9 June and the final report[68] was presented on 8 October 1970. The Memorandum and proposals which the Commission submitted to the Council on 29 October 1970 were based on this Werner Report. The Commissioner's proposals contained a draft Resolution and two draft decisions.

2–157. In a Resolution of 22 March 1971,[69] the Council and the Representatives of the Governments of the Member States expressed their political will to establish a political and monetary union according to a plan in phases starting on 1 January 1971.

The final objective is the establishment of an area within which persons, goods, services and capital will freely move forming an individualised entity within the international system and having in the economic and monetary field, powers and responsibilities allowing its institutions to administer the union. Community instruments will be created whenever necessary.

The resolution contains provisions relating to the realisation of the first stage starting on 1 January 1971 and ending on 31 December 1973:

- the strengthening of the co-ordination of short-term economic policies;
- the accelerated establishment of effective freedom of movement of persons, goods, services and capital *inter alia* by approximation of certain taxes, of the structure of company taxes, and by the adoption of a directive concerning the issue of shares, etc.;
- measures in the regional and structural fields;
- the reinforcement of co-ordination of monetary and credit policies;

[68] Both reports are published in the Bulletin, see Nos. 7 and 11–70, and in J.O. C 94, 1970 and C 136, 1970.

[69] J.O. C 28, 1971.

- the adoption of joint positions in monetary relations with third countries;
- an invitation addressed to the Central Banks to narrow the fluctuations of exchange rates;
- the possible establishment of a European Fund for monetary co-operation.

2–158. As for the Council's *decision concerning the strengthening of co-ordination of the short-term economic policies of the Member States*[70] it provides for three annual Council meetings devoted *inter alia* to defining quantitative guidelines for the national budgets before these are adopted.

2–159. In its *decision concerning the strengthening of co-ordination between the Central Banks of the Member States*, the Council invites them *inter alia* to establish the general principles to be followed by each one of them in regard to bank liquidity, credit conditions and levels of interest rates.

2–160. On 22 March 1971 the Council also adopted a *decision concerning medium-term financial assistance*; it provides that when a Member State encounters balance of payment difficulties it can ask for this assistance; the Council decides by qualified majority. According to the European Communities Bill, the United Kingdom has accepted a maximum lending obligation under this scheme of 250 million pounds.

These various measures constitute a beginning of closer co-operation not only within the Community, but also in regard to relations with third countries as was shown by the various decisions taken by the Council in the second half of 1971 following the dollar crisis.[71]

(l) *Approximation of laws* (Arts. 100–102)

" the approximation of laws of Member States to the extent required for the proper functioning of the common market " (E.E.C., Art. 3(*h*)).

2–161. There exists a fundamental distinction between E.E.C.,

[70] J.O. L 73, 1971.
[71] See Fifth General Report, 1971, ss. 190 *et seq.*

Art. 100 which provides for approximation of laws which directly affect the establishment or functioning of the common market and the Articles 101 and 102 which provide for the elimination of distortions of the conditions of competition in the common market resulting from differences between national legislations.

Free movement of goods is hampered, even after abolition of all customs barriers, by fiscal barriers. Here also, as with all measures which discriminate according to country of origin, a distinction must be made between specific distortions which are prohibited by E.E.C., Arts. 95–99 and general distortions which can only be abolished through approximation of legislation in pursuance of E.E.C., Arts. 100–102. General distortions however do not result from fiscal measures alone, there are many domains in which existing national legislation creates differences of treatment which prevent a proper functioning of the common market: this is the case with technical obstacles to trade, with legislation concerning patents, trade-marks, etc.

For each one of these domains the Commission has submitted to the Council working programmes and often also formal proposals for measures to be adopted.

2–162. Not only is approximation of legislation required for the establishment of the common market, but also for its proper functioning. In the section devoted to competition policy, it was shown how the capacity of an undertaking to compete on the market is partly determined by the " economic climate " in which it operates; this climate is the sum of all the legislative, administrative and other measures which influence its production costs such as: prices, salaries, system of credit, rebates, rates of interest, depreciation, taxation, etc. It is clear that as long as the national measures regarding these elements have not been harmonised, there will not exist a real unified market. E.E.C., Art. 100 refers to " provisions laid down by law, regulation and administrative action " in Member States (which) directly affect the establishment or functioning of the common market." When amendment to national legislation as distinguished from mere administrative regulations is involved the Assembly and Economic and Social Committee must be consulted. Since the powers conferred on the Community institutions by E.E.C., Art. 100 are very broad and general, the procedural requirements laid down are far more stringent than those presented by Article 101 which is limited to cases of distortion of competition.

Also, the directives provided for under Article 100 are addressed to several Member States; in the case of Article 101, only one Member State may be concerned.

2–163. When the differences between the national laws not only affect the establishment or functioning of the common market, but are "distorting the conditions of competition in the Common Market and . . . need to be eliminated" then the Council can, acting on a proposal from the Commission which has first tried to have the Member States voluntarily eliminate the distortions, issue the necessary directives by a qualified majority (E.E.C., Art. 101); it will be remembered that for "approximation" of laws under Article 100 a unanimous vote is required; in the case of distortions (Article 101) of competition there is no reference to "approximation" of laws, only to elimination of the distortion in question.

As was pointed out above in section (c) concerning the abolition of obstacles to freedom of movement for persons, services and capital, approximation of law, or at least of administrative measures and practices, is also required to ensure the abolition of existing restrictions on freedom of establishment within the Community (E.E.C., Art. 54); the same applies to freedom to supply services (E.E.C., Art. 63). Both articles provide, as do Articles 100 and 101, for the Council to issue directives after consultation of the Economic and Social Committee.

Lists of the directives issued by the Community are to be found in the yearly General Reports; they cover a wide variety of matters, such as production activities, including farming, processing, contractors, wholesale and retail trade, insurance and banking, personnel and business services, the technical, medical, legal and cultural professions, free movement of workers, fiscal laws, social laws, food legislation and last but not least company law.

(m) *Social policy* (Arts. 117–128)

"the creation of a European Social Fund in order to improve employment opportunities for workers and to contribute to the raising of their standard of living" (E.E.C., Art. 3(*i*)).

2–164. The second and third paragraphs of the Preamble to the E.E.C. treaty refer to "social progress" and to the fact that "the essential objective of the efforts of the Member States is the constant improvement of the living and working conditions of their peoples."

It follows that this is also the essential objective of the European Communities as such, their underlying and constant preoccupation in all their activities: what is indeed the use of steady expansion, balanced trade, fair competition, economic development if the ensuing prosperity is not going to increase the well-being of the peoples concerned.[72] Therefore, if the words " social," " welfare " or " well-being " do not appear in the great majority of the treaty provisions, it is not because this aspect was overlooked, but simply because it " goes without saying " that all the activities and measures provided for are aimed at improving the living conditions, not only of the peoples of the Community, but also of others and in the first place of the associated " overseas countries." Essential in this respect is therefore the correlation between social policy and the other Community policies; an overall picture of the Community's manifold economic activities with social implications and the work being done in regard to them is given in the reports submitted by the Commission to the Assembly.[73]

But beside this general, more human, objective, there are specific social problems whose solution should be made easier by the establishment and functioning of a common market.

2–165. E.E.C., Art. 117 assigns as an objective of the social measures to be enforced at Community level, the improvement of working conditions and of the standard of living for workers. The instruments for achieving this aim are

– the harmonisation of social systems through the functioning of the common market: it was seen above how the " freedom of movement of workers " is one of the elements making up the common market and although this abolition of all obstacles to free movement of workers was based on purely economic reasons, it is clear that when implemented, it will have improved the working conditions by widening the choices for employment and permitting close co-operation between trade unions which should strengthen their bargaining position.[74] Mention was already made of the regulations concerning social security

[72] See Third Medium-term Economic Policy Programme which refers to " lasting betterment of the welfare of the Community's citizens, J.O. L 49, 1971.

[73] See for instance Fourth General Report 1970, sections 102 *et seq.*

[74] It is surprising however how little actual co-operation has been achieved between the various national workers' organisations.

of migrating workers: Regulation No. 3 was completely revised in 1971 and became Regulation 1408/71[75]; the revision of the implementing Regulation No. 4 has not yet been completed, thus preventing the Regulation 1408/71 from becoming effective;

- the procedures provided for in the treaty: Article 118 for instance provides for the Commission to promote close co-operation between Member States in the social field, particularly in matters relating to employment, labour law and working conditions, social security, right of association, etc. To facilitate this co-operation, the Commission shall make studies, deliver opinions and arrange consultations.

  Relations with management and labour are understandably of the utmost importance in this respect for the Community: in this framework the Commission set up the Standing Committee on Employment[76];

- the approximation of provisions laid down by law, regulation or administrative action; as was seen in the preceding section, this can be done in pursuance of either E.E.C., Art. 100 or 101.

2–166. Another important social provision is to be found in Article 119 which imposes upon the Member States to ensure and maintain the application of the principle that men and women should receive equal pay for equal work. Although the treaty has set a time limit for fulfilling this obligation (first stage) it appears to be an area where traditionalism presents a barrier.

To underline the importance of the Community's social policy, Article 122 requires the Commission to include a separate chapter on social developments within the Community in its annual report to the Assembly.

2–167. E.E.C., Art. 128 provides for a "*common vocational training policy*" capable of contributing to a harmonious development both of the national economies and of the common market. General principles were laid down by the Council acting on a proposal from the Commission and after consultation with the Economic

[75] J.O. L 149, 1971.
[76] See Fourth General Report, 1970, section 103.

and Social Committee, in 1963.[77] Mention should also be made of the European career brief on the training of skilled machine-tool operators, of minimum levels of training for drivers of goods and passenger vehicles, etc.[78]

2–168. On 26 July 1971 the Council adopted " guidelines for the elaboration of a programme of activities at Community level, in the field of vocational training " and on the basis of these guidelines the Commission has started in close liaison with the Member States to establish such a programme.

THE EUROPEAN SOCIAL FUND (Arts. 123–127)

2–169. The task of the Fund is to render the employment of workers easier and to increase their geographical and occupational mobility within the Community. The Social Fund is the instrument by which the Community can implement some of the objectives assigned to it by the treaty, just as the European Investment Bank which will be examined hereafter constitutes an instrument for implementing some of the economic objectives.

The financial means of the Fund are provided via the Community's budget by the Member States, previously according to a special scale (see E.E.C., Art. 200(2)) and special weighted votes of the members of the Council (see E.E.C., Art. 203(5)), but since 1 January 1971 the Fund is financed first in part and from 1975 on entirely by the Community's own resources.[79]

The Fund's task is rather limited since most of its interventions are dictated by actions of the Member States. Indeed, its main function is limited to paying 50 per cent. of the expenditure incurred by a State or a body governed by public law for the purpose of ensuring re-employment or aiding the unemployed (E.E.C., Art. 125(1)). The refunding takes place under the conditions provided in implementing provisions laid down by the Council in pursuance of Article 127.[80] In 1971 refunds totalled 56.5 million units of account. Only in regard to " granting aids for the benefit of workers whose employment is reduced or temporarily suspended, in whole or in

77 J.O. 1338/63.
78 For more information on all these subjects, consult the General Reports on the activities of the Community.
79 See Chap. 5: Financial Provisions.
80 See Reg. 9/60, J.O. 1189/60, modified by Reg. 47/63, J.O. 1605/63 and by Reg. 12/64, J.O. 537/64. See also decision of the Commission implementing Art. 18 of Reg. 9/60, J.O. L 44, 1968.

part, as a result of the conversion of an undertaking to other production" does the Commission play a certain role, since aids are only paid when the Commission has approved the conversion.

In pursuance of Article 126(*b*) which provides that the Council may assign new tasks to the Fund, the Commission submitted proposals on 4 June 1969. On 1 February 1971 the Council formally confirmed its decision of 26 November 1970[81] concerning reform.[82] The Fund is now assigned two separate functions with separate implementing arrangements: on the one hand to facilitate the carrying out of Community policies in accordance with *ad hoc* Council decisions and on the other hand to help overcome current difficulties hindering the smooth development of the Community; at least 50 per cent. of the money will be employed for these purposes.

(n) *The European Investment Bank* (Arts. 129–130)

"the establishment of a European Investment Bank to facilitate the economic expansion of the Community by opening fresh resources" (E.E.C., Art. 3(*j*)).

2–170. Article 129 establishes a European Investment Bank with legal personality, whose members are the Member States. The statute which was laid down in a Protocol annexed to the E.E.C. treaty was extensively amended by the treaty of accession, Protocol No. 1.[83]

The Bank operates on a non-profit making basis: it grants loans and gives guarantees to facilitate the financing in all sectors of the economy:

(a) of development projects in less developed regions,

(b) of the modernisation or conversion of undertakings or for the development of fresh activities which cannot be financed by the various means available in the individual Member States and

(c) of projects of common interest to several Member States.

Before deciding on the financing of a given project, the Bank must secure the opinion of the Commission (Protocol on the Statute, Art. 21(2)); when the Commission delivers an unfavourable opinion, the Board of Directors may not grant the loan or guarantee unless its

[81] J.O. L 28, 1971.
[82] See Bulletin 9/10–70, Pt. I, Chap. III.
[83] Cmnd. 4862–I, 77.

decision is unanimous (the director nominated by the Commission abstaining).

2–171. The Bank is directed and managed by a Board of Governors, a Board of Directors and a Management Committee. The Board of Governors consists of the Ministers designated by the Member States and exercises the powers provided in Article 9(3) of the Statute. It also lays down general directives for the credit policy of the Bank (Statute, Art. 9(2)) and may decide that the Member States shall grant the Bank interest-bearing loans (Statute, Art. 6). Voting by the Board of Governors is the same as for the Council (E.E.C., Art. 148, and Act of accession, Art. 14).

The Board of Directors consists of twelve directors and twelve alternates (Statute, Art. 11); under the treaty of accession this becomes Articles 19 and 10 (Protocol No. 1, Art. 6). The Board of Directors has sole power to take decisions in respect of granting loans and guarantees, raising loans and fixing interest rates.

As for the management committee, it consists of a President and two Vice-Presidents appointed for six years by the Board of Governors (four Vice-Presidents under Article 9 of Protocol No. 1 to the Act of accession).

According to its last report, the Bank has granted loans for a total sum of 2.316 million units of account, divided among 269 projects.

2–172. The capital of the Bank is of one thousand million units of account subscribed by the Member States as provided for under Article 4(1) of the Statute. The second paragraph of said Article provides that " the admission of a new member shall entail an increase in the subscribed capital corresponding to the capital brought in by the new member." According to the European Communities Bill, the United Kingdom will make a contribution equal to those of France and Germany. These payments will be made in sterling in five equal instalments over a period of two and a half years from the date of accession, and are estimated to amount to about £55 million.

(o) *Association with overseas countries* (Arts. 131–136)

" the association of the overseas countries and territories in order to increase trade and to promote jointly economic and social development " (Art. 3(*k*)).

2–173. According to paragraph 7 of the Preamble to the E.E.C. treaty, the Member States intend " to confirm the solidarity which binds Europe and the overseas countries " and desire " to ensure the development of their prosperity, in accordance with the principles of the Charter of the United Nations." Consequently, the Member States decided to " associate with the Community the non-European countries and territories which have special relations with Belgium, France, Italy and The Netherlands " (Norway and the United Kingdom are added by Act of accession, Art. 24(1)). These countries and territories are listed in Annex IV to the E.E.C. treaty (this list is extended under Act of accession, Art. 24(2)). Written at a time when most of these countries and territories were dependent, the principle of association was maintained after they gained independence.

2–174. The second Yaoundé Convention,[84] concluded with these countries in 1969, entered into force on 1 January 1971.[85] Basically this convention is the same as the First Yaoundé Convention which became effective on 1 June 1964. The institutions are the Association Council, the Association Committee and the Parliamentary Conference of the Association. Besides provisions concerning the right of establishment, it provides mainly on the one hand for the establishment of a free trade area between the Community and the Associated States, each side reserving the right to make some exceptions (this entitles the Associated State to reimpose duties and quantitative restrictions or even to suspend imports of a particular product), and on the other hand for financial and technical cooperation. The aim of the latter is to give aid for investments in the form of loans from the European Development Fund and of ordinary loans from the European Investment Bank; the five-year appropriation amounts to 918 million units of account. Together with the Convention an Internal Agreement on the financing and administration of Community Aid was signed.

In pursuance of Articles 109 and 115(1) of the Act of accession, the above mentioned Convention is not to apply between the new Member States and the States associated with the Community, until 31 January 1975. For the interim period see Articles 109 to 114 of said Act.

[84] See Third General Report, 1969, section 348.

[85] This Convention is referred to as " Convention of Association between the European Economic Community and the African and Malagasy States associated with that Community."

2–175. Similar Conventions were concluded between the E.E.C. and the *United Republic of Tanzania, the Republic of Uganda and the Republic of Kenya* (24 September 1969); together with this Association the parties also signed an Internal Agreement on measures to be taken and procedures to be followed for implementing the agreement establishing the said Convention.

Another association agreement signed with Nigeria never became effective.

(p) *External relations*

2–176. Although mentioned neither in the Preamble of the treaty, nor in Article 3 which enumerates the activities of the Community, the relations of the Community with third countries constitute one of its more important activities. The relations examined under the previous section constitute since the associated states have become independent " external relations " identical to those with other third countries.[86] Relations with non-member countries are referred to in Articles 113, 114, 228 to 231 and 238. In its judgment of 31 March 1971 (case 22–70) the Court of Justice held that " in the field of external relations, the Community enjoys the capacity to establish contractual links with third States within the whole scope of the field covered by the objectives specified in the first part of the treaty and of which the sixth part constitutes the prolongation . . . that such a competence does not only follow from an explicit attribution under the treaty – as in the case under Articles 113 and 114 for tariff and commercial agreements and under Article 238 for agreements of association – but can also follow from other treaty provisions and acts of the institutions based upon these provisions."[87]

2–177. *Article* 228 lays down the procedure to be followed for the conclusion of agreements between the Community and one or more States or international organisations: they are negotiated by the Commission and concluded by the Council, acting unanimously, after consultation of the Assembly " when required by this Treaty." An example is the first agreement with Israel.[87a]

[86] The question whether the Yaoundé Conventions were concluded under Art. 136 or under Art. 238 was never settled. The Conventions simply refer to the treaty.
[87] Rec. XVII, 274 (case 14–16).
[87a] J.O. 1517/64; see also J.O. L 183, 1970.

2–178. *Article* 229 instructs the Commission to maintain relations with the organs of the United Nations, its specialised agencies and with the General Agreement on Tariffs and Trade and generally with all international organisations, whilst *Articles* 230 *and* 231 provide for co-operation with the Council of Europe and the Organization for European Economic Co-operation.

Under those Articles agreements were concluded with the International Labour Office,[88] the Central Commission for Navigation on the Rhine,[89] the Food and Agricultural Organization[90] and the Committee of Ministers of the Council of Europe.[91]

2–179. *Article* 238 turned out to be the most important of all these provisions; it provides for the conclusion of agreements *inter alia* with a third State establishing " an association involving reciprocal rights and obligations, common action and special procedures." These agreements are concluded by the Council acting unanimously after consulting the Assembly.

In fact two kinds of association have been established (1) those with countries which are expected to become full members in due course (this is presently the case with Greece[92] and Turkey[93] and probably in the near future with the EFTA-countries which do not become members of the Communities), and (2) those with less-developed countries for whom membership is not envisaged; see agreements with Morocco,[94] Tunisia,[95] and Malta.[96]

Mention must also be made of the Memorandum on a Community policy for co-operation in development[97] and of various commercial agreements based upon article 113 such as those with Iran,[98] the Lebanon[99], Argentine[1] and Spain.[2]

2–180. Article 108 of the Act of accession provides that from the date of accession, the new Member States shall apply the pro-

[88] J.O. 521/59.
[89] J.O. 1027/61.
[90] See Sixth General Report, section 256.
[91] Not yet published.
[92] J.O. 294/63.
[93] J.O. 3687/64.
[94] J.O. L 197, 1969.
[95] J.O. L 198, 1969.
[96] J.O. L 61, 1971.
[97] See Fifth General Report, section 433.
[98] J.O. L 262, 1971.
[99] J.O. L 181, 1971.
[1] J.O. L 249, 1971.
[2] J.O. L 182, 1970.

visions of the agreements concluded with Greece, Turkey, Tunisia, Morocco, Israel, Spain and Malta, taking into account the transitional measures and adjustments which may appear necessary and which will be the subject of protocols to be concluded with the co-operating third countries and annexed to those agreements.

CHAPTER 3

THE INSTITUTIONS OF THE COMMUNITIES

3–1. The first European Institutions – Assembly, Council, High Authority and Court – were set up under the Paris treaty of 1951 and although the centre of gravity originally vested in the High Authority – an institution composed of independent members – has shifted to the Council, composed of national cabinet Ministers, a similar structure was set up by the Rome Treaties for the E.E.C. and for Euratom. The result would therefore have been three Assemblies, three Councils, three Commissions (High Authority) and three Courts, had not a Convention[1] signed the same day as the Rome treaties provided for only one Assembly and one Court for both the E.E.C. and Euratom[2] and for this single Assembly and single Court to replace the E.C.S.C. Assembly and Court.[3] None the less, this left three Councils and three Commissions (High Authority) beside the one Court and one Assembly: a total of eight institutions. A further rationalisation was introduced by the Merger treaty of 1965, entering into force on 1 July 1967 a year before the completion of the Customs Union; Articles 1 and 9 provide for the establishment respectively of "a Council of the European Communities" and "a Commission of the European Communities," taking the place of the existing Councils and Commissions (High Authority) of the E.C.S.C., E.E.C. and Euratom, and exercising "the powers and competences devolving upon these institutions under the conditions laid down in the treaties establishing respectively the E.C.S.C., the E.E.C. and the Euratom." The treaty of accession of 22 January 1972 has not modified that structure in any way; it only provides for increases in the number of members of each institution in order to accommodate nationals from the new Member States.

[1] Convention relating to certain Institutions common to the European Communities of 25 March 1957.
[2] *Ibid.*, Arts. 1, 3.
[3] *Ibid.*, Arts. 2, 4.

I. THE ASSEMBLY (EUROPEAN PARLIAMENT)

3–2. All the above mentioned treaties[4] (E.C.S.C., E.E.C., Euratom, Merger and Accession) refer to an " Assembly " which shall exercise advisory and supervisory powers. In a resolution of 30 March 1962[5] the Assembly decided to call itself " European Parliament " and within the Communities themselves all the Institutions, except the Council, have adopted that name; so does the British Government in its White Papers.[6] Even the Court in its judgments has, since 1959,[7] used the term " Parliamentary Assembly " or " Parliament."

Whether the Assembly was well advised in changing its name can be questioned, not so much because this institution lacks the powers that are characteristic of democratic parliaments, *i.e.* the powers to legislate and to raise taxes, besides controlling the Administration, but by doing so it has created the illusion that democratic control already exists within the Communities, while on the other hand this same institution has been clamouring for years to get real powers. As it happens it is precisely the Council, the only institution opposed to enlarging the powers of the Assembly – since this could only be done at the cost of the Council's own powers – which by constantly referring to the " Assembly " reminds everybody of the fact that there is not sufficient democratic control within the Community. If this last statement is largely correct, the political weight of the Assembly should not however be entirely overlooked.

1. Members of Parliament

3–3. The Assembly consists, according to E.E.C., Art. 137[8] " of representatives of the peoples of the States brought together in the Community." The Court of Justice considered this fact when it

[4] See also the treaty amending certain Budgetary Provisions of the Treaties establishing the European Community and of the Treaty establishing a Single Council and a Single Commission of the European Communities. Cmnd. 4867, 1972.

[5] J.O. 1045/62. Earlier, on 20 March 1958, the Assembly had decided to call itself " European Parliamentary Assembly," J.O. 6/58.

[6] See for instance Cmnd. 4289, para. 8 and Cmnd. 4715, para. 72. There is no reference to the Assembly in the European Communities Bill.

[7] Opinion of 17 December 1959, Rec. V, 562.

[8] Identical provisions are to be found in the other two European treaties establishing the E.C.S.C. (Art. 20) and Euratom (Art. 107); since this is the case for most provisions regarding the institutions, reference will only be made hereinafter to the E.E.C. Treaty.

found that the E.E.C. treaty was " more than an agreement creating mutual obligations between the contracting states "; this opinion was confirmed – in the view of the Court – by the " Preamble to the Treaty which beyond the governments, addresses itself to the peoples . . . [and] that furthermore one must note that the citizens of the States brought together in the Community are called upon to participate, by means of the European Parliament and the Economic and Social Committee, in the activities of this Community."[9] But are the citizens really represented in the Assembly, do they really participate in the Community activities? Indirectly, yes, directly, no. And indeed, E.E.C., Art. 138 provides that " the Assembly shall consist of delegates who shall be designated by the respective Parliaments from among their members[10] in accordance with the procedure laid down by each Member State." In The Netherlands for instance a royal decree of 11 February 1958 provides that the delegates shall be nominated by both Houses, according to a procedure jointly laid down by them; in fact, the members of parliament empowered the speakers to define this procedure and nominations are made purely on party lines, each party[11] receiving a quota reflecting its actual strength in Parliament, taking into account furthermore the relative number of members of Senate and Chamber of Representatives. But whatever the technicalities of the procedures, in each country it is the relative strength of the national political parties which determines the number of " their " European delegates and therefore it is actually the national political parties which are represented in the Assembly of the European Communities and not the citizens. The European delegates then have no direct mandate

[9] Rec. IX, 23 and C.M.L.Rev. 1963, 129.

[10] The question has been asked whether or not a delegate to the Assembly who ceases to be a member of the national Parliament automatically loses his membership of the European Assembly; one answer is that the treaty only seems to require national membership at the time of nomination; but Art. 5(1) of the rules of procedure of the Assembly provides that membership ceases with the end of the national mandate. But these rules cannot modify a treaty provision! In practice, delegates who lose their quality of national M.P. no longer attend the sessions in Strasbourg. Another question is whether the Assembly has the right to challenge the right of delegates to sit in the Assembly once they have been designated by their national Parliament. The answer seems to be negative and the provisions of Art. 4 of the rules of procedure therefore appear as a pure formality.

[11] Except for Italy since 1968, no Member State allows their Communist Party to send members to Strasbourg, the reasoning behind this being, that these parties had vowed to destroy the Communities and it would therefore have been contradictory to send them to the Assembly to participate in the activities of the Communities.

to sit in Strasbourg; their election to the national parliament had nothing to do with the concrete problems of the European Communities which are to be discussed by the Assembly.

3–4. The draftsmen of the European treaties were of course conscious of this discrepancy and they provided, therefore that " the Assembly shall draw up proposals for elections by direct universal suffrage in accordance with a uniform procedure in all Member States " (E.E.C., Art. 138(3)). Although the subject is regularly brought up[12] and proposals have been laid before the Council,[13] no action has been taken as yet. It is the Council which must, acting " unanimously, lay down the appropriate provisions which it shall recommend to Member States for adoption in accordance with their respective constitutional requirements " (E.E.C., Art. 138(3)). The provisions of Article 138(3) call for two remarks: (1) there is no time-limit laid down in the E.E.C. treaty for making this recommendation and (2) since the elections must be organised in accordance with a uniform procedure there is no use in submitting to national parliaments' procedures for direct election which are not accepted by all the Member States. Even if a national parliament were to decide that the Assembly delegates from their country would be directly elected, the individuals so chosen could not sit in Strasbourg unless they were at the same time members of the national parliament (E.E.C., Art. 138(1)); this would limit eligibility in these elections to national M.P.s and this in turn raises the question whether such elections would be " elections by direct universal suffrage " (E.E.C., Art. 138(3)). The answer is negative.

As for the number of delegates, Article 10[14] of the Act of accession provides that Germany, France, Italy and Great Britain will each have thirty-six, Belgium and The Netherlands fourteen, Denmark, Ireland and Norway ten and Luxemburg six, the total being 208. As mentioned before, the provisional seat of the Assembly is in Strasbourg, but the General Secretariat and its services are established in Luxemburg![15] Under the E.E.C. treaty, Germany, France and

[12] On 22 October 1958, the Political Commission of the Assembly created a " Working Group for European Elections."

[13] On 17 May 1960 the Assembly adopted a draft convention for election of the European Parliament by direct universal suffrage, this draft convention was then sent to the Council, J.O. 834/60.

[14] This Art. 10 at the same time abolishes E.C.S.C., Art. 21, E.E.C., Art. 138(2), and Euratom, Art. 108.

[15] See Arts. 4 and 12 of the Decision of the Representatives of the Governments of the Member States on the provisional location of certain institutions and departments of the Communities, of 8 April 1965, Cmnd. 4866, 23.

Italy have thirty-six delegates, Belgium and The Netherlands fourteen and Luxemburg six.[16]

3–5. The internal organisation of the Assembly is comparable to that of any national parliament; it is based on a double structure: the political parties and the parliamentary commissions. In the Assembly of the Six there are four political groups, from left to right, the Socialists (thirty-seven in February 1972), the Christian Democrats (fifty-one), the Liberals with affiliates (twenty-four) and the European Democratic Union established by the Gaullist delegates (nineteen); nineteen delegates are not affiliated with a group. The rules of procedure[17] of the Assembly require a minimum membership of fourteen for the formation of a political group.[18] This explains why there is no Communist group.

With regard to the parliamentary commissions, Article 37 of the rules of procedure provides for standing or temporary, general or special commissions which can be set up by the Assembly which determines their task. At the moment there are twelve standing commissions.[19]

3–6. The Assembly holds "an annual session," it "meets automatically on the second Tuesday in March" (Merger treaty, Art. 27(1)). Article 9 of the Protocol attached to the Merger treaty provides that "Members of the Assembly shall not be subject to any form of inquiry, detention or legal proceedings in respect of opinions expressed or votes cast by them in the performance of their duties." Furthermore, by virtue of Article 10 of the same treaty, they shall enjoy "during the sessions of the Assembly" in the territory of their own State, the immunities accorded to members of their parliament." This added protection can be very useful as two Luxemburg M.P.s found out when a case was brought against them in a Luxemburg court at a time when their national parliament was not in session; they claimed immunity under the above mentioned

[16] This relatively large number of delegates for small countries was accepted in order to allow most national political parties to be represented.

[17] See E.E.C., Art. 142, "The Assembly shall adopt its rules of procedure, acting by a majority of its members."

[18] See Art. 36(5) of the rules of procedure, J.O. 2437/62, which provides that 17 members are required; this number was later reduced to 14 to accommodate the Gaullists, J.O. 280, 1967. Latest modification to be found in J.O. C 55, 1971.

[19] The political Commission, the economic –, the finance and budget –, the agricultural –, the social and public health –, the external economic relations –, the legal –, the Commission for energy, research and nuclear questions –, the transport –, the Commission for the association with Greece, *idem* for Turkey and the Commission for the relations with the African countries and Madagascar.

provisions although the European Assembly had not been actually convened in Strasbourg at the time the action for which they were being sued took place. The question arose whether the Assembly could nevertheless be considered to be in session. The question was referred to the European Court which decided that subject to the opening and closing dates Parliament must be considered " in session," even when it is not in fact assembled, until the yearly or extraordinary sessions are closed.[20]

2. Powers of the Assembly

3–7. The Assembly – according to E.E.C., Art. 137 – shall exercise the advisory and supervisory powers which are conferred upon it by the treaty. It follows, as was pointed out above, that " unlike a Parliament, it has no power to legislate and thus to impose its policy," nor does it possess " the power of the purse " in the parliamentary sense.[21]

When the Assembly exercises its powers, it acts, except when otherwise provided for in the treaty,[22] by an absolute majority of the votes cast (E.E.C., Art. 141); the required quorum[23] is laid down in the rules of procedure. What are exactly those advisory and supervisory powers? The Assembly fulfils an *advisory* function each time it uses its right to express *opinions* and make recommendations. Since E.E.C., Art. 137 refers to the advisory powers " which are conferred upon it by the Treaty," the question can be asked whether the Assembly does have the power to deliver opinions also in cases not explicitly mentioned in the treaty, the more so since Article 155 which refers to the powers of the Commission provides for the right to formulate recommendations or give opinions on matters within the scope of this treaty, " if it expressly so provides or if the Commission considers it necessary." Furthermore, as expressed by the terms " within the terms of the Treaty " (E.C.S.C., Art. 8) and " under the conditions . . . envisaged in this Treaty " (E.E.C.,

[20] Judgment of 12 May 1964, Rec. X, 381, case 101–63.
[21] Stein and Hay, *Law and Institutions in the Atlantic Area*, 1967, 100.
[22] See E.C.S.C., Art. 95 and E.E.C., Art. 144.
[23] Art. 33(2) of the rules of procedure provides that there is a quorum when the majority of the members is present; but, knowing by their national experience how difficult it is to assemble so many members, the next paragraphs provide that votes, except the nominal votes, are always valid whatever the number of voters, when the speaker has not been formally requested before the vote to ascertain the number of members present.

Art. 3), it is a fundamental treaty rule that the institutions only have those powers which are explicitly provided for. It is true that the Court of Justice has, in one or two instances, admitted that " without indulging in extensive interpretation," one can apply a principle of interpretation admitted both in international and in national law according to which rules established by international agreement or by law are considered to imply those rules without which the first either would have no sense or could not be reasonably or successfully applied,"[24] but the principle remains. However, it seems that what the above mentioned rule refers to is powers to bind Member States, individuals or enterprises and therefore not " opinions " and " recommendations " which according to E.E.C., Art. 189 " have no binding force." The conclusion therefore is that the Assembly is free to formulate recommendations and to deliver opinions whenever it considers this necessary. Generally speaking this is done in the form of " resolutions."

3–8. The advisory powers of the Assembly also play an important role in the decision-making process of the Communities. There are for instance twenty-three cases in which the E.E.C. treaty[25] requires *consultation* of the Assembly as part of the process leading to a formal decision, regulation or directive of the Council. Generally speaking the treaty provides for consultation on all important matters such as Community policies (agriculture, transport, competition, etc.); there is no consultation however on the admittance of new members to the Community. It is up to the Council to consult the Assembly on the proposals which are submitted to it by the Commission. This requirement is one of the " basic procedural rules " referred to in E.E.C., Art. 173 and violation of such rules is a ground for annulment of decisions, directives and regulations.[26] For this reason also the treaty provides that these acts " shall refer[27] to any proposals or opinions which were required to be obtained pursuant to this

[24] Judgment of 29 November 1956, Rec. II, 305, case 8–55. Another example can be found in a judgment of the same date, Rec. II, 360, case 9–55.

[25] See E.E.C. treaty, Arts. 7, 14(7), 43(2), 54(1), (2), 56(2), 57(1), (2), 63(1), (2), 75(1), 87(1), 100, 106(3), 126, 127, 133(2), 201, 212, 228(1), 235, 236 and 238. In the Euratom treaty consultation must take place under Arts. 31, 32, 76, 85, 90, 96, 98, 173, 186, 203, 204 and 206. The E.C.S.C. treaty does not provide for consultation of the Assembly. The Council has often consulted the Assembly in cases where this was not required by the treaty.

[26] See Chap. 5, I, for further details about these acts.

[27] The simple reference is not necessarily sufficient, the Court may also examine whether the Assembly has indeed been consulted on all the points which were to be submitted; see judgment of 11 February 1955, Rec. I, 221, case 6–54.

treaty " (E.E.C., Art. 190). The opinions thus expressed by the Assembly are given further weight by E.E.C., Art. 149: " As long as the Council has not acted, the Commission may alter its original proposal, in particular where the Assembly has been consulted on that proposal." The role of the Assembly in the decision-making process of the Communities is thus clearly defined, but also the limitations of this role: indeed the Commission is " free " to take the expressed opinion into account and consequently in case of a negative opinion to modify its original proposal, but it is in no way bound to do so. Nor does the Commission (or the Council for that matter) have to explain why it does not heed the opinion of the Assembly and finally, if mention must be made of the fact that the Assembly was consulted, the treaty does not require the decision-making institution to mention whether the expressed opinion was positive or negative or to refute, in case of a negative one, the arguments brought forward by the Assembly. This was clearly stated by the Court of Justice in one of its earlier judgments.[28] Finally, it should be noted that if the Commission does not itself modify its proposal on the basis of the Assembly's opinion, the Council can do so, but then only with a unanimous vote, since E.E.C., Art. 149 provides that " where, in pursuance of this treaty, the Council acts on a proposal from the Commission, unanimity shall be required for an act constituting an amendment to that proposal."

3–9. If the Assembly has no real powers when it acts in its advisory capacity, it has, on the other hand, real *supervisory* powers with regard to the Commission. Not only must the Commission " reply orally or in writing to questions put to it by the Assembly or by its members " (E.E.C., Art. 140) and not only must the Commission " publish annually, not later than one month before the opening of the session of the Assembly, a general report on the activities of the Community " (E.E.C., Art. 156) which is discussed in open session by the Assembly (E.E.C., Art. 143), but the " European Parliament " can force the members of the Commission to resign as a body (E.E.C., Art. 144) and finally, should the Council or the Commission, in infringement of the treaty, fail to act, the Assembly may, under E.E.C., Art. 175 " bring an action before the Court of Justice to have the infringement established."

[28] See judgment of 11 February 1955, Rec. I, 220, case 6–54.

3–10. The right to *put questions* has been widely used[29] and their influence on the outlining of the Community policies should certainly not be underestimated. It is nevertheless difficult to compare the Community's practice with the national parliamentary procedures, since most questions put by members of the Assembly are in writing – this is due to the fact that the European Parliament assembles in Strasbourg only during a few days every year so that oral questions to the Commission or Council[30] are necessarily very limited; answering a written question is a cumbersome procedure, since it must be prepared by the staff, formally accepted by the Commission or Council (only the Institution itself has legal and political existence, not its members who therefore, unlike cabinet ministers, cannot answer written questions), translated into three other languages (soon six), informally discussed with the other institution, Council or Commission, and finally sent to the Assembly and published in the Official Journal: very cumbersome and time-consuming indeed.

3–11. As for the yearly discussion of the Community's general report, it has no real political or other consequences, but it gives the Assembly a good opportunity for a general discussion during which it can voice its desires, criticisms and preoccupations with regard to specific activities of the Institutions. On the other hand, it should be noted that these general reports are an invaluable source of information for students of the Communities not only as to facts but also with regard to policies, programmes and forecasts; it is surprising how much information is actually made available in these reports.

3–12. By far the most impressive power vested in the European Assembly is its right to force the resignation of the Commission at any time[31] by a *motion of censure*. E.E.C., Art. 144 provides that " if a motion of censure on the activities of the Commission is tabled before it the Assembly shall not vote thereon until at least three days

[29] Several hundred questions are asked every year which might seem a very small number indeed compared to the thirty thousand which are according to William Pickles, raised in the House of Commons during a normal year (Cox, " Study of European Institutions, *etc*.") quoted by Stein and Hay, *op. cit*., 102.

[30] E.E.C., Art. 140 provides that the Commission shall reply to the questions put to it and no mention is made of the Council, but Arts. 44, 45 and 46 of the Assembly's rules of procedure refer to the right to put questions also to the Council. In practice, the latter has never refused to answer questions of the Assembly; one can therefore consider this as a common law development within the Communities.

[31] Under the E.C.S.C. treaty such a vote could only be taken on the annual general report submitted by the High Authority, see E.C.S.C., Art. 24.

after the motion has been tabled and only by open vote." This procedure underlines the gravity of the consequences of such a vote by giving members " time to reflect "; other essential requirements are a two-thirds majority of the votes cast and the presence[32] of a majority of the members. Drastic as it sounds, even this power is more apparent than real since it only concerns the Commission. The consequences are twofold: in the first place, it is not the Commission who bears the ultimate responsibility for the Community's decisions, but the Council, and although in most instances the latter can only act on the basis of a proposal put before it by the Commission, the Council is not entirely bound by the contents of the proposal since it may adopt amendments to that proposal unanimously (E.E.C., Art. 149); therefore, although the Council is the decision-making institution, it remains outside the Assembly's control. In the second place, a vote of censure might very well remain without any practical consequences: E.E.C., Art. 144 provides that after the members of the Commission have been forced to resign as a body " they shall continue to deal with current business until they are replaced in accordance with Article 158." Pursuant to this article the members of the Commission are appointed by common accord of the Governments of the Member States. Therefore, if the origin of the motion of censure is an act of the Council which the Assembly is thus trying to reach through the Commission, it could very well be that the Governments, whose representatives form the Council, refuse to designate new members for the Commission or simply re-appoint the same Commissioners. In the first case the Commission would then be reduced to deal with current business only and in the second case the motion of the Assembly will have had no effect whatsoever except that in both instances the final result would be a loss of prestige for the Community as a whole. The motion of censure of the European Assembly, although analogous to a vote of confidence known in national parliaments, can thus not have the same effects.

3–13. The real influence of an institution can of course not be judged on the basis of legal provisions alone. As it appears, the political groups in the Assembly have over the years developed policy positions and " a number of representatives have acquired

[32] E.E.C., Art. 144 refers to a two-thirds majority of the votes cast " representing a majority of the members of the Assembly "; since, according to Article 34 of the rules of procedure, the right to vote is a personal right and cannot be delegated, the majority of the members has to be personally present to carry a motion of censure.

considerable expertise and, as a result some Assembly Committees are capable of producing policy reports whose impact promises to exceed that which the formal powers of the Assembly would give them."[33] Nevertheless it is doubtful whether the delegates of the European Assembly have as such played an important role in Community affairs, and if some do take an active and influential part in the Community's activities it might very well be because of the role they play in their own parliament: indeed the cabinet Ministers who form the Council cannot simply ignore the position taken by people they will have to face in their own parliaments under sometimes very different conditions indeed. For its own status it seems therefore that the present composition (*i.e.* members of the national parliaments) of the European Assembly confers upon this institution practical political powers which it might very well no longer enjoy if its members, because of direct popular election, were to be chosen outside the traditional political parties whose backing they would then lack. It follows that election by universal suffrage only has sense if at the same time the formal powers of the Assembly are increased; this however seems unlikely to happen very soon.

3–14. The conclusion is that at the present time there exists, within the European Communities, a not too effective democratic (= parliamentary) control over the activities of the institutions; this role is to be fulfilled by the national parliaments in as much as the national ministers are responsible before them for their actions as members of the Council. However, owing to the fact that the Communities were entrusted with limited powers and especially in view of the strict legal control exercised by the Court over every activity of the institution, it does not seem that the present structure of the European Communities constitutes a great danger to democratic traditions.

II. The Council

3–15. At the beginning of this Chapter 3 it was mentioned that with the E.E.C. and Euratom treaties the centre of gravity shifted from the institution composed of independent members to the Council, composed of representatives of the Governments of the Member States (Merger treaty, Art. 2). This shift results from the

[33] Stein and Hay, *op. cit.*, p. 100–101.

various provisions describing the tasks of the institutions: under the E.C.S.C. treaty it is " the duty of the High Authority to ensure that the objectives set out in this Treaty are attained in accordance with the provisions thereof" (E.C.S.C., Art. 8), while the Council exercises its powers "in particular in order to harmonize the action of the High Authority and that of the Governments which (since the E.C.S.C. treaty only integrates two economic sectors) are (= remain) responsible for the general economic policy of their countries" (E.C.S.C., Art. 26). For the E.E.C. treaty it is the responsibility of the Council " to ensure that the objectives set out in this Treaty are attained" (E.E.C., Art. 145), while the Commission simply is " to ensure the proper functioning and development of the common market"; it follows that the establishment of the common market and of the other policies rests with the Council.

1. Members of the Council

3–16. E.E.C., Art. 146 was abolished by the Merger treaty of 1965 and replaced by Article 2 of said treaty; the first paragraph of both articles are identical: " The Council shall consist of representatives of the Member States. Each Government shall delegate to it one of its members." The only problem that could arise concerns the question who is a member of a government since most continental governments have what is known as "*secrétaires d'état*"; in practice, it is up to each Member State to determine who is and who is not a " member," since there are no " credentials."

As for the term " one " in this Article 2, it simply indicates that each Member State normally[34] has one vote[35] and not that only one member of the Government may attend the sessions of the Council; in fact, at the so-called " general " Council meetings, Member States are generally represented by two or three ministers while the special council meetings (agriculture, transport, etc.) are attended by one member of each government. Consequently, it is not unusual to have various council meetings going on at the same time.

The second paragraph of Article 2 of the Merger treaty as modified by Article 110 of the Act of accession provides that " each member of the Council in turn in the following order of Member

[34] See para. 3 below: Voting procedure.

[35] Any member of the Council may act as proxy for not more than one other member (E.E.C., Art. 150).

States: Belgium, Denmark, Germany, France, Ireland, Italy, Luxemburg, Netherlands, Norway, United Kingdom" shall hold the office of President for a term of six months.

2. Tasks of the Council

3–17. The Council exercises the powers and jurisdiction conferred on the E.C.S.C., Euratom and E.E.C. Councils under the conditions laid down in the treaties establishing respectively the E.C.S.C., Euratom and the E.E.C. (Merger treaty, Art. 1(2)). The E.E.C. treaty describes the tasks of the Council in its Article 145: "To ensure that the objectives set out in this Treaty are attained, the Council shall in accordance with the provisions of this Treaty:

- ensure co-ordination of the general economic policies of the Member States;
- have power to take decisions."

It was pointed out above that the first sentence of this article entrusts the Council with the main task in implementing the European treaties and also that this task may only be carried out in accordance with the treaty provisions. As with the other Community institutions, the Council has no general law-making power ("power to take decisions") it may use to fulfil its mission, but only those powers which are explicitly provided in the various treaty provisions.

It will be remembered that in Chapter 2, IV, (a), the analysis of E.E.C., Art. 2 showed that the treaty provides for two means to fulfil the various tasks assigned to the Community and that one of these is the approximation of the economic policies of Member States, the other being the establishment of a common market. For the latter the treaty itself provides numerous more or less precise rules of a rather technical nature whose implementation automatically entails the "establishment" of the common market. When this implementation calls for "legislation" it is generally speaking up to the Council to use its "power to take decisions" and to issue the necessary decisions, regulations and directives[36] and it is the Commission's main task to ensure that this common market, once established in accordance with the Treaty provisions, works efficiently and develops satisfactorily (E.E.C., Art. 155). Roughly speaking

[36] See Chap. 5, IV.

the corresponding activities of the institutions are dealt with in Part Two of the E.E.C. treaty: " Foundations of the Community." It was also pointed out that the approximation of economic policies is much less defined and is a question of policy, rather than of law-making. It is this policy-making which is described as the main task of the Council under E.E.C., Art. 145, and once again roughly speaking, the corresponding activities of the Community are spelled out in Part Three of the E.E.C. treaty: " Policy of the Community," which covers such topics as approximation of laws, policy relating to economic trends, commercial policy and social policy. All these activities have been examined in some detail in the previous Chapter.

3. Voting procedure

3–18. The basic rule is that " the Council shall act by a majority of its members " except where otherwise provided for in the treaty (E.E.C., Art. 148). Since most provisions do provide otherwise, the general rule is in fact the exception; the other voting procedures are (1) a qualified majority when acting on a proposal from the Commission, (2) a qualified majority when acting without such a proposal and (3) the unanimous vote. In many cases the treaty provides for a unanimous vote during a certain period after the date of entry into force of the treaty and a qualified majority vote afterwards.[37]

3–19. Where the Council is required to act by a *qualified majority*, the votes of its members shall be weighted as follows: Germany, France, Italy and the United Kingdom each ten, Belgium and the Netherlands five, Denmark, Ireland and Norway three and Luxemburg two; total sixty-one.[38] Now, when the treaty requires that the act of the Council be taken on a proposal from the Commission – as was seen this is normally the case – and the voting calls for a qualified majority the adoption shall require forty-three votes. This means that the " big four " can never impose their will, but also that two big member states can veto any decision, in other words can never be overruled. When, on the other hand, the treaty does

[37] This was the case under E.E.C., Arts. 28, 33, 42–44, 54, 56, 57, 63, 69, 75, 87, 101 and 111–114.

[38] Under E.E.C., Art. 148 the votes are weighted as follows: France, Germany and Italy 4, Belgium and the Netherlands 2, Luxemburg 1, the special majority being 12 votes or 12 votes cast by 4 members.

not provide for a Commission proposal,[39] the required qualified majority is still forty-three, but votes must then be cast by at least six members, in other words a majority of the Member States.

3–20. Finally, in those cases where a *unanimous vote* is required,[40] the treaty specifies that " abstentions by members present in person or represented shall not prevent the adoption by the Council of acts which require unanimity " (E.E.C., Art. 148(3)). As was pointed out above, unanimity is also required when the Council acting on a proposal from the Commission, wants to amend it (E.E.C., Art. 49).

3–21. At this point mention must be made of an arrangement regarding majority voting adopted by the Council at its meeting of 28 and 29 January 1966[41] in Luxemburg, normally referred to as the " Luxemburg Agreement." This agreement ended the most serious crisis the Communities have known in their twenty years of existence, which occurred in June 1965 when the Commission submitted a rather ambitious proposal to the Council providing for the definitive establishment of the common agricultural policy linked with the introduction of direct revenue for the Communities and increased budgetary powers for the Assembly. For various reasons the French Government (read: De Gaulle) took offence and embarked upon the so-called " empty-chair " policy (absence from all non-technical meetings). This Luxemburg agreement concerns both the collaboration between the Council and the Commission and majority voting; the latter is recorded in full hereafter:

1. In the event of decisions that can be adopted by majority on the proposal of the Commission, when very important interests of one or several partners are at stake, the members of the Council will attempt, within a reasonable period of time, to arrive at solutions that could be adopted by all members of the Council in respect of their mutual interest and those of the Community, in accordance with Article 2 of the treaty.

2. With regard to the preceding paragraph, the French delegation considers that, when very important interests are at stake, discussion must be continued until unanimous agreement has been reached.

3. The six delegations acknowledge that a difference of opinion

[39] This is the case for instance under Arts. 73(2), 106(2), 108(2) and (3), 109(3), 111, 113, 114, 154 and 206.
[40] For instance Arts. 14(7), 45(3), 59, 76, 93(2), 136, 188, 200, 223, 227.
[41] See Bulletin No. 3, 1966, 5.

remains on what should be done in the event conciliation cannot be fully attained.[42]

4. The six delegations nonetheless consider that this difference of opinion does not prevent the resumption, according to normal procedure, of the Community's work.

There seems to be no doubt about the content of the agreement, namely that on very important questions, the Member States should try to reach unanimity; the disagreement concerns the next stage, *i.e.* what happens if after a reasonable time-limit unanimity is not reached? For five Member States the rules of the treaty then apply and decisions can be taken with qualified majority; for France discussion should continue until unanimity exists.[43] It is obvious that in taking this position France is refusing to apply the treaty rules and thus violating its obligations, although technically speaking there is no violation in the sense of E.E.C., Art. 169 as long as such a decision has not been adopted with a qualified majority and France has refused to abide by it. Such a case has not yet presented itself. But the whole attitude is clearly one of refusing to observe the rules previously agreed upon.

3–22. From the brief description of the Council's tasks it follows that the governments of the Member States have retained very wide powers indeed in regard to Community affairs; one might even wonder whether the transfer of sovereign powers to which the Court of Justice referred in several judgments has really taken place since Member States are in fact never overruled. The answer simply is that political reality cannot be moulded by legal formulæ. There is no doubt that a strict application of the latter could in certain cases lead to majority decisions imposing upon a Member State obligations which it deems contrary to its material interest, but no provision can force the other Member States to take such a majority decision if they prefer, for political reasons, to arrive at a unanimous one. And unanimous decisions require mutual concessions; whether or not those can be made is a political decision which every government

[42] This is why this agreement was called an " agreement to disagree."

[43] There seems therefore to be an error of interpretation in the statement of the British Government according to which " on a question where a Government considers that vital national interests are involved it is established that the decision should be unanimous " (Cmnd. 4715, 29). It might be so that in the past questions that were implicitly recognised as being important were always decided by unanimous vote, but is it " established " that it should be so? The statement under para. 70 of the same document is therefore more correct: "... where Member States' vital interests are at stake, it is Community practice to proceed only by unanimity."

must make in view of its Community obligations and its domestic political position.

4. The permanent representatives[44]

3–23. The Committee of Permanent Representatives moved in a few years from semi-obscurity to full limelight; it fulfils a task which even the wording of the Merger treaty does not adequately express. In the E.C.S.C. treaty there is no mention whatsoever of such a Committee, but from 1953 on there existed a co-ordination Committee (C.O.C.O.R.) composed of civil servants which met to prepare the Council meetings and fulfilled an important role. The E.E.C. and Euratom treaties mention under Article 151 (121) that the Council shall lay down its rules of procedure and that these rules " may provide for the setting up of a committee consisting of representatives of the Member States. The Council shall determine the duties and powers of that committee." This was done in Article 16 of the rules of procedure: the task of this committee is to prepare the activities of the Council and to implement the mandates of the Council; it can create working groups; the Commission is invited to be represented at its meetings and it is chaired by the delegate of the Member States whose representative exercises the office of President of the Council.

3–24. The Committee of Permanent Representatives is a subordinate organ of the Council and not a gathering of deputies of the members of the Council; in other words, it has no powers of decision on the Community level and the Council cannot delegate such powers to it. Van der Meulen, who has been the Belgian Permanent Representative for many years, describes the members of the Committee as high civil servants with the rank of ambassador; they represent their country but unlike the members of the Council, they are not members of their government. Therefore they are not political figures.[45]

3–25. The essential task of the Committee is, as was mentioned earlier, to prepare the work of the Council; it is of interest to know

[44] For more details, see Noel, " The Committee of Permanent Representatives," *Journal of Common Market Studies*, V, 3, 1967, 1167.

[45] Van der Meulen, " la Commission de Coordination, le Comité des Représentants Permanents et le Secrétariat Général du Conseil," *Droit des Communautés Européennes*, 1969, § 709.

that this preparation is carried out in close co-operation with the Commission on the one hand and national civil servants on the other. The importance of this preparatory activity is stressed by the fact that when agreement is reached at the ambassador's level, the points in question are submitted to the Council as " point A "; the custom is that the Council then broadly accepts all the solutions arrived at and thereby transforms them into legal acts as provided for under E.E.C., Art. 189. It must however be underlined that the Council is in no way bound to accept the " A points " and any member is free to ask for a discussion of any subject, in which case, that subject is placed on the agenda of the next meeting. Once again there exists no decision-making power of the Permanent Representatives not even by way of the indirect approach of the " A points."

Generally speaking it can be said that the Permanent Representative fulfils a double function: he defends the national interest of his country within the Communities and at the same time he fights for the Community's viewpoint at home: he is thus the link between the national administration and the European institutions.

5. The powers of the Council

3–26. The decision-making powers of the Council are mainly used in the following areas: legislation, finance and international agreements.

When the Council enacts Community *legislation*, through regulations, directives and decisions,[46] it in fact continues the work of the draftsmen of the treaties. This is particularly true for the E.E.C. treaty which in many respects contains no more than general principles to guide the Community law makers and the necessary rules of procedure. Examples are the agricultural policy: E.E.C., Art. 39 sets out the " objectives " of the common agricultural policy, while Article 43 provides that " the Council shall on a proposal from the Commission and after consulting the Assembly, acting unanimously . . . make regulations, issue directives, or take decisions "; the free movement of labour: E.E.C., Arts. 48, 49; the right of establishment: E.E.C., Art. 54; the freedom of supply of services: E.E.C., Art. 63; the free movement of capital: E.E.C., Art. 69; transport: E.E.C., Art. 75; the rules of competition: E.E.C., Art. 87; the approximation of laws: E.E.C., Art. 100.

[46] See Chap. 5, I.

The powers of the Council in *financial* (budgetary) matters will be examined in some detail in the next Chapter (Chapter 4: Financial Provisions).

As for the *international agreements* to be entered into by the Communities, E.E.C., Art. 228 provides that agreements between the Community and one or more states or an international organisation shall be negotiated by the Commission, but " concluded by the Council "; these agreements are " binding on the Institutions of the Community and on the Member States " (E.E.C., Art. 228(2)).

Also with regard to new members, it is by now well known that applications must be sent to the Council which " shall act unanimously after obtaining the opinion of the Commission " (E.E.C., Art. 237).

Finally, mention should be made of the fact that the Council must also lay down its rules of procedure (Merger treaty, Art. 5). This was done on 15 April 1958 (not published in the Official Journal). The rules provide among other things that the Council meetings are not public (Art. 3(*a*)); that the Commission is normally present unless the Council decides otherwise (Art. 3(*b*)); indications of the form any measures should take (Arts. 10–14); that the discussions are secret (Art. 18).

III. The Commission

3–27. The task, powers and composition of the Commission of the European Communities are defined in E.E.C., Art. 155 and Merger treaty, Arts. 9–19 as modified by the Articles 15 and 16 of the Act of accession. The present Commission which, since 1 July 1967, has replaced the High Authority of the E.C.S.C. and the E.E.C. and Euratom Commissions, exercises the powers and jurisdiction conferred on those institutions in accordance with the provisions of the treaties establishing the E.C.S.C., the E.E.C. and the E.A.E.C., and of the Merger treaty (Merger treaty, Art. 9).

1. The European Commissioners

3–28. The High Authority was composed of nine members (E.C.S.C., Art. 9), the E.E.C. Commission of nine also (E.E.C., Art. 157) and the Euratom Commission of five (Euratom, Art. 126). This total of twenty-three Commissioners was reduced to fourteen by the Merger treaty (Art. 32) when the above mentioned institutions were replaced by the Commission of the European Communities (1 July 1967). Three years later this number was reduced to nine (Merger treaty, Arts. 10 and 32). At the time the treaty of accession enters into force (1 January 1973) the number of Commissioners will be modified once more: Article 15 of the Act of accession, which substitutes a new paragraph for Article 10(1) of the Merger treaty, provides that " the Commission shall consist of fourteen members, who shall be chosen on the grounds of their general competence and whose independence is beyond doubt."[47] They are appointed by " common accord[48] of the Governments of Member States " and " their term of office shall be four years.[49] It shall be renewable." (Merger treaty, Art. 11).

3–29. *The requirements for designation* as European Commissioner are very generally defined; besides the fact that the members of the Commission must have the nationality[50] of one of the Member States and that they are not eligible when already two compatriots are members, the treaty provides that members shall " be chosen on the grounds of their general competence " – this obviously has no precise meaning – " and whose independence is beyond doubt " – (Merger treaty, Art. 10(1)).

All the European treaties are very explicit indeed with regard to the conditions required for the *performance of duties*. This is particularly important, since it underlines the independence the Commission as such must have within the institutional framework of the Communities: the Commission represents the Communities' general

[47] Art. 10(1) provides furthermore that " the number of members of the Commission may be amended by the Council, acting unanimously."

[48] There are two well known cases where such agreement was not reached: the first concerned Mr. Hirsch, President of Euratom, of French nationality and whose mandate the French Government refused to renew, although the other five member states wanted to do so. The second case concerns Herr Hallstein who after the 1965 " crisis " became " *persona non grata* " for the same government, again against the wish of the other partners.

[49] The mandate of the members who were appointed on 1 July 1970 was therefore to expire on 1 July 1974, but since the Commission is to be enlarged following the accession of four new Member States on 1 January 1973, the members " volunteered " to jointly resign on 31 December 1972, thereby giving the governments a free hand in their choice of the 14 members.

[50] The treaty also requires that " the Commission must include at least one national of each of the Member States" (Merger treaty, Art. 10(1)); this raises the question whether the Commission's activities could be blocked by a Member State refusing to designate one of its nationals; the answer simply is that this requirement is not a conditio sine qua non for the functioning of this institution. The same applies when no agreement can be reached on the designation of certain members.

interests and must be in a position to take a stand against any government which tries to put national interests first. This function can only be accomplished when the members of the Commission are totally independent of national governments, especially their own.[51] It must be remembered that it is in connection with this independent position that the E.C.S.C. treaty used the term " supranational ": the members of the High Authority " will refrain from any action incompatible with the supranational character of their duties. Each Member State undertakes to respect the supranational character . . ." (E.C.S.C., Art. 9).[52] And although the word did not reappear in later European treaties the substance of the concept as described in the E.C.S.C. treaty was never modified. Article 10 of the Merger treaty uses the same words to specify what is meant by " independence ": " the members of the Commission shall in the general interest of the Communities, be completely independent in the performance of their duties. In the performance of these duties, they shall neither seek nor take instructions from any Government or from any other body. They shall refrain from any action incompatible with their duties." Consequently " the members of the Commission may not, during their term in office, engage in any other occupation, whether gainful or not."[53] And again to underline the importance of these obligations, the members of the Commission, " when entering upon their duties, shall give a solemn undertaking[54] that, both during and after their term of office, they will respect the obligations arising therefrom." Finally, the treaty even provides that " in the event of any breach of these obligations, the Court of Justice may on application by the Council or the Commission, rule that the member concerned be, according to the circumstances, either compulsorily

[51] It is the author's opinion that the present system is not ideal in this respect and that total independence of the Commission's members – whose mandate can only be prolonged if their government so desire and all the others concur – could be better guaranteed if the Commission's members were to be paid full salaries in case of non-renewal of their mandate, until they found an equivalent position elsewhere.

[52] It is the only European treaty provision using this term which has raised so many controversies; but here again it is not the word which counts but the concept it tries to express.

[53] If participating in national elections is not an " occupation " in the sense of Merger treaty, Art. 10(2), one may wonder however whether or not this action is " incompatible " with the nature of their duty. The same applies to the Commission's civil servants.

[54] This undertaking is given by the new members during a special session of the Court of Justice, which adds solemnity to the occasion.

retired . . . or deprived of his right to a pension or other benefits in its stead " (Merger treaty, Art. 10(2)). See also Merger treaty, Art. 13 concerning the competence of the Court to compulsorily retire a member in case of serious misconduct. Nowhere else do the treaties go into such details with regard not only to the duties of office of members of institutions but also to the obligations of the Member States themselves: " Each Member State undertakes to respect this principle (of independence) and not to seek to influence the members of the Commission in the performance of their tasks" (Merger treaty, Art. 10(2), 2nd para.). The reason for all this " concern " is, as was pointed out above, the fact that the independence of the Commission and its role as guardian of the general interest of the Communities plays a role in the determination of the voting procedure in the Council: when the treaty requires a proposal of the Commission for the Council to act, a majority of twelve (after accession forty-three) weighted votes is sufficient; if no proposal is required then twelve (forty-three) cast by four (six) Member States are needed (E.E.C., Art. 155 as amended by Act of accession, Art. 14).

3–30. A President and three (after accession five) Vice-Presidents are appointed from among the members for a period of two years by common accord of the Governments of the Member States. Their appointment may be renewed (Merger treaty, Art. 14).

2. The Commission's task and powers

3–31. Generally speaking the task of the Commission is " to ensure the proper functioning and development of the common market " (E.E.C., Art. 155). To accomplish this task the Commission

(1) watches over the application of the Community legislation;
(2) may formulate recommendations and deliver opinions;
(3) takes decisions and participates in the decision-making process of the Council;
(4) exercises the powers conferred on it by the Council.

3–32. The principal function probably is *to ensure that the Community provisions are applied.* Since the European treaties and the acts taken by the institutions under these treaties impose obligations on the Member States and the undertakings operating within the Community,[55] the Commission was given certain powers with regard to the Member States as well as the undertakings. So, when the Commission finds that a Member State has not fulfilled an obligation under the Community legislation, it will in the first place remind the Government in question of its duties and request it to take the measures necessary to ensure conformity with treaty provisions. If this informal approach remains unsuccessful, the Commission will start a formal procedure against the Member State, in accordance with E.E.C., Art. 169. This procedure develops in three stages. First, the Commission will formally (by letter) state that it considers that the Member State has failed to fulfil such or such obligation arising out of the treaty or another binding act and give the state a short period (usually one month) to submit its comments. Secondly, if the Member State does not answer, or does not give a satisfactory answer, the Commission issues a " reasoned " opinion on the matter, ordering the State to fulfil its obligations within a certain time-limit. Thirdly, if the Member State does not comply with the terms of such opinion within the period laid down by the Commission, the latter may refer the matter to the Court of Justice (E.E.C., Art. 169). If the Court of Justice finds that the Member State has indeed failed to fulfil any of its obligations[56] under the treaty, such state is bound to take the measures required for the implementation of the judgment of the Court (E.E.C., Art. 171). The next step is left to the Member State concerned, since there are no ways to force a Member State to fulfil its obligations under the treaty, at least no legal coercive ways.[57] However, the more advanced the economic integration of the Member States, the more difficult it becomes for one of them to break the rules, since each Member State is in some way or other dependent on the good will of its partners for implementing the various common policies. If the violation were to cause severe damage to the economy of another Member State, one could imagine certain protective measures being taken by the latter, but as to the question whether or not it could invoke the " principle of reciprocity " in a case before the Court, in the sense

[55] See for instance Chap. 2, IV, 2, Competition policy. For a definition of " undertaking " see also E.E.C., Art. 58.

[56] In the past 20 years 19 of such judgments have been rendered by the Court; see Fifth General Report, Chap. VII.

[57] Some kind of coercive measures are provided for by the E.C.S.C. treaty, but they were never applied; see E.C.S.C., Art. 88.

that the Member State could justify its violation on the ground that a Community institution or a Member State has not fulfilled its own obligation, the answer will be negative.[58]

In certain cases the procedure set out above is slightly modified; so for instance when the Commission after having given notice to the parties concerned to submit their comments, finds that "aid granted by a State or through State resources is not compatible with the common market within the meaning of Article 92, or that such aid is being improperly used"; the Commission shall then decide that the State concerned shall abolish or modify such aid within a set time-limit. "If the State concerned does not comply with the decision within the prescribed time, the Commission . . . may, in derogation from the provisions of Article 169 . . . refer the matter directly to the Court of Justice" (E.E.C., Art. 93(2)). Basically, however, this procedure is the same as the one provided in E.E.C., Art. 169.

3–33. With regard to undertakings, the powers of the Commission are of a quite different nature: indeed the Commission can impose fines or penalties upon undertakings which violate obligations arising for them under the treaties. The E.C.S.C. treaty has conferred this power upon the Commission (High Authority) in many instances: Articles 47 (refusal to furnish information), 54 (resort to resources other than own funds to carry out investments when it is found that these would require subsidies), 58 (violation of production quotas), 59 (allocation of coal and steel resources), 64 (violation of the provisions concerning prices), 65–66 (violation of competition rules) and 68 (violation of directives[59] concerning wages).

In the E.E.C. treaty the right for the Commission to impose fines and daily penalties is explicitly provided only in Article 87(2) (rules of competition).[60] Another article, E.E.C., Art. 79, provides that the Council shall lay down rules for implementing the provisions of paragraph 1 and may "in particular lay down the provisions needed to enable the institutions of the Community to secure compliance with the rule laid down in paragraph 1 . . ." On the basis of

[58] See judgment of 13 November 1964, Rec. X, 1231, cases 90 and 91–63.

[59] The E.C.S.C. treaty calls these acts "Recommendations," but they are identical with the directives of the E.E.C. and Euratom treaties.

[60] See Reg. 17 of 1962, J.O. 204/62.

this provision, the Council issued Regulation 11/60,[61] which in its Article 18(1) and (2) empowers the Commission to impose fines.

Writers do not agree as to whether or not E.E.C., Art. 172 implies a general competence to provide for the imposition of fines: "regulations made by the Council pursuant to the provisions of this treaty, may give the Court of Justice unlimited jurisdiction[62] in regard to the penalties provided for in such regulations." If the answer to this question were to be negative, it seems that there still is another possibility to provide penalties, namely on the basis of E.E.C., Art. 235: " if action by the Community should prove necessary to attain in the course of the operation of the common market, one of the objectives of the Community and this treaty has not provided the necessary powers, the Council shall, acting unanimously on a proposal from the Commission and after consulting the Assembly, take the appropriate measures."

Other cases where penalties for enterprises are explicitly provided are Articles 83 and 145 of the Euratom treaty.

3–34. To fulfil its task the Commission shall furthermore " formulate *recommendations* or deliver *opinions* on matters dealt with in this treaty, if it expressly so provides or if the Commission considers it necessary " (E.E.C., Art. 155). Such an opinion is for instance required by E.E.C., Art. 237: " any European State may apply to become a member of the Community. It shall address its application to the Council, which shall act unanimously after obtaining the opinion of the Commission." An example where a Commission recommendation is required is to be found in Article 111(2): " the Commission shall submit to the Council recommendations for tariff negotiations with third countries in respect of the common customs tariff." It must be remembered that, in accordance with E.E.C., Art. 189, " recommendations and opinions shall have no binding force." Where the Council is required to consult the Commission, the position of the latter is comparable to that of the Assembly and the weight its advice will carry entirely depends on its political stature.

3–35. Legally more important is the fact that the Commission

[61] J.O. 1121/60.

[62] Unlimited jurisdiction confers on the Court the power to vary and suspend such penalties.

has " its own power of *decision*[63] and participate[s] in the shaping of measures taken by the Council and by the Assembly in the manner provided for in this Treaty." In other words the Commission participates in the decision-making process of the Communities by making proposals to the Council, when this is a necessary step in said process; this power is generally referred to as the exclusive right of initiative in the law-making process. But, E.E.C., Art. 155 in the first place entrusts the Commission with an autonomous power to take decisions; the legislative power within the Communities is thus shared by two institutions: the Council and the Commission, although the former undoubtedly has by far the larger share. The last sub-paragraph of E.E.C., Art. 155 provides furthermore that the Commission shall exercise the powers (of decision) conferred upon it by the Council for the implementation of the rules laid down by the latter (delegated decision-making power).

In certain cases the Commission when exercising its right to take decisions has a choice as to the form of the measures: Article 90(3) mentions " appropriate directives or decisions to the Member States," in others no form is prescribed: E.E.C., Art. 10(2), " the Commission shall determine the methods of administrative cooperation "; in other cases a certain type of measure is required: E.E.C., Art. 45(2), " directives drawn up by the Commission." An example of a delegated power is to be found in Regulation 19/65,[64] whereby the Council empowered the Commission to declare, by regulation and in accordance with Article 85(3), that Article 85(1) is not applicable to certain groups of agreement.

If the legislative power is thus divided between two institutions, it should be clear however that the Commission's decisions mainly concern individual cases such as authorisations under specific treaty provisions (E.E.C., Art. 226 or Act of accession, Art. 38(3) and (4)). Into this category fall all the decisions the Commission takes in accordance with E.E.C., Art. 85, 86, 90 or 93.

3–36. Next to its function of watchdog over the application of

[63] Decisions of the Commission are taken by a majority of the members (E.E.C., Art. 163); this implies that the Commission may not delegate power of decision to anyone of its members or to one of its civil servants; neither can the Commission delegate such powers to more or less autonomous organs (see Rec. IV, 9, case 9–56). See however the decision of the Commission of 3 April 1968, concerning authorisation for certain measures pertaining to the administration of market organisations, J.O. L 115, 1971. Owing to the constant increase of administrative tasks this inability to delegate has imposed on the Commission a more and more impossible task. Amendment of the Treaties on this point is urgent.

[64] J.O. 533/65.

the European treaties, the main task of the Commission is to initiate legislation. Numerous treaty provisions contain the standard expression: " the Council shall, on a proposal from the Commission, issue. . . ." There are cases where the Commission is bound *to make proposals*, as for instance under E.E.C., Art. 21(2): " before the end of the first stage the Council shall, acting by a qualified majority on a proposal from the Commission, decide . . ."; not only must the Commission make a proposal but it must also be done in time to permit the Council to act within the given time-limit. In case the Commission fails to act " the Member States and the other institutions[65] of the Community may refer the matter to the Court of Justice in order to have the infringement established " (E.E.C., Art. 175)[66]; if the Court of Justice declares the failure to act to be contrary to the provisions of the treaty, the Commission " shall be required to take the necessary measures to comply with the judgment of the Court of Justice " (E.E.C., Art. 176). In other cases the Commission must use its own judgment as to the opportuneness of making a proposal: E.E.C., Art. 94: " the Council may, acting by a qualified majority on a proposal from the Commission, make any appropriate regulation." When the Commission in such a case does not take the initiative, there is no recourse to the Court of Justice under the E.E.C. treaty,[67] however the Council " may request the Commission . . . to submit to it any appropriate proposals " (E.E.C., Art. 152). Of course, this is only a request, not legally binding upon the Commission, but it is generally considered that when the Council (composed of representatives of the Member States) puts such a request to the Commission, it becomes politically very difficult to refuse.

3–37. It has become good practice within the Commission carefully to prepare the various proposals in close consultation with representatives of the Member States. When required,[68] the Commission, before submitting proposals to the Council, consults the Economic and Social Committee (E.E.C., Art. 198); unlike consultation of the European Assembly which only the Council can do,

[65] This is the only case where the Assembly can initiate a Court action.

[66] This and other provisions are reviewed in more detail in the next section concerning the Court of Justice.

[67] Under the E.C.S.C. treaty, it was possible but then, to be successful one had to prove " détournement de pouvoir " (E.C.S.C., Art. 35).

[68] When consultation of the Committee is required by the treaty, failure to do so is a ground for annulment of the act by the Court of Justice, since it would constitute a violation of a basic procedural rule (E.E.C., Art. 173).

the Economic and Social Committee gives opinions to both the Council and the Commission. Together with this opinion the proposal is sent by the Commission to the Council; if during the ensuing discussions with various sub-organs of the Council the Commission considers it desirable to modify its original proposal, it may do so " as long as the Council has not acted" (E.E.C., Art. 149). The question has been asked whether the Commission may also withdraw its proposal thereby making it impossible for the Council to act; the Commission might want to do this for instance when on the basis of the above mentioned discussions, it fears that a final decision, totally unacceptable from a Community point of view, is on the point of being enacted – it will be remembered that the Council may adopt amendments to the Commission's proposals by unanimous vote. There are cases in which proposals have been withdrawn.

3–38. There also is a problem with regard to the extent of the amendments the Council may adopt: how much of the original proposal must be left to remain within the treaty requirement of the Council acting " on a proposal from the Commission." The institutional structure and balance of powers within the Community clearly implies that the Council is bound by the general lines of the Commission's proposal; the latter is not a mere signal empowering the Council to enact whatever measure it wishes. And indeed the treaty refers in Article 149 to " amendment to that proposal," which is quite different from modifying the essence of it. It is also considered that when the Council's amendment is substantial, a new consultation of the Assembly is required; it is indeed on the original proposal that the consultation took place and there must be some analogy between this draft and the final text, unless the consultation of the European Assembly is to be considered a real farce.

3–39. The Commission's activities are not limited to the internal life of the Communities; the Commission is also responsible for the maintenance of all appropriate relations with the organs of the United Nations, of their specialised agencies and of the General Agreement on Tariffs and Trade and more generally speaking the Commission shall ensure appropriate relations with all international organisations[69] (E.E.C., Art. 229). But, as mentioned above, agree-

[69] See also exchange of letters between the President of the Commission and the President of the Central Commission for Navigation on the Rhine, J.O. 1027/61, and the Agreement concerning relations between the International Labour Organizations and the Community, J.O. 521/59.

ments between the Community and one or more States or an international organisation must be concluded by the Council, although they are negotiated by the Commission (E.E.C., Art. 228(1)). One could say therefore that external relations are the responsibility of both the Council and the Commission. The same prevails within Euratom, although there the emphasis is rather more on the Commission's role (Euratom, Art. 100). In regard to foreign missions accredited to the Communities, since the crisis of 1965 " letters of credence of Heads of Missions accredited to the Community by non-Member States will be presented to the President of the Council and to the President of the Commission meeting together for that purpose " (Point 4 of the Council's decision on arrangements regarding co-operation[70] between the E.E.C. Council of Ministers and the Commission[71]).

3. The Commission's staff

3–40. In Article 162 one finds the first treaty reference to the Commission's staff: " the Commission shall adopt its rules of procedure so as to ensure that both it and its departments operate in accordance with the provisions of this Treaty. It shall ensure that these rules of procedure are published."[72] Other references to the staff can be found in E.E.C., Art. 179 (jurisdiction of the Court of Justice in disputes between the Community and its servants), Merger treaty, Art. 24(1) (Staff Regulations laid down by the Council for Officials of the European Communities and Conditions of Employment of other servants of the Communities).[73] E.E.C., Art. 214 (Professional secrecy of officials and other servants of the Community) and Chapter Five of the Protocol on the Privileges and Immunities of the E.E.C.

The Commission's staff[74] (before the merger the staff of the High Authority, the E.E.C. Commission and the Euratom Com-

[70] It should be noted that E.E.C., Art. 162 provides that " the Council and the Commission shall consult each other and shall settle by common accord their methods of co-operation." The above mentioned Council decision is not of course a " common accord "; nevertheless, some of its clauses, such as Point 4 have been faithfully implemented by both institutions.

[71] See E.E.C. Bulletin No. 3, 1966, 5.

[72] J.O. L 147, 1967, modified by the Commission's Decision of 26 May 1971, J.O. L 145, 1970.

[73] Regulation 259/68, J.O. L 56, 1968, which refers to the basic regulation J.O. 1385/62.

[74] In 1972 about 8,100 persons.

mission) is divided into over twenty-two Departments[75] (Directorates-General, Services or Groups) which more or less correspond to the main subdivisions of the treaty provisions; a " Directorate-General " is composed of several " Directorates " which in turn contain three or four " Divisions." The staff is recruited directly by the Commission without interference from the Member States and is not, contrary to general belief, exclusively or even mainly composed of national civil servants. Article 27 of the Statute of Service provides that the Community's civil servants will be recruited " on as large a geographical basis as possible among the nationals of the Member States "; the same provision adds that " no post may be reserved for a given nationality." In practice, there exists a tendency to consider certain Directorate's-General posts as "French," or "German," etc. and it must be admitted that since there is a general equilibrium, especially among the higher posts (generally speaking France, Germany, Italy and the Benelux, each claim a fourth of the total number), in case one post becomes vacant, it is extremely difficult to nominate someone from another nationality lest this equilibrium, painfully attained, be upset. The Court, which has had to pronounce judgment in quite a few cases concerning disputes between the Community[76] and its personnel, has admitted that nationality be taken into account for the selection of candidates with equal qualifications.[77] The Community's civil servants pay no national income tax and the Court has decided that their Community income may not be taken into account for the calculation of their domestic income tax[78]; they pay a Community income tax which in the highest bracket is 45 per cent.[79]

3–41. Through its powers of daily administration the Commission

[75] The Directorates-General are: External Relations; Economic and Financial Affairs; Industrial, Technological and Scientific Affairs; Competition; Social Affairs; Agriculture; Transport; Development Aid; Personnel and Administration; Press and Information; External Trade; Dissemination of Information; Internal Market and Approximation of Legislation; Regional Policy; Energy, Safeguards and Control of Euratom; Credit and Investments; Budgets; Financial Control; then there are 4 other units of equal importance: the Secretariat of the Commission, the Legal Service, the Spokesman's Group and the Statistical Office. There are also the Administration of the Customs Union, the Joint Research Centre, the Euratom Supply Agency, the Security Office and the Office for Official Publications of the European Communities.

[76] Between 1953 and 1971, 266 cases had been submitted to the Court, which pronounced 164 judgments.

[77] See Rec. X, 73, case 15–63.

[78] See Rec. VI, 1127, case 6–60.

[79] See J.O. L 56/9, 1968.

has a more direct impact on the life of the Community's citizens than the other institutions. Particularly in the fields of Agriculture and Competition the Commission, as was mentioned in Chapter 2, wields large and direct powers. Accession of new Member States to the Communities will therefore mean that for certain matters which directly interest people living in these countries, the centre of decision will be displaced from the traditional and therefore well-known ones to Brussels; it is there that they will, in the future, have to make their representations if they want action, it is there also that they must seek to obtain, if need be, special consideration in the implementation of Community law.

Farmers who want higher prices for their products or lower levies on their imported animal feed, will turn to the Commission and urge it to make proposals accordingly.

Companies which seek exemption from the prohibitions on certain agreements with other companies will send their requests to the Commission.

Undertakings which feel that their position on the market is threatened by some illegal actions of certain governments or enterprises can request the Commission to take the necessary steps even against their own Government to remedy this situation, where previously they might have been powerless. But the Commission is also a new organ to be reckoned with, since it will ensure the application of certain Community provisions through the imposition of fines and daily penalties which the national " strong arm " will collect at its first request.[80]

IV. The Court of Justice[81]

3–42. The short and sibylline text of E.E.C., Art. 164 ill prepares the newcomer to the European Communities for the essential role played by this institution in regard to the interpretation, implementation and creation of Community law and thereby in the development of the European Communities and in a certain way in the shaping of the common policies. The Court of Justice, according to the

[80] See Chapter 5, IV: Enforcement.

[81] Literature: Bebr, *Judicial Control of the European Communities*, 1962; Valentine, *The Court of Justice of the European Communities*, 1965; Brinkhorst/Schermers, *Judicial Remedies in the European Communities*, 1969.

European treaties,[82] must ensure that in the interpretation and application of these treaties the law is observed. In fact, the Court of Justice is the only totally independent institution whose sole objective is the Community's interests. This aspect is the more important since, as was explained before, the Council acts most of the time as an intergovernmental conference where every member fights for his country's interests, the Assembly has none of the powers required for exercising a democratic control and the Commission, if beside its overwhelming administrative tasks it wants to fulfil a political function, is bound to accept compromises with regard to the implementation of the treaty provisions by the Member States.

3–43. The Court's task is extremely varied since it has to act in several capacities: administrative court (legality of Community measures, compensation for damages caused by wrongful Community acts, unlimited jurisdiction in regard to penalties), penal court (dismissal of Commissioners), internal administrative tribunal (appeals by civil servants), international court (conflicts between Member States and between the Commission and Member States), constitutional court (conformity of international agreements with the treaties) and civil jurisdiction (attribution of competence in contracts concluded by the Community). It is also complicated by the fact that the basic Community law is " economic " law which furthermore is only partly drafted with sufficient precision. It has been pointed out on several occasions that by and large the E.E.C. treaty contains two sets of rules: the first pertains to the establishment and functioning of the common market and more particularly of the Customs Union; the second to the approximation of economic policies. For this second category, the treaties only contain some very general principles and entrusted to the institutions the task of finishing the work started by the treaty draftsmen. The only guidelines in these cases are the objectives of the treaty as specified in the E.E.C., Arts. 2, 3. This explains why the Court of Justice when called upon to state what the law of the Community is in a given field, has nearly always sought to interpret and create by reference to these objectives. And indeed, the task of the Court of Justice is not only to interpret the existing rules, but also to state what the law is when the existing Community legislation does not explicitly provide for it. This, of

[82] This basic text regarding the Court's role is practically identical in the E.C.S.C. (Art. 31), E.E.C. (Art. 164) and Euratom (Art. 136) treaties.

course, is not unique to the Court of Justice: " wherever there are courts, the law grows in the hands of the Judges,"[83] but it is particularly appropriate in the case of the Communities, not only because, as was said before, the treaties contain mainly economic law which by definition is essentially evolutive and in constant need of adaptation, but also because it was out of the question to regulate the economic policies of six countries in a document containing less than 250 provisions. The Court of Justice has been well aware of this fundamental " obligation " on its part: in a judgment of 12 July 1957, the Court held in regard to the possibility of revoking an individual administrative act that " this is a problem of administrative law well known in the case-law and doctrine of all the countries of the Community, but for whose solution the treaty does not provide rules. That therefore the Court, unless it were to deny justice, is obliged to solve this problem on the basis of the rules recognized by the laws, the doctrine and the judgments of the Member States."[84]

The Court of Justice can only express itself in judgments and when called upon to do so; nevertheless, it was able, over the years, to build a set of rules which were of prime importance in shaping the evolution of the Communities themselves; this happened not so much when the Court was called upon to control the legality of Community acts but mainly when giving rulings concerning the interpretation of Community legislation at the request of national courts which were confronted with questions of interpretation in cases pending before them. These rulings enabled the Court to affirm *inter alia* the direct applicability of a certain number of treaty provisions, the existence of Community law alongside international law and the internal laws of the Member States and especially the supremacy of Community law above national law[85]; in each case the main argument was that there could be no question of a " Common Market " if all those who operate in this market were not throughout the Community and at all times subjected to similar rules, and that this in turn could not be the case if national authorities were free to interpret and apply Community legislation in conformity with national doctrine and legislation.[86]

[83] Schwarzenberger, *International Law*, p. 24.
[84] Rec. III, 114, joint cases 7–56 and 3 to 7–57.
[85] These questions were discussed in detail in Chap. 1.
[86] See Rec. X, 1159, case 6–64.

1. The Court's jurisdiction

3–44. Proceedings may be initiated by Member States, institutions of the Community and under certain conditions by natural or legal persons; they may be directed at Member States for alleged violation of their treaty obligations or at an institution of the Community for acts or omissions. Proceedings against Member States and against institutions and the Court's preliminary ruling will be successively examined, followed by a survey of the other most important cases in which the Court has jurisdiction.

(a) *Proceedings against Member States*

3–45. Proceedings against Member States may be initiated under the European treaties either by the Commission (E.E.C., Art. 169) or by a Member State (E.E.C., Art. 170).

The proceedings of the *Commission* have already been briefly mentioned in this Chapter 3, under Section IV, concerning the Commission. It was pointed out that the main task of the Commission is to ensure the application of the treaty and other Community provisions and that for that purpose it can bring a Member State before the Court. According to E.E.C., Art. 169, " if the Commission considers that a Member State has failed to fulfil an obligation under this Treaty, it shall deliver a reasoned opinion on the matter after giving the State concerned the opportunity to submit its observations." This first paragraph thus provides for two procedural phases[87]:

(1) giving the Member State concerned the opportunity to submit its observations and

(2) the delivery of a reasoned opinion.

The wording of this first paragraph does not seem to leave much room for the exercise of discretionary power in case the violation is obvious, unless one admits that the Commission is free to consider that a measure which objectively violates a treaty rule (for instance the introduction of a customs duty on imports from other Member States) can nevertheless, owing to special circumstances, be considered as not constituting a violation. Obviously this cannot be. But there are cases where violation is a question of appreciation and it

[87] Exactly the same procedure is provided for under E.E.C., Art. 93(2), although it constitutes an exception to E.E.C., Art. 169. A real exception is to be found in E.E.C., Art. 225.

is then up to the Commission to decide whether or not it is to be considered as such.[88]

Once this decision has been taken, the procedure laid down in Article 169 must be initiated and if the Commission were to hesitate in doing so, other Member States or institutions (Council and Assembly) could refer the Commission's omission to the Court (E.E.C., Art. 175, see below).

If the Member State considered by the Commission to have violated the treaty does not submit its observations within the time-limit set by the Commission, or if the submitted observations are not satisfactory in the Commission's opinion, the latter " shall deliver a reasoned opinion on the matter." Here again if no observations are received, it seems there is no other solution but to deliver an opinion; it is only when observations are received that the Commission is to decide whether or not they are satisfactory and consequently whether or not to pursue the procedure.

3–46. The reasoned opinion is a decisive step since the merits of the case, if it reaches the Court of Justice, will be decided exclusively upon the reasons put forward in the opinion.[89] As to the reasons, the Court decided that an opinion under Article 169 must be held to contain legally sufficient grounds when it presents a coherent statement of the reasons which convinced the Commission that the State in question failed in its obligations.[90] According to the second paragraph of E.E.C., Art. 169 the opinion must also contain the period within which the State concerned should comply with the Commission's terms.

If the State does not comply, the Commission " may bring the matter before the Court of Justice." The treaty clearly leaves the decision entirely to the Commission and if the latter decides not to pursue the case although the State in question did not conform to the Commission's ruling, there is nothing that can be done under the E.E.C. treaty, since E.E.C., Art. 175 only provides for an action should the Commission fail to act in infringement of this treaty; clearly there can be no violation when there is no obligation. The situation is different under the E.C.S.C. treaty, where even enterprises can bring such an omission to the attention of the High

[88] In a judgment of 1 March 1966, the Court states that Art. 169 " empowers the Commission to set in motion a procedure that can lead to a Court action," Rec. XII, 39, case 48–65.

[89] Rec. XI, 1069, case 45–64.

[90] Rec. VII, 654, case 7–61.

Authority, if the latter " where empowered by this treaty . . . to take a decision or make a recommendation, abstains from doing so and such abstention constitutes a misuse of power " (E.C.S.C., Art. 35). If then at the end of a period of two months the High Authority has not taken any decision proceedings may be instituted before the Court against the implied decision of refusal which is to be inferred from the silence of the High Authority on the matter.[91]

3–47. If the Commission does decide to refer the matter to the Court of Justice and the latter " finds that [the] Member State has failed to fulfil any obligation under this treaty, the State shall be required to take the necessary measures to comply with the judgment of the Court " (E.E.C., Art. 171). In other words the judgment of the Court is of a purely declaratory nature and the next step is therefore, as was pointed out above, left to the good sense if not the good faith of the Member State concerned.[92] Owing to the political " give and take " upon which much of the bargaining leading to many an important decision is based, the breaking of the rules by one of the partners will not go " unpunished " forever, not to mention the claims for damages which might be recognised by national courts at the suit of aggrieved individuals against governments whose acts or omissions the Court of Justice has declared illegal.

3–48. Besides the proceedings by the Commission, any *Member State* " which considers that another Member State has failed to fulfil an obligation under the Treaty may bring the matter before the Court of Justice " (E.E.C., Art. 170). Although Member States have undertaken " not to submit a dispute concerning the interpretation or application of this Treaty to any method of settlement other than those provided for therein " (E.E.C., Art. 219), no case has ever been brought before the Court under E.E.C., Art. 170. In the first place the six governments are bound constantly to work so close together that court actions for infringements might endanger the badly needed good-will and co-operation, and in the second place

[91] See for instance joint cases 7 and 9–54 in which the Luxemburg steel industries lodged a complaint based on E.C.S.C., Art. 35 on the ground that the High Authority had failed to initiate proceedings against Luxemburg. The Court held that in such a case plaintiff could appeal in accordance with E.C.S.C., Art. 35. Rec. II, 53.

[92] In theory the situation is different under the E.C.S.C. treaty: Art. 88 provides that " if the State does not fulfil its obligations . . . the High Authority may with the assent of the Council acting by a 2/3 majority (a) suspend the payment of any sums it may be liable to pay to the State in question . . . (b) take measures or authorize the other Member States to take measures by way of derogation from the provisions of Article 4, in order to correct the effects of the infringement of the obligation."

the Member States rely upon the Commission to take action, the more so since before referring a violation to the Court, the Member State which intends to institute proceedings must first " refer the matter to the Commission " (E.E.C., Art. 170).

(b) *Proceedings against an institution*

3–49. These proceedings can be initiated by Member States, other institutions and, under certain conditions, by natural and legal persons. Action can be brought " against " an institution either to obtain annulment of binding acts[93] issued by this institution, or to obtain a judgment declaring a failure of the institution to act contrary to the provisions of the treaty, or also to obtain compensation for damage caused by an illegal act of an institution. There also is the possibility for civil servants of referring to the Court any dispute with their institution.

APPEALS FOR ANNULMENT

3–50. The purpose of these appeals is to supervise the legality of the acts of the institutions and thereby the Court not only protects all those who are subject to Community law against arbitrary action of the institutions (when it acts as an administrative court), but also restrains the Community's activities within the boundaries laid down by the treaties and more particularly ensures that each institution respects the balance of powers within the Community and thus acts as a constitutional court.

WHO MAY LODGE AN APPEAL FOR ANNULMENT?

3–51. In all the Member States there prevails a general rule with regard to the admissibility of court actions, well coined in French as " *pas d'intérêt, pas d'action* "; the same principle is applied in

[93] E.E.C., Art. 173 refers to " acts of the Council and the Commission other than recommendations or opinions "; these acts are mainly regulations, directives and decisions (see Chap. 5: Acts of the Institutions), but are in no way limited to those forms, see judgment of the Court of Justice of 31 March 1971 (case 22–70): " the appeal for annulment must be available with regard to all provisions enacted by the institutions, whatever their nature or form, which aim at producing legal effects," Rec. XVII, 277 (42).

E.E.C., Art. 173: Member States and the Community institutions are considered to be the guardians of the general interest and therefore have, subject to a two month time-limit, an unlimited right to initiate proceedings aimed at control of the legality of Community acts; natural and legal persons on the other hand must prove their interest in such a control. In this respect it is assumed that acts having a general application concern everybody, but nobody in particular and therefore cannot be challenged in Court by individuals, unless those acts contain provisions which in reality have an " individual " rather than a " general " application: " any natural or legal person may . . . institute proceedings against a decision addressed to that person or against a decision which, although in the form of a regulation or a decision addressed to another person,[94] is of direct and individual concern to the former" (E.E.C., Art. 173, 2nd para.). In this connection the Court has clarified several important points:

- it is not the form of an act which determines its nature, but rather its substance (Rec. V, 181, case 20–58 and VIII, 918, case 16, 17–62), although " the judicial protection necessary for all interested parties, implies that they must be able to identify by its very form[95] a decision which entails such serious judicial consequences."[96] See also the judgment of 15 March 1967 wherein the Court defined a binding act as one which produces " legal effect on the interests of the enterprises concerned and (imposes) obligations on them "[97];
- an act can contain provisions of differing nature: certain may be generally applicable, others may be directed to an individual (Rec. VIII, 918, case 16, 17–62);
- an act is of direct and individual concern to someone

[94] " Another person " can according to the Court (Rec. IX, 222, case 25–62) include Member States since no limitations as to the meaning of these words are to be found in the treaty. Individuals can therefore attack decisions of the institutions addressed to a Member State when they are directly concerned.

[95] This is the reason why the High Authority defined " in a binding way the form of the decisions . . . so that all interested parties can ascertain, on the basis of objective and clear criteria, whether these acts constitute decisions as provided for by the Treaty " (J.O. 1248/60). See also the Council's internal regulation Arts. 9 *et seq.* (This regulation has not been published in the J.O.)

[96] Rec. IX, 507, joint cases 53 and 54–63.

[97] Rec. XIII, 117, joint cases 8 to 11–66.

" only if the act touches him because of certain qualities particular to him or because of a factual situation which characterizes him in regard to other persons and thereby singles him out in a way comparable to that used for the addressee " (Rec. IX, 223, case 25–62);

– a decision (as opposed to a regulation) is " characterized by the limited number of persons to whom it is addressed " (Rec. IX, 223, case 25–62).[98]

The opportunities for private parties to appeal for annulment are thus much more limited than for Member States and Community-institutions. However, there exist other means whereby persons and enterprises may obtain a Court ruling on the legality of Community acts; see below: preliminary ruling, exception of illegality and non-contractual liability.

GROUNDS FOR ANNULMENT

3–52. All three European treaties provide the same four grounds for annulment which find their origin in French administrative law.

(a) *Lack of jurisdiction*: this is the expression in juridical terms of the general principle mentioned before, namely that the Community's institutions only have the powers that have explicitly been attributed to them by the provisions of the various treaties. The consequence of the judicial system as provided by the treaties could result in a situation where a measure was taken by an institution not having the necessary power to do so, but if no appeal for annulment is filed with the Court within the set time-limit of two months (dating from publication or notification, as the case may be)[99] this measure will forever remain in force.[1]

This question was in effect raised but answered ambiguously in the joint cases 6 and 11–69, *Commission* v. *French Republic*. Although the time-limit for appealing against the Commission's decision had expired, the French Government invoked the Community's Public Policy (" *Ordre public communautaire* ") and expressed the opinion

[98] See also Rec. X, 823, case 1–64 where the Court admits that this plaintiff is "directly" and " individually " concerned.

[99] Art. 173, last para.

[1] If, however, in a court case involving this measure, a party invokes the exception of illegality (E.E.C., Art. 184) the Court might declare the act inapplicable.

that too exclusive an attachment to formalities would be as contrary to the real Community spirit as their violation. The French Government contended that the decision had been taken in a domain which was reserved solely to the Member States. It seems that this is a typical case of " lack of jurisdiction " and falling within the rules of E.E.C., Art. 173. However the Court of Justice found that " if this contention is well founded, the decision in question would lack all legal basis in the Community legal order " and that therefore it was a requirement of the legal order for the Court to examine whether or not this was the case.[2] What the Court did not clearly say is what the consequences would have been in regard to the decision had the Court accepted the French Government's contention (which it declined to do): would the decision have been considered null and void – something that is not contemplated by the European Treaties – or would the decision have been " voidable " for lack of jurisdiction, in conformity with E.E.C., Art. 173? The former solution seems to be implied by the Court's decision and if this is correct one might wonder in which cases lack of powers could result in " voidability " and in which others in " nullity." The difference is important since the Court of Justice can find an act void at any time, while it may only annul (voidability) when a request to do so has been filed within the time-limit set by E.E.C., Art. 173.

3–53. (b) *Violation of basic procedural rules.* As was mentioned above under Sections I and III, if the Council were to take a decision without consulting the Assembly (when this is required under the treaties) or if the Commission were to make a proposal to the Council without asking for the opinion of the Economic and Social Committee,[3] when required to do so, each institution would violate a procedural rule and therefore an appeal for annulment could be lodged against the measures they issued. The same applies when an act of an institution is not sufficiently reasoned.[4]

3–54. (c) *Infringement of the treaty or of any rule of law relating to its application.* It could of course be argued that the above mentioned grounds refer also to violations of the treaty and that this ground in fact covers all possible illegalities. It has therefore been suggested that at the first opportunity the draftsmen would do well to simplify the text by mentioning only that the Court supervises the

[2] Rec. XV, 540 (12–13).
[3] For more details see Chap. 5 and Rec. I, 31, case 1–54.
[4] For more details see Chap. 5 and Rec. I, 31, case 1–54; also Rec. III, 220, cases 1 and 14–57.

legality of the acts of the Council and the Commission.[5] The four grounds for annulment mentioned in the treaties are four different aspects of what in French administrative law is referred to as " *excès de pouvoir* " and this distinction between various grounds has a special significance under the E.C.S.C. treaty, since general binding decisions can only be challenged by enterprises when they can invoke a " *détournement de pouvoir* " (one of the four grounds). But under the E.E.C. treaty, where the admissibility of an appeal for annulment depends on the nature of the act and the standing of the plaintiff, the distinction between the four grounds seems rather senseless.

However, the present treaties provide for four grounds and accordingly these must here be examined. In the expression " violation of the Treaty," treaty must be understood as referring also to the Protocols annexed thereto (E.E.C., Art. 239), while the expression " rules of law relating to its application " refers not only to the secondary Community law (regulations, directives, decisions and other Acts), but also to agreements concluded by the Community, international law[6] and the general principles of law[7]; it also covers of course the treaties that were concluded by the Six or by the Ten to modify the existing European treaties, such as the Treaty of accession.

3–55. (d) *Détournement de pouvoir* (*misuse of power*).[8] There is *détournement de pouvoir* when an authority uses its lawful powers to attain an objective for which the powers were not intended. Although this ground has been invoked over and over again, right from the beginning,[9] never yet has the Court of Justice based annulment on *détournement de pouvoir*. As was mentioned, this ground played a major role under the E.C.S.C. treaty, since in accordance with Article 33 " undertakings . . . may institute proceedings . . . against general decisions . . . which they consider to involve a misuse of power affecting them." The Court held it to be sufficient for the admissibility of an appeal against a general decision that the plaintiff

[5] See *La Fusion des Communautes Européennes*, Université de Liége, 22, 1965, 110–111.

[6] See Rec. II, 305, case 8–55, and Rec. VIII, 22, case 10–61.

[7] See for instance Rec. VIII, 104, case 13–61 (legal certainty); Rec. IV, 247, case 8–57 (equality before the law); VII, 159, case 42, 49–59 (lawfulness); VII, 338, joint cases 14, 16, 17, 24, 26, 27–60 and 1–61 (equal sharing of public burdens).

[8] For a comparative study, see conclusions of the Advocate-General in the case 3–54, Rec. I, 149.

[9] See Rec. I, 13, case 1–54.

formally alleges a *détournement de pouvoir* concerning him while specifying the reasons which in the plaintiff's opinion give rise to this détournement.[10] Under the E.E.C. and Euratom treaties this ground no longer fulfils this particular role.

CONSEQUENCES OF ANNULMENT

3–56. In accordance with E.E.C., Art. 174 " if the action is well founded, the Court of Justice shall declare the act concerned to be void." This annulment need not necessarily affect the entire measure: if the Court " considers this necessary, [it can] state which of the effects of the regulation which it has declared void shall be considered as definitive." This possibility does not apply to directives and decisions.

Once a measure has been declared void, it is up to the institution responsible for the measure in question – and not to the Court – to take the necessary measures to comply with the judgment of the Court of Justice (E.E.C., Art. 176 and E.C.S.C., Art. 34). It is only when " unlimited jurisdiction " has been conferred upon the Court that it may decree which measures will apply instead of the abolished one, but otherwise it may not: " the Court, if it grants the appeal, is not competent to dictate to the High Authority the decisions to which the judgment of annulment should lead, but will have to limit itself to referring the matter to the High Authority."[11]

APPEALS AGAINST COMMISSION

3–57. Proceedings against institutions can be based as was just seen, on a measure or a positive act of the institutions, but it can also be initiated because of their failure to act: " should the Council or the Commission in infringement of this Treaty, fail to act, the Member States and the other institutions of the Community may bring an action before the Court of Justice to have the infringement established " (E.E.C., Art. 175).

Any natural or legal person may also bring proceedings before the Court of Justice on the ground that one of the institutions has

[10] See Rec. I, 138, case 3–54.
[11] See Rec. VII, 36, case 30–59.

failed to address to him an act other than a recommendation or an opinion (E.E.C., Art. 175, last para.; see also E.C.S.C., Art. 75).

The action of Member States and institutions is not limited to cases in which the Council or Commission had to take a binding measure: if the Commission fails to send a proposal to the Council when this is required by the treaty, action under this article is also possible; not so for natural or legal persons: only when an institution fails to address a binding act (since the addressee is a person, it can only be a decision) may persons bring proceedings.

3–58. Proceedings for omission are only admissible when the institution called upon to act has not defined its position within two months (E.E.C., Art. 175, para. 2). If under E.C.S.C., Art. 35 many appeals against omissions were brought before the Court,[12] only very few were lodged under E.E.C., Art. 175.[13] Mention must be made of one of those, since plaintiffs brought action because the Commission had not reacted to their request to withdraw a measure they considered illegal; the Court held that since the treaty provides, in particular[14] in Article 173, for actions against measures considered illegal, " to accept, as requested by the plaintiffs, that interested parties could ask the institution responsible for said act, to revoke it, and in case of inaction, refer this omission to the Court of Justice, would result in opening proceedings which would run parallel to those of Article 173 without being submitted to the conditions laid down in the treaty."[15] In a recent case under E.C.S.C., Art. 35 the Court held the plea inadmissible on the ground that eighteen months had elapsed between the moment the Dutch Government (plaintiff) was notified of the Commission's position and the moment the Commission was invited to act, the more so, added the Court " since the notification brought nothing that was not already known."[16]

When the Court declares a failure to act " contrary to the provisions of this treaty [the institution] shall be required to take the necessary steps to implement the judgment of the Court " (E.E.C., Art. 176).

[12] For instance: Rec. V, 14, case 17–57; V, 275, joint cases 32 and 33–58; VI, 579, joint cases 24 and 34–58; VI, 994, joint cases 41 and 50–59.
[13] Rec. XII, 28, case 48–65; XVI, 818, case 6–70 and XVI, 975, case 15–70.
[14] Other possibilities are, as already mentioned: the preliminary ruling, the exception of illegality and the action for non-contractual liability; see below.
[15] Rec. XV, 483 (17), joint cases 10 and 18–68.
[16] Rec. XVII, 654 (22), case 59–70.

(c) *Preliminary ruling*

3–59. The preliminary ruling is the ideal instrument in the hands of the Court to define and develop Community law: when the Court interprets a provision of Community law, more likely than not this interpretation will be accepted by the national courts called upon to ensure the application of this provision and parties invoking it will be hesitant to contest such interpretation although they remain, of course, free to do so.

3–60. As was pointed out under Chapter 1, the European treaties provide for a " division of labour " between the Court of Justice and the national courts: by and large, the latter are responsible for applying Community law, the former has exclusive competence to interpret its provisions. The object of E.E.C., Art. 177 is to ensure uniform interpretation within the community, *conditio sine qua non* for the very existence of a common market. The first paragraph of Article 177 provides that the Court of Justice shall be competent to give preliminary rulings concerning *inter alia* the validity and the interpretation of the treaties and of acts of the institutions of the Community. That this competence is not exclusive results from the second paragraph: " where such a question is raised before any court or tribunal of a Member State, the court or tribunal may, if it considers that a decision on the question is necessary to enable it to give judgment, request the Court of Justice to give a ruling thereon." The last paragraph of Article 177 is slightly different from the second in that it provides that when the national court or tribunal is the highest domestic jurisdiction, in the sense that there is no judicial remedy against its decisions, " that court or tribunal shall bring the matter before the Court of Justice." Much has been written about the precise meaning of the words " where such a question is raised ": what is a " question " and when is it " raised "? It seems that these terms must be interpreted together in the following way: a question regarding interpretation of Community law is raised when it appears during the proceedings in the national court that a difference of opinion exists as to the exact meaning of the Community provision which is to be applied.[17] Such difference can exist either between the parties[18] or between the parties and the national

[17] This implies therefore that the Community rule about whose interpretation there is a difference of opinion, is " self-executing " Rec. XVI, 839 (6), case 9–70.

[18] See for instance case 26–62, Rec. IX, 5.

judge; it may indeed very well be that the parties agree on the meaning of such a provision, but that the judge does not concur. A third possibility is that the national judge[19] or the parties do not agree with an interpretation previously given by the Court of Justice.

This does not mean, of course, that as soon as one of the parties claims that a certain treaty provision does apply in the case before the national court and expresses a view of its meaning which differs from that of the other party, the judge must then immediately suspend the proceeding and refer the matter to the Court of Justice. Not only does the obligation to refer not exist unless the national judge " considers that a decision on the question is necessary to enable [him] to render judgment," but as is generally admitted, it is also within the discretionary powers of the judge to decide whether a question is raised in good faith or whether it is a purely procedural move initiated by a party for instance to delay judgment.[20] There is therefore nothing automatic in the procedure of E.E.C., Art. 177.

3–61. In regard to the jurisdiction of the Court of Justice under E.E.C., Art. 177 the following statements made by the Court of Justice are important for the interpretation of Article 177 itself:

(a) the Court cannot examine a concrete case and determine for instance whether an export prohibition in an agreement between undertakings is contrary to E.E.C., Art. 85(1) (*Bosch* case[21] and *ENEL* case[22]);

(b) "the motives which guided the national court in the choice of its questions and the relevance it intends to give to these questions in the case pending before it, are outside the Court's appreciation " (*Van Gend en Loos* case[23] and *ULM* case[24]);

(c) the national judge is free in the formulation of his question leaving it to the Court to express its opinion within the limits of its jurisdiction (*Bosch* case)[25]; the Court of Justice must isolate from the

[19] Rec. XIV, 225: a German court asked the Court of Justice whether it " maintained its ruling given on 16 June 1966 in case 57–65, that Article 95, paragraph 1, of the E.E.C. Treaty is directly applicable," (case 28–67).

[20] See conclusions of the Advocate-General in the same sense: Rec. X, 1181, case 6–64.

[21] Rec. VIII, 106, case 13–61.

[22] Rec. X, 1157, case 6–64; see also Rec. XIII, 267, case 2–67.

[23] Rec. IX, 22, case 26–62.

[24] Rec. XII, 357, case 56–65.

[25] Rec. VIII, 102, case 13–61.

formulation of the national courts those elements which come under its jurisdiction (case 5–69[26]);

(d) the Court of Justice cannot examine the motives that made the national judge consider that a decision on the question is essential to enable him to render judgment (case 56–65[27]);

(e) when deciding under E.E.C., Art. 177, the Court limits itself to deduce the meaning of the Community rules from the letter and the spirit of the treaty, while the application of the rules thus interpreted to the concrete case is reserved to the national judge (joint cases 28 to 30–62[28]);

(f) once a treaty provision has been interpreted by the Court of Justice, the obligation imposed upon national courts to refer it for interpretation under E.E.C., Art. 177(3) may lose its basis (*Da Costa*[29] and " *Rotterdam* " cases[30]); the national court remains free of course even when an interpretation has already been given, to refer the question once more to the Court[31];

(g) the Court of Justice may not, under E.E.C., Art. 177, express an opinion on the regularity of a national rule (case 100–63[32]);

(h) whether or not a national organ which refers a question to the Court of Justice is a " court of law " must be determined in accordance with national law (case 61–65[33]);

(i) the Court of Justice may not examine whether or not a national court is competent to refer a question under E.E.C., Art. 177 (case 19–68[34]);

(j) the fact that the interpretation of a Community rule is referred to the Court under E.E.C., Art. 177 implies that this rule is self-executing, otherwise it could not be invoked by a person in a national court (case 9–70[35]);

(k) the Court of Justice may not pass judgment on the compatibility of a national law with a Community measure (cases 30–70[36] and 10–71[37]);

[26] Rec. XV, 302; see also Rec. XVI, 1026 (2), case 28–70.
[27] Rec. XII, 357; see also Rec. XIV, 672, case 13–68.
[28] Rec. IX, 76.
[29] Rec. IX, 75, joint cases 28 to 30–62.
[30] Rec. X, 25, joint cases 73 and 74–63.
[31] See also case 29–68, Rec. XV, 180 (3).
[32] Rec. X, 1121.
[33] Rec. XII, 394.
[34] Rec. XIV, 698.
[35] Rec. XVI, 839 (6).
[36] Rec. XVI, 1206 (4).
[37] Rec. XVII, 729 (7).

(l) the Court of Justice acting under E.E.C., Art. 177 may not interpret national law (case 78–70[38]).

3–62. It is clear from the abundance of questions of interpretation put to the Court of Justice that here lies an essential function, not only in regard to the development of Community law, but also as an instrument put at the disposal of natural and legal persons when confronted with self-executing Community measures whose legality they cannot directly challenge in the Court of Justice.

(d) *The exception of illegality*[39]

3–63. " Notwithstanding the expiry of the period laid down in the third paragraph of Article 173, any party may, in proceedings in which a regulation of the Council or of the Commission is in issue, plead the grounds specified in the first paragraph of Article 173, in order to invoke before the Court of Justice the inapplicability of that regulation " (E.E.C., Art. 184).[40]

As the Court of Justice clearly stated in its judgment of 14 December 1962,[41] this provision does not confer on any person the right to refer to the Community Court a question concerning the applicability of a regulation. It is true that E.E.C., Art. 184 does not specify before which particular court the legal proceedings must have been instituted, but the wording and content of this provision clearly suggest that it only concerns a plea for inapplicability raised in a dispute before the Court of Justice based on another article and then only incidentally and with limited effect. In fact, Article 184 does not provide a means for escaping the prescribed time limits of Article 173; its only aim is to protect parties against enforcement of illegal regulations, without thereby in any way raising the question of the validity of the regulation itself.

This provision has found little application in practice, although in theory one could easily imagine cases where undertakings would be fined for violation of a regulation (which, as was said, they can only challenge when it affects them directly and personally); they would then appeal to the Court of Justice for annulment of the

[38] Rec. XVII, 498 (3).
[39] Bebr, " Judicial Remedy of Private Parties against Normative Acts of the European Communities," C.M.L.Rev. 1966–1967, 7.
[40] A similar provision is to be found in E.C.S.C., Art. 36.
[41] Rec. VIII, 979, joint cases 31 and 33–62.

individual decision imposing the fine and thereby submit to the Court that the regulation in question is inapplicable. If the Court were to find that indeed the regulation violates treaty rules, it would hold this measure non-applicable in the case under review; the Court cannot annul the regulation but it appears that application to other cases either by the Community institutions or by national courts would at least become questionable.

(e) *The action for non-contractual liability*

3–64. " In the case of non-contractual liability, the Community shall, in accordance with the general principles common to the laws of the Member States, make good any damage caused by its institutions or by its servants in the performance of their duties " (E.E.C., Art. 215). The E.C.S.C. treaty contains two provisions in regard to liability: Article 34 refers to " direct and special harm . . . by reason of a decision or recommendation held by the Court to involve a fault of such nature as to render the Community liable "; in such case " the High Authority shall . . . take steps to ensure equitable redress for the harm resulting directly from the decision declared void . . ."; the other provision, Article 40, confers upon the Court of Justice " jurisdiction to order pecuniary reparation from the Community . . . to make good any injury caused in carrying out this Treaty by a wrongful act or omission on the part of the Community in the performance of its functions."

In one of its first judgments (14 July 1961) concerning claims for redress, the Court of Justice held that pecuniary reparation can be sought under E.C.S.C., Art. 40 independently of the appeal for annulment (*Vloeberghs* case, 9 and 12–60).[42] In a later judgment (15 July 1963) the Court of Justice seems to have reversed its position: " an administrative measure which has not been annulled could not in itself constitute an offence causing prejudice to persons under the administration's jurisdiction; that the Court cannot via an action for liability, decide on measures which could cancel the legal effects of such a measure which was not annulled " (*Plaumann* case 25–62[43]).

However, in more recent judgments, concerning E.E.C., Art. 215,

[42] Rec. VII, 425.
[43] Rec. IX, 225. See also *Leroy* case, Rec. IX, 420, joint cases 35–62 and 16–63, and *Van Nuffel* case, Rec. X, 1002, case 93–63.

the Court of Justice seems to have modified its position. In its judgment of 2 December 1971, in the case 5–71,[44] the Court of Justice had to decide on a claim brought by a German firm against the Council for damages allegedly inflicted by Regulation 769/68 (J.O. L 143, 1968). The Council requested the Court to declare the appeal inadmissible because it tended in fact to annul the legal effects of the contested measure and because in case the claim were considered admissible it would constitute a violation of the appeals system set up under the treaty in particular by Article 173(2) according to which persons cannot request annulment of regulations. The Court of Justice held that " the appeal for damages under Articles 178 and 215(2) of the treaty provides for an autonomous appeal fulfilling a particular role within the appeals system and for which have been established conditions for admissibility which are in accordance with its specific aim; that this appeal differs from the appeal for annulment in that it does not aim at annulment of certain measures, but at compensation of damages caused by an institution " (sections 4–7 of the motives).

The Court of Justice thus admits the possibility of liability for a measure which has not previously been annulled. Here again – just as was the case with the exception for illegality – the consequence of a decision of the Court of Justice granting damage for an act of a Community institution would virtually render it inapplicable.

3–65. This conclusion is important for natural and legal persons whose right of direct appeal against Community acts is rather limited, but who have several other opportunities to bring their case before the Court of Justice.

(f) *Other cases within the Court's jurisdiction*

3–66. In the present Section IV of Chapter 3 were successively examined: (a) the proceedings against Member States initiated either by the Commission or by a Member State, (b) proceedings against an institution: appeals for annulment and appeals against inaction, (c) the preliminary ruling, (d) the exception of illegality and (e) the action for non-contractual liability.

The European treaties provide for a number of other cases where the Court of Justice is competent either exclusively or through attribution of competence.

[44] Rec. XVII, 975.

3–67. E.E.C., Art. 179 confers upon the Court of Justice exclusive " jurisdiction in any dispute between the Community and its servants[45] within the limits and under the conditions laid down in the Staff Regulations or the Conditions of Employment."[46] Mention should be made here of a well known case involving a Community official, although not in a dispute with a Community institution, but with a Member State: the *Humblet* case.[47] In its judgment of 16 December 1960, the Court of Justice clearly stated that it has absolutely no jurisdiction over national legal or administrative rules. It concerned Article 16 of the Protocol on Privileges and Immunities of the Community attached to the E.C.S.C. treaty; this is the only Community provision which empowers a natural person to appeal directly against a measure of a Member State.

Usually the cases brought by servants are decided upon by one of the chambers consisting of three judges and one Advocate-General set up under E.E.C., Art. 165.[48]

3–68. E.E.C., Art. 181 provides that " the Court of Justice shall have jurisdiction to give judgment pursuant to any arbitration clause contained in a contract concluded by or on behalf of the Community whether such contract be governed by public law or private law "; this so-called "arbitration clause " which is a contractual provision attributing to the Court of Justice exclusive competence in case of a dispute between the parties to a contract, is necessary to establish the Court's jurisdiction, since E.E.C., Art. 183 provides that the fact that the Community is party to a contract is not sufficient to exclude it from the jurisdiction of national courts. Such clauses have been included in many contracts by the Communities, for instance all the research contracts concluded under Euratom treaty, Art. 10.[49]

3–69. The Court of Justice is also competent to decide any dispute between Member States connected with the subject of the treaties, if the dispute is submitted to it under a special agreement between the parties (E.E.C., Art. 182). If Member States have undertaken not to submit a dispute concerning the interpretation or application of the treaties to any method of settlement other than those provided for in the treaties (E.E.C., Art. 219) they remain free

[45] By the end of 1971, 266 cases had been submitted to the Court of Justice by Community civil servants; the Court of Justice rendered 164 judgments.
[46] See Art. 91 of the Statute, J.O. 1387/62.
[47] Rec. VI, 1131, case 6–60.
[48] See also Art. 15 of the Statute of the Court of Justice.
[49] See P. Mathijsen, " Some Legal Aspects of Euratom," C.M.L.Rev. 1965–1966, 342.

to submit to other tribunals disputes that are no more than " connected " with the treaties; here again, jurisdiction may be attributed to the Court of Justice. This provision has not yet been applied.

3–70. Under Article 186 the Court of Justice may, in cases referred to it, prescribe necessary interim measures; the Court of Justice may also order that an act referred to it be suspended if it considers that circumstances so require (E.E.C., Art. 185). Only once was such a request put to the Court of Justice, but without success.[50]

2. The judges and the Advocates-General

3–71. The Court of Justice consists of seven judges (eleven under Article 17 of the Act of accession) and is assisted by two (three) Advocates-General (E.E.C., Arts. 165, 166). The origins of the latter must be found in the " *commissaire du gouvernement* " of the French *Conseil d'Etat*; his role has been compared with that of a public prosecutor,[51] or, in an English Court, with an *amicus curiae*; in fact he advises the Court. His duty is to make in open Court reasoned submissions (conclusions) on all matters referred to the Court of Justice, in order to assist the Court to achieve the task assigned to it (E.E.C., Art. 166). (See below under 3 for the part played by these submissions within the Court procedures.) The Advocate-General is not a member of the Court (see E.E.C., Arts. 165, 166)[52]; he does not participate in the drafting of the judgments neither in the discussions that lead to the Court's decisions. This independent position allows him to carry out his own personal examination and study of the case in much more detail than the Court itself; he is free also to examine any related question even when it was not brought forward by the parties. Although his submissions do not reflect the Court's views, they often give some indication as to the reasoning which was followed by the Court.

3. The procedure

3–72. According to E.E.C., Art. 188, the Court of Justice must

[50] Case 50–69 R, Rec. XV, 449.
[51] See Advocate-General Gand in *Droit des Communautés Européennes*, 1969, p. 299.
[52] This last provision was included in order to permit two judges in the E.C.S.C. Court of Justice who had no formal legal training to remain on the bench.

lay down its rules of procedure[53] which require the unanimous approval of the Council. The basic rules however are to be found in the Statute of the Court of Justice annexed to the treaties by a special Protocol. The Protocol provides that the Rules of procedure of the Court shall contain, " apart from the provisions contemplated by the Statute, any other provisions necessary for applying and, where necessary, for supplementing it " (Statute, Art. 44).

The procedure before the Court is in two stages: one written and the other oral (Statute, Art. 18). The language of the proceedings must be one of the official languages of the Community[54] and is determined by the plaintiff (Rules of procedure, Art. 29(2)).

3–73. The *written procedure* starts with the submission to the Court of a formal Request which must contain the name and " domicile "[55] of the plaintiff and the status of the signatory, the name of the party against whom the request is lodged, the subject matter of the dispute, the relief sought and a short summary of the main argument on which the petition is based. The Request must be accompanied by other documents such as the act of which annulment is sought; in case the plaintiff is an undertaking, the articles of the company and the powers of attorney of the legal adviser who must necessarily be a practising member of the Bar (Statute, Art. 17). If those documents are not attached the Registrar must request the parties to produce them within a reasonable period; if they are not produced the Court of Justice may declare the request non-admissible (Rules of procedure, Art. 38(7)). But much more important is the provision according to which the Request must contain a short summary of the main arguments: since parties may not at a later stage bring forward other arguments (Rules of procedure, Art. 42(2)).

Essential also is the time-limit within which the Request must be filed: appeals for annulment must be " instituted within two months of the publication of the measure, or of its notification to the plaintiff, or in the absence thereof, of the day on which it came to the

[53] See J.O. 17/60 and Additional Rules 1113/62. For English text see *The Rules of Procedure of the Court of Justice of the European Communities*, Leyden, 1962.

[54] After accession the official languages will be: Danish, German, English, French, Italian, Dutch and Norwegian; see Cmnd. 4862–II, 134.

[55] See Art. 38(2) of the Rules of procedure: each party has to designate an address at the place where the Court has its seat; it is there that the Court sends all the documents; usually this domicile is a lawyer's office in Luxemburg and a fee must be paid for this.

knowledge of the latter, as the case may be " (E.E.C., Art. 173). This time-limit was extended for all parties living outside Luxemburg.[56]

The request is notified to the other party who then has one month to file a Reply. After that each party may submit one more formal document, for which a time-limit (usually two months) is set by the President. An extension of those time-limits can be obtained with valid reasons. Before formally closing the written stage of the procedure, the Court may, at the suggestion of the judge-rapporteur or the advocate-general, decide to " instruct " the case, *i.e.* interrogate the parties, request information, hear witnesses, etc. The Rules contain several provisions in regard to witnesses: the Court may impose penalties in case of default (Statute, Art. 24), the Court may have a witness heard by the judicial authorities of his place of residence (Statute, Art. 26), Member States must treat violation of an oath by a witness in the same manner as if the same offence had been committed before a domestic court dealing with a case in civil proceedings. Member States must prosecute before the competent domestic court any violation reported by the Court of Justice[57] (Statute, Art. 27).

3–74. The *oral procedure* consists of the reading of the report presented by the judge acting as rapporteur, the hearing by the Court of agents, legal advisers or counsel and of the submissions of the advocate-general (Statute, Art. 18). These submissions are usually read during a separate court session and indicate the end of the oral procedure. The judgment of the Court is, in turn, read a few weeks later.[58] This judgment always contains a decision regarding the costs which are normally paid by the losing party whether Member State, undertaking or Community Official.

3–75. The Statute of the Court of Justice and the Rules of Procedure contain provisions for various special proceedings such as the summary procedure, intervention, retrial and interpretation or review of judgment.

Lawyers who hope to act as counsel in proceedings before the Court would do well to pay special attention to Articles 32 to 36 of the Rules of procedure.

[56] See J.O. 378/59.

[57] See European Communities Bill, cl. 11.

[58] On the average it takes a year between the moment the Request is filed and the judgment is read.

V. Other Organs of the European Communities

1. The Economic and Social Committee

3–76. On several occasions mention was made of this Committee with regard to the decision-making process within the Communities; as was pointed out also, this Committee, contrary to the Assembly, is consulted both by the Commission and the Council (E.E.C., Art. 198). This consultation, when provided for by the treaty, must necessarily take place lest the decision might be annulled by the Court of Justice for " violation of basic procedural rules " (E.E.C., Art. 173); an appeal for annulment may not however be lodged by the Committee itself, since it is not an " institution of the Communities " and only Member States, institutions and, under certain conditions, undertakings and individuals can do so.[59] Furthermore such consultation when required must be referred to in the regulations, directives and decisions of the Council and of the Commission[60] (E.E.C., Art. 190). The Committee may also be consulted by the Council and the Commission in all cases where they deem it appropriate (E.E.C., Art. 198).

The Economic and Social Committee has a purely consultative status and although the Court of Justice in its judgment in the *Van Gend en Loos* case mentioned that through the Assembly and this Committee the citizens of the Member States participate in the Community activities,[61] the Committee in fact plays a minor role within the Communities. It consists of 101[62] " representatives of the various categories of economic and social activity, in particular, representatives of producers, farmers, transport operators, workers, merchants, artisans, the professions and representatives of the general interest " (E.E.C., Art. 193). The Committee must be so composed as to ensure adequate representation of the various categories of economic and social activity (E.E.C., Art. 195). Presently there are three groups in the Committee: as provided for by Article 19 of the Rules of Procedure[63]: Employers (thirty-one members: thirteen for private industry, three state industry, five

[59] See however judgment of the Court of Justice of 7 July 1971, Rec. XVII, 689.
[60] See below, Chap. 5, acts must be reasoned.
[61] Rec. IX, 23 and [1963] C.M.L.R., 129.
[62] Germany, France, Italy (and Great Britain) have 24 members each, Belgium and The Netherlands 12, (Denmark, Ireland and Norway 9) and Luxemburg 5 (6). The figures in brackets are those provided for in the Act of accession, Art. 21.
[63] E.E.C., Art. 196; J.O. L 42, 1968.

transport, four agriculture, two chambers of commerce, two commerce, one medium and small undertakings and one banking), Employees (thirty-six members affiliated to christian, socialist and communist trade unions) and various activities (thirty-four persons: nine agriculture, six medium and small undertakings, four consumers and family, four professions, two managers, four commerce and five various interests).

The representatives are appointed by the Council in their personal capacity and may not be bound by any mandatory instructions; they are appointed for four years, renewable (E.E.C., Art. 194). Details as to the appointment procedure are to be found in E.E.C., Art. 195.[64]

2. The Consultative Committee of the E.C.S.C.

3–77. The E.C.S.C. treaty provides for the creation of a Consultative Committee consisting of not less than thirty and not more than fifty-one members (under Article 22 of the Act of accession these figures become respectively sixty and eighty-four) made up of an equal number of producers, workers and consumers and dealers. They are appointed for two years by the Council from lists drawn up by representative organisations also designated by the Council (E.C.S.C., Art. 18).

The function of the Consultative Committee is in all points comparable to that of the Economic and Social Committee (E.C.S.C., Art. 19).

3. The Scientific and Technical Committee of Euratom

3–78. The twenty (twenty-eight under Article 23 of the Act of accession) members are appointed for five years by the Council after the Commission has been consulted; like the other two committees it has a consultative status (Euratom, Art. 134).

3–79. At the end of this Chapter concerning the Community's institutions it might be of interest to reflect on the relations the individual citizen is likely to have with them. Those relations will not in fact be any different from those he has at home with his own

[64] Each Member State provides the Council with a list containing twice as many candidates as there are seats allotted to its nationals (see E.E.C., Art. 194 and Act of accession, Art. 21).

national institutions. A citizen does not often deal direct with the legislature, unless it is through his M.P. Since the legislative power in the European Communities is not in the hands of the (parliamentary) Assembly whose members are also (at least for the time being) members of the national parliaments, the contacts a normal citizen has with his representative are of no avail in this field. There is, on the other hand, ample opportunity for communication between him and at least one of the " legislative " and " executive " institutions of the Communities, the Commission. Where the latter is concerned, useful contacts can be established by undertakings or individuals having a legitimate case either directly or through the representatives of the various industrial organisations represented in Brussels. Since the Commission has the right of initiating legislation, such contacts can be particularly useful.

There is however a field in which natural and legal persons established in the Member States have direct dealings with the Commission, namely " competition "; it has been explained in Chapter 2 that the Articles 85 and 86 directly impose obligations on the undertakings and that, consequently, the Commission enforces those rules without interference from the Member States. It is important for companies located in Great Britain to realise that after 1 January 1973 they must reckon with this Community institution (see Chap. 2, (f) dealing with the rules of competition).

3–80. Probably more important for persons and enterprises is the Court of Justice to which, as was seen, they can appeal either directly or through their national courts. The judicial protection thus given to the citizens of the Member States, especially in regard to the self-executing provisions of Community law might very well become the most tangible aspect of the European Communities.

British citizens who from the time of accession will have to comply with Community measures either directly addressed to them or published in the Official Journal, which shall be " admissible as evidence of any instrument or other act thereby communicated of any of the Communities or of any Community institution " (European Communities Bill, Cl. 3(2)), will also be able to request British courts to " enforce " such legislation (European Communities Bill, Cl. 2(1)) and to appeal against such acts in the Court of Justice of the European Communities (E.E.C., Art. 173) in cases which they deem unlawful. When doing so they will find at least one British judge on the bench of this Court, they will be able to express themselves in English and they will be assisted, if they so wish, by British lawyers who are members of the Bar in the United Kingdom; they will by doing so, be submitted to rules of procedure of the Court, and so will be their lawyers; false evidence given by them on oath before this Court will constitute a criminal offence under the applicable national law (European Communities Bill, Pt. II).

They can also challenge the validity of Community acts in their national courts when those courts are requested to apply these acts in cases in which they are a party and when a dispute arises over the exact meaning of such acts they may request that the national judge ask the Court of Justice to rule on the interpretation of such acts (E.E.C., Art. 177). And when they find Community acts have caused them injury, they may go to the Court of Justice and seek reparation under E.E.C., Art. 215.

As will be seen in the last chapter, the fines imposed upon natural or legal persons by the European Commission will be enforceable in the United Kingdom (E.E.C., Art. 191) in accordance with local rules; such enforcement may only be suspended by a decision of the Court of Justice, while national courts will have jurisdiction over complaints that enforcement is being carried out in an irregular manner. As for the fines, being acts of the European institutions their legality can of course also be challenged in the Court of Justice.

4. Future developments

3–81. " Reinforcement of the Institutions " is a recurring phrase in many official statements. Does this mean that the present institutional set-up of the Communities is not adequate to cope with the problems of an ever growing and developing Community? It might seem unrealistic to try to answer this question at all. However, it is fair to say that the adequacy of institutions, especially in the interstate sphere, depends not upon the formal powers and procedures provided for, but exclusively on the political will of the Member States and also to a very large degree upon the personality and quality of the individuals who compose the institutions. In this respect the European Communities are probably not much different from national institutions. Most of the achievements – customs union, agricultural policy and competition policy – are due in large part to the initiatives and urgings of the Commission; the failure of progress in other fields practically always finds its cause in the inability of the inter-governmental body, the Council, to reach agreement: transport policy, regional policy, industrial policy, social policy, commercial policy. From past experience one might therefore conclude that the future of European integration certainly does not lie in giving more power to the intergovernmental procedures, especially not when for important matters only unanimous voting is accepted; rather it appears that more decision-making power within the framework of general lines defined by the Council should be attributed to a Commission manned by political figures. But this Commission must then be allowed to delegate some of its administrative work to one or a group of its members and to its top civil servants. This, in turn, requires of course a more effective democratic control.

CHAPTER 4

FINANCIAL PROVISIONS

4–1. On 22 April 1970 the Six signed at Luxemburg a treaty " amending certain Budgetary Provisions of the Treaties establishing the European Communities and of the Treaty establishing a Single Council and a Single Commission of the European Communities."[1] This treaty became effective on 1 January 1971. In pursuance of Article 10 of said treaty, the revenue and expenditure of the three European Communities, " with the exception of that of the Supply Agency[2] and the Joint Undertakings,"[3] are shown in the " budget of the European Communities."[4] This single budget replaced the E.C.S.C. administrative budget, the E.E.C. budget and the Euratom operating and research and investment budgets.

The basic principle of the European budget is that it must be in balance as to revenue and expenditure. Until recently, the revenue consisted for the E.E.C. and Euratom mainly in contributions of the Member States, on a scale provided for in the treaty[5]: Germany, France and Italy paid 28 per cent. each, Belgium and The Netherlands 7.9 and Luxemburg the remaining 0.2; in the Coal and Steel Community the revenue came from the levies imposed on the production of coal and steel.[6] The latter was not modified by the Merger treaty which repealed E.C.S.C., Art. 78[7] nor by the treaty amending certain Budgetary Provisions.[8]

4–2. As for the E.E.C. and Euratom, the treaty of 22 April 1970 and the related Council decisions of 21 April 1970 introduced important changes since the decisions provide for the replacement of financial contributions from Member States by the Communities' own resources. This replacement was provided for by the original

[1] See Cmnd. 4867 and J.O. L 2, 1971.
[2] See Euratom, Art. 54: " The Agency shall have legal personality and financial autonomy."
[3] See Euratom, Arts. 45–51.
[4] Also excluded from the joint budget are the financial activities of the European Investment Bank and of the European Development Fund.
[5] See E.E.C., Art. 200 and Euratom, Art. 172.
[6] See E.C.S.C., Arts. 49, 78.
[7] See new Art. 78(6) established by Merger treaty, Art. 21.
[8] See Art. 2(8) of that treaty.

European treaties: " the Commission shall examine the conditions under which the financial contributions of Member States provided for in Article 200 could be replaced by the Communities' own resources, in particular by revenue accruing from the common customs tariff when it has been finally introduced. To this end the Commission shall submit proposals to the Council. After consulting the Assembly on these proposals the Council may, acting unanimously, lay down the appropriate provisions, which it shall recommend to the Member States for adoption in accordance with their respective constitutional requirements " (E.E.C., Art. 201).[9] It will be noticed that this treaty provision only refers to customs duties; however, Regulation 25[10] on financing the common agricultural policy stipulates in its Article 2(1) that at the single market stage revenue from agricultural levies shall be allocated to the Community and appropriated to Community expenditure. Also in pursuance of this Regulation the European Agricultural Guidance and Guarantee Fund forms part of the Community budget and Regulation 130 of 1966[11] provided that 90 per cent. of all the levies collected by a Member State must be contributed to the Guarantee Section of the Agricultural Fund, the remaining revenue coming from contributions from Member States on a special scale which applies equally to the Orientation Section. This situation prevailed until the end of 1969. For 1970 a purely temporary scale of contributions to the Agricultural Fund was established.[12] On 1 January 1971 the provisions recommended by the Council decision of 21 April 1970 became effective.[13] This decision provides for an interim-period (1971–1974) and a definitive period (beginning on 1 January 1975). During the interim-period the total revenue from agricultural levies shall be entered in the budget and the revenue from customs duties shall progressively be thus allocated (Decision, Art. 3(1)). During the same period the financial contributions from Member States required in order to ensure that the budget is in balance are appointed on a scale which differs slightly from the one provided in E.E.C., Art. 200: instead of contributing 28 per cent. each, Germany, France and Italy now pay respectively 32.9, 32.6 and 20.2 per cent., whilst

[9] See also Euratom, Art. 173.
[10] J.O. 991/62.
[11] J.O. 965/66.
[12] Reg. 728/70 of the Council, 21 April 1970, J.O. L 94, 1970.
[13] Cmnd. 4867, 19 and J.O. L 94, 1970.

Belgium and The Netherlands now contribute 6.8 and 7.3 instead of 7.9 per cent.

4–3. From 1 January 1975 the budget of the Communities shall, irrespective of other revenue (such as fines and penalties, taxes on the salaries of the Communities' civil servants, sales of publications, etc.), be financed entirely from the Communities' own resources, *i.e.* the total revenue from agricultural levies and from customs duties and also those resources " accruing from the value added tax and obtained by applying a rate not exceeding 1 per cent. to an assessment basis which is determined in a uniform manner for Member States according to Community rules. The rate shall be fixed within the framework of the budgetary procedure " (Decision of 21 April 1970, Art. 4(1)). In other words, by 1975 the value added tax will be levied on a uniform basis of assessment throughout the Community and a percentage thereof (not to exceed one point) will accrue to the Community.

National administrations will remain responsible for collecting the revenue in question but it will belong wholly to the Community. As was pointed out by the Commission, " the application of such a system of administrative co-operation cannot fail to raise legal problems of a more or less novel character in the life of the Communities."[14]

4–4. The creation of Community resources produced some institutional changes. For years, the question of an increased parliamentary control over the Communities' finances was discussed, not only by the European Assembly itself but also by the other institutions and by the Governments of the Member States. It will be remembered that the crisis that rocked the E.E.C. in 1965–66 was caused by the Commission proposals concerning the financing of the common agricultural policy linked with the introduction of direct revenue for the Community and increased budgetary powers for the Assembly.[15] But it was only by a resolution annexed to the Treaty of 22 April 1970 that the Council expressed willingness to associate Parliament more closely with the elaboration of the Communities' budget. This was the direct consequence of the allocation to the Communities of their own resources: since democratic control can no longer be exercised at the national level, it became indispensable

[14] Fourth General Report, 1970, 395.
[15] See Chap. 3, II, 1, above.

to establish it at Community level. From fiscal year 1975 onwards, the Assembly will possess a genuine power of decision over expenditures other than those necessarily resulting from the treaties or from acts adopted thereunder, the latter being referred to as "*dépenses fatales*."[16] The Assembly will not only have the right to amend the draft budget (by a majority vote) but also the right to take the final decision (majority vote, including three-fifths of the votes cast) whenever its own amendments have been altered by a qualified majority vote of the Council.[17]

Finally the treaty of 22 April 1970 provides that henceforth the Assembly and the Council shall be jointly responsible for giving discharge to the Commission in respect to the implementation of the budget.[18]

In 1971 the Communities' budget was made up as follows[19]

	£ million
European Agricultural Fund	1,096
Community administrative costs	62
Repayment to Member States to cover costs of collecting levies and duties	56
Euratom research and investment	28
European Social Fund	23
Food Aid	8
	1,273

4–5. In the July 1971 White Paper the British Government summarised as follows how United Kingdom contribution to the Community budget will be established: "a percentage or 'key' has been set, broadly corresponding to our present share of the total gross national product (GNP) of the ten countries likely to form the enlarged Community. This will represent the proportion of the budget which we should *nominally* be expected to pay in the first year of membership. This key will increase marginally in each of the four subsequent years . . . (1973: 19.19 per cent. and 20.56 per cent. in 1977). However, we shall pay only a portion of our *nominal* contribution over these first five years. The proportion will increase

[16] These "*dépenses fatales*" amount to about 97 per cent. of the budget; this means that the Assembly's powers are limited to the remaining 3 per cent.

[17] Compare with the procedure provided for in E.E.C., Art. 203(3) and (4).

[18] For more details see Fourth General Report, 1971, 396.

[19] Cmnd. 4715, 42.

in annual steps (1973: 45 per cent. of 19.19 per cent. and in 1977: 92 per cent. of the 20.56 per cent."

Or, to put it more simply, in 1973 the United Kingdom will be expected to pay 8.64 per cent. of the budget of the enlarged Community and 18.92 per cent. in the fifth year or, assuming that the budget will amount to £1,600 million in 1977, the size of Britain's gross contribution would be £300 million and its receipts £100 million.

Chapter 5

ACTS OF THE INSTITUTIONS

I. General

5–1. E.E.C., Art. 189 (Euratom, Art. 161) provides that " in order to carry out their task the Council and the Commission shall, in accordance with the provisions of this Treaty, make regulations, issue directives, take decisions, make recommendations or deliver opinions." The E.C.S.C. treaty refers in its Article 14 to decisions, recommendations and opinions; from Article 33 it follows that E.C.S.C. decisions are either " general " or " individual "; the former correspond to the " regulations " of the Rome treaties and the latter to the " decisions," while E.C.S.C. recommendations are similar to " directives." In the following pages reference will be made only to the E.E.C./Euratom terminology. Whether an act is a regulation rather than, for instance, a decision is relevant in more than one respect. Each category fulfils a specific function in the development of Community law and the European treaties therefore explicitly provide in several cases, which kind of act must be adopted. Different procedural rules apply to the various categories and, which is more important, the extent of legal protection afforded individuals under the treaties varies widely from one category to another as was explained in Chapter 3, IV. As the Court clearly stated on several occasions, it is not the name given by the institutions to an act which classifies it in one of the above mentioned categories, but rather the contents and objective of its provisions.[1] The Court has also admitted that the same act can contain provisions of different categories: a regulation for instance can contain provisions which by their very nature constitute individual decisions.[2]

5–2. A *regulation* has general application. It is binding in its entirety and directly applicable in all Member States (E.E.C., Art.

[1] Rec. V, 181, case 20–58 and Rec. VIII, 918, joint cases 16 and 17–62.

[2] Rec. VIII, 918, joint cases 16 and 17–62. In its judgment of 13 March 1971, joint cases 41 to 44–70, the Court of Justice found that regulation 983/70 was not a provision with general application but a series of individual decisions; Rec. XVII, 422 (21), joint cases 41 to 44–70.

189). Regulations are by far the most important source of secondary legislation of the European Communities. In regard to " general application," the Court of Justice stated in its judgment of 11 July 1968[3] that the act in question " constitutes a measure with general application as provided for under Article 189, since it applies to situations which are objectively defined and has legal effect for categories of individuals which are defined in a general and abstract way."[4]

Previously the Court of Justice had defined E.C.S.C. general decisions (regulations) as " quasi-legislative acts issued by a public authority and having normative effect *erga omnes*."[5]

Regulations, according to E.E.C., Art. 189 are binding in their entirety. This distinguishes them from directives which are only binding as to the results to be achieved. In this respect it is of interest to know that E.E.C., Art. 174 provides that if an action for annulment is well founded the Court of Justice which then declares the act concerned to be void, can " in the case of a regulation, . . . if it considers this necessary, state which of the effects of the regulation which it has declared void shall be considered as definitive." In other words, since all the provisions of a regulation are binding, the Court can declare that certain remain in force although the act has in fact become void.

Reference was made in Chapter 1 to the fact that regulations are " directly applicable " and it was pointed out that such Community law provisions create rights and obligations not only for the Member States but also, without further enactment or interference from national authorities, for the citizens; the latter can request the national courts to uphold these rights and national judges must apply these Community provisions, even if they conflict with national laws. However, the expression " directly applicable " in E.E.C., Art. 189 does not mean that this is the case for all the provisions of every single regulation. Here again it depends on the nature of each provision and whether or not the criteria specified by the Court of Justice for direct applicability are fulfilled.[6] Many provisions contained in Community regulations need implementation by national provisions before they can be applied; but, the regula-

[3] Rec. XIV, 605, case 6–68.
[4] See also Rec. XIV, 180, case 30–67.
[5] Rec. II, 227, case 8–55; see also Rec. IX, 455, cases 23, 24 and 52–63.
[6] See above, Chap. 1.

tion as such does not have to be transformed into national law by a national measure to become " applicable."[7]

Finally, the description given by E.E.C., Art. 189 of a regulation refers to direct applicability " in all Member States "; these words are important: they should be understood as meaning that the binding force and the applicability is identical in the whole Community. In its judgment of 18 February 1970 (case 40–69), the Court of Justice held that " since in pursuance of Article 189(2), E.E.C. Regulation No. 22/62 is directly applicable in all Member States, it is excluded (unless otherwise provided) that they enact measures for its implementation whereby its application is modified or whereby provisions are added to it."[8]

5–3. A *directive*, according to E.E.C., Art. 189 shall be binding, as to the results to be achieved, upon each Member State to which it is addressed,[9] but shall leave to the national authorities the choice of form and methods. Directives can be issued by the Council[10] or by the Commission[11] and constitute the appropriate measure when existing national legislation must be modified or provisions enacted: Member States are for instance free to decide whether these provisions will be legislative or administrative in nature.

For many years writers[12] discussed the question whether or not directive provisions could be directly applicable, *i.e.* create rights without national implementing legislation. In a judgment of 6 October 1970, the Court of Justice decided that " if, in accordance with Article 189, regulations are directly applicable and consequently are, by their very nature, capable of producing direct legal effects, it does not follow that the other acts mentioned in this Article can never have similar effects "[13] and the Court concluded that " the provisions of the decision and of the directive, taken together, produce direct effects in the relations between the Member States

[7] See for instance Regulation 22/62, J.O. 959/62.

[8] Rec. XVI, 80(4); it should however be noted that the applicability in all Member States does not necessarily mean that every regulation does always apply in every Member State: Reg. 125/64 for instance only applies to the price of rice in France.

[9] Act of accession, Art. 149 provides that " fiom accession, the new Member States shall be considered as being addressees . . . of directives within the meaning of Article 189 . . . provided that these directives . . . have been notified to all the original Member States."

[10] See for instance E.E.C., Arts. 21(1), 54(2), 57(1), 63(2), 100.

[11] See for instance E.E.C., Art. 13(2).

[12] See M. Waelbroeck, " The application of E.E.C. law by national courts," *Stanford Law Review*, 1967, 1274.

[13] Rec. XVI, 838 (5), case 9–70.

and their citizens and create for the latter the right to invoke them before the courts."[14] The Court of Justice based its conclusion *inter alia* on E.E.C., Art. 177, which does not distinguish between the various categories provided for under E.E.C., Art. 189 and thereby implies that all these acts can be invoked in the national courts.

5–4. As for the *decision*, it is " binding in its entirety upon those to whom it is addressed " (E.E.C., Art. 189). The addressee can be a Member State or a legal or natural person and decisions can be taken by the Council and by the Commission: decisions are generally administrative decisions implementing Community law: granting of exceptions or authorisations, imposition of fines or obligations, etc. In several cases the Court of Justice had to decide whether or not a certain act of a Community institution constituted a binding decision; in the case 54–56 the Court of Justice held that " a decision must appear as an act of a competent organ, destined to produce legal consequences and bringing to a close the internal proceeding of said organ through which the latter rules definitively in a form which permits identification of its nature."[15] In other words, a decision settles a concrete individual case and must be recognisable as a binding act.[16]

5–5. E.E.C., Art. 189 (Euratom, Art. 161) also mentions " recommendations " and " opinions " and simply states that they " have no binding force "; the main consequence is that they cannot be reviewed by the Court of Justice (E.E.C., Art. 173, and Euratom, Art. 146). When the powers of the Assembly[17] were examined, it was pointed out that it was not clear whether or not an institution could make recommendations or deliver opinions when it is not explicitly provided for by the treaties. The question arises because E.E.C., Art. 189 (Euratom, Art. 161) states that the Council and the Commission shall enact the various measures referred to " in accordance with the provisions of the Treaty " and this expression is generally read to mean that only when expressly called for can the institutions issue such measures or, in other words, the powers of the institutions to act are not general but are specifically attributed by the treaties. Writers have accepted the idea that this limitation only applies to binding acts, *i.e.* " acts of the Council and the Commission other

[14] *Ibid.* (10). Rec. XVI, 838 (10).
[15] Rec. XII, 280.
[16] Rec. IX, 481 (case 28–63) and 507 (case 53 and 54–63).
[17] See above, Chap. 3.

than recommendations or opinions " (E.E.C., Art. 173 – Euratom, Art. 146).

Generally speaking " recommendations " aim at obtaining a certain action or behaviour from the addressee while " opinions " express a point of view at the request of a third party; this distinction however is legally irrelevant.

II. Acts must be Reasoned

5–6. " Regulations, directives and decisions of the Council and of the Commission shall state the reasons on which they are based and shall refer to any proposals or opinions which were required to be obtained pursuant to this Treaty " (E.E.C., Art. 190, Euratom, Art. 162 and E.C.S.C., Art. 15).

If an act is not or not sufficiently reasoned, this constitutes an " infringement of an essential procedural requirement " which can be a ground for an action in which the Court of Justice has jurisdiction to review the legality of such an act and to annulment of it in case the action is well founded (E.E.C., Arts. 173, 174; Euratom, Arts. 146, 147 and E.C.S.C., Art. 33). At one point the Court even held that the absence of reasons entailed the non-existence of the act[18]; this rather extreme position was not confirmed in later judgments. In the conception of the Court, that a decision shall be " reasoned " means that (1) the legal ground, (2) the reasons which motivated the institution to act and (3) the proposals and opinions concerning the act must be mentioned.

5–7. The fact that the legal grounds, that is the legal provisions empowering the institution to act, must be referred to stems from the basic principle – already mentioned several times, according to which the Community institutions only possess those powers which have been explicitly conferred to them by the European treaties or other acts (" conferred powers "). Every regulation, directive or decision must therefore necessarily refer to one of the treaties and more specifically to one or more provisions thereof.[19] In this respect attention must be drawn to E.E.C., Art. 235 (Euratom, Art. 203;

[18] Judgment of 10 December 1957 (cases 1 and 14–57), Rec. III, 220.

[19] Some indications as to the precise form of Community acts are laid down in the rules of procedure of the Council, Art. 11: Council regulations contain: (a) . . . (b) the indication of the provision by virtue of which the regulation is enacted starting with the word " considering "; (c) the mention of proposals, opinions and consultations which must be requested; (d) the reasons for the regulation, starting with the word " whereas "; Decision of the Council of 15 April 1958 (not published).

E.C.S.C Art. 95): " if action by the Community should prove necessary to attain, in the course of the operation of the Common Market, one of the objectives of the Community and this Treaty has not provided the necessary powers, the Council shall, acting unanimously on a proposal from the Commission and after consulting the Assembly, take the appropriate measures." By thus providing the possibility to " create " additional powers in case of need, the draftsmen of the treaties have shown unusual foresight since they recognised the fact that they might have overlooked some essential elements and furthermore that especially in the field of economics, no rule, however cleverly drafted, can provide solutions for all future contingencies. And they were proved right since many a regulation is based, at least partially, on E.E.C., Art. 235.

This provision should not, however, be considered as opening unlimited opportunity to increase the powers of the Communities, although it does constitute a way of supplementing the treaty provisions without going through the usual (cumbersome) procedures. First, appropriate measures may only be taken on the basis of E.E.C., Art. 235 when action is necessary to attain "one of the objectives of the Community," which clearly indicates that the powers granted by this provision are purely complementary. Also, the required unanimous vote of the Council should provide the necessary guarantee since any extension of the Communities' powers will, generally speaking, reduce in the same proportion the powers of the Member States.[19a]

Related to this principle of " conferred powers " is the question of " implied powers." As was mentioned before, in two cases the Court of Justice admitted that " rules established by international agreement or by law are considered to imply these rules without which the first either would have no sense or could not be reasonably or successfully applied."[20] This prudent approach to a controversial question cannot be considered as opening the door to extensive treaty interpretation, in regard to the powers of the Community institutions; the principle of " conferred powers " therefore remains.

5–8. Besides the legal grounds, the binding acts of the Com-

[19a] The application of Article 235 of the E.E.C. treaty is further limited by the existence of Art. 236 which provides for formal amendment of the treaty. The Merger treaty of 8 April 1965 and the treaty amending certain budgetary provision constitute amendments provided for under E.E.C., Art. 236 (E.C.S.C., Art. 96 and 204, Euratom, Art. 204).

[20] Rec. II, 305 and 359 (cases 8–55 and 9–55); see case 22–70, Rec. XVII, 263.

munities must also mention the reasons which motivated the institutions to act. In the case 14–61, judgment of 12 July 1962 the Court of Justice held that this condition is fulfilled " when it is possible for the interested parties and for the Court to reconstruct the essential elements of the High Authority's reasoning."[21] The Court was more explicit in its judgment of 4 July 1963 in the case 24–62: " whereas by imposing upon the Commission the obligation to indicate the reasons for its decision, Article 190 does not only satisfy a formal need, but aims at permitting the parties to defend their rights, the Court to exercise its control and the Member States, and in the same way all interested citizens, to know the conditions under which the Commission has applied the Treaty; and that, to attain these objectives, it was sufficient for the decision to state explicitly, even if concisely but clearly and pertinently, the main legal and factual elements supporting the decision and necessary to understand the reasoning which prompted the Commission."[22] An extensive indication of reasons is especially required when the institution exercises discretionary powers, since in such cases the judicial control of the Court of Justice is limited and the decision to act is based upon the institution's appreciation.[23]

In short, the foregoing means that all the main elements of a binding act must be " explained " in the recitals.

5–9. As for the reference to the proposals and opinions, a simple mention is considered sufficient. The Court of Justice decided on 11 February 1955 that the institution is not required to indicate whether or not the advice was favourable and certainly not to refute dissenting opinions.[24]

III. Publication and Entrance into Force

5–10. E.E.C., Art. 191, para. 1 (Euratom, Art. 163 and E.C.S.C., Art. 15) provides that " regulations shall be published in the Official Journal of the Community.[25] They shall enter into force on the date specified in them, or, in the absence thereof, on the twentieth day following their publication." A typical example of the latter case is

[21] Rec. VIII, 523.
[22] Rec. IX, 143.
[23] See judgment of 15 July 1960 (joint cases 36, 37, 38 and 40–59), Rec. VI, 897.
[24] See judgment of 11 February 1955 (case 4–54), Rec. I, 196.
[25] On 15 September 1958, the Council decided to " consolidate " the existing E.C.S.C. Official Journal and the E.E.C. and Euratom Official Journal. See J.O. 390/58.

Regulation 17 (giving effect to the principles set out in E.E.C., Arts. 85, 86): this regulation was adopted on 6 February 1962 by the Council, published in the Official Journal of 21 February 1962 and since it did not mention the date of entry into force, became effective on 13 March 1962.

The Official Journal is presently published in Dutch, French, German and Italian; it is understood that " authentic English texts which will apply after the United Kingdom's accession to the Communities will be published in due course in an English Language Edition of the Official Journal of the European Communities."[26] And indeed Council Regulation No. 1 of 15 April 1958[27] will be modified in pursuance of Article 29 of the Act of accession, together with Point XIV (1) of Annex I to said Act in such a way that from accession on its Article 1 will read: " The official languages and the working languages of the institutions of the Community shall be Danish, German, English, French, Italian, Dutch and Norwegian." Furthermore, Article 155 of the Act of accession provides that: " the texts of the Acts of the institutions of the Community adopted before accession and drawn up by the Council or the Commission in the Danish, English and Norwegian languages shall, from the date of accession, be authentic under the same conditions as the texts drawn up in the four original languages. They shall be published in the *Official Journal of the European Communities* if the texts in the original languages were so published."[28]

The second paragraph of E.E.C., Art. 191 (Euratom, Art. 163; E.C.S.C., Art. 15) provides that " directives and decisions shall be notified to those to whom they are addressed and shall take effect upon such notification." It follows that these acts do not have to be published and this was confirmed by the Court of Justice (joint cases 73 and 74–63) in its judgment of 18 February 1964. The Court added however " that it appears desirable that a decision of this nature which affects the rights and interests of the citizens of several Member States does not remain unpublished when in analogous cases publication is guaranteed."[29] And indeed, since the Court of Justice can, in pursuance of E.E.C., Art. 173 (Euratom, Art. 146;

[26] *European Communities, Secondary Legislation*, English text.
[27] J.O. 385/58.
[28] See Reg. 857/72 of the Council of 24 April 1972 concerning the establishment of special editions of the *Official Journal of the European Communities*, J.O. L 101, 1972. See also Cmnd. 4862–II, 134.
[29] Rec. X, 28

E.C.S.C., Art. 33) review the legality of decisions at the request of parties which are not addressees of said acts when the latter are of " direct and individual concern " to them, it is important that they be informed of the contents of all such decisions.[30] This explains why most decisions are actually published in the Official Journal of the Communities.

IV. Enforcement

5–11. Decisions of the Council or of the Commission which impose a pecuniary obligation[31] on persons other than States and judgments of the Court of Justice are enforceable under the conditions laid down in E.E.C., Art. 192 (Euratom, Art. 164; E.C.S.C., Art. 92). These conditions are, generally speaking, that " enforcement shall be governed by the rules of civil procedure in force in the State in the territory of which it is carried out." The procedure provided for under the European treaties is the following:

The beneficiary of a decision or judgment must in the first place obtain a certified copy from the Council, Commission or Court of Justice. The party concerned then presents this copy to " the national authority which the Government of each Member State shall designate for this purpose and shall make known to the Commission and to the Court of Justice"[32] and applies for implementation of the formalities provided in E.E.C., Art. 192. To do this, the national authority only has to verify the authenticity of the decision, nothing more; thus no *ex equatur* as in the case of a foreign judgment. To verify the authenticity means, in practice, checking whether or not the signatures appearing on the document are authentic: to this end the Community institutions have sent specimens of the signatures of their members to the national authorities.

Once the authenticity is established " the order for its enforcement shall be appended to the decision " by said authority. How this

[30] See submissions in the case 69–69, Rec. XVI, 397.

[31] For instance, decisions imposing fines pursuant to Art. 15 of Reg. 17, J.O. 204/62.

[32] The Netherlands: Law of 24 February 1955, Stb 73, modified by Law of 13 January 1960, Stb 15: Minister of Justice is addressee of request; Greffier of Hoge Raad implements. Belgium: Law of 6 August 1967: Greffier en Chef of the Court of Appeal at Brussels. France: Décret No. 57/321 of 13 March 1957, *Journal Officiel*, 19 March 1957, 2885, designates (1) persons who have received delegation from the Prime Minister and (2) Secrétariat Général du Comité Interministériel. Germany: Bundesgesetzblatt, 3 February 1961, II, 50: Minister of Justice. Italy: Decree of 2 December 1960, Official Gazetta, 21 February 1961, No. 46, 738: Minister of Foreign Affairs. Luxemburg: Reg. of 17 October 1962, Memorial of 31 October 1962, No. 58, 1028: verification by Minister of Foreign Affairs, and order for enforcement appended by Minister of Justice.

is done varies from State to State; in The Netherlands for instance the formula " in the Queen's name " is written on the document itself, which thereby acquires the same legal force as a national Court or administrative order.

The party concerned can then proceed to enforcement in accordance with national law, by bringing the matter directly before the competent national authority. From this moment on the national rules of civil procedure apply with the exception that suspension of the enforcement may only be decided by the Court of Justice.

V. Other Community Acts not provided for under E.E.C., Art. 189

5–12. Regulations, directives and decisions are not the only binding acts provided for in the European treaties. Community law can also be created for instance by agreements concluded by the European Communities with third States or with international organisations,[33] agreements concluded by the Member States among themselves regarding matters connected with the treaties, either in pursuance of the latter[34] or on their own initiative and, finally, decisions of the representatives of the Governments of the Member States meeting in Council. Typical examples of the latter are the so-called acceleration decisions by which the Member States agreed to establish the Customs Union within a shorter time-limit than provided for under the E.E.C. treaty.[35]

All these acts prevail over regulations, directives and decisions and constitute rules of law relating to the application of the treaties within the meaning of E.E.C., Art. 173; Euratom, Art. 146 and E.C.S.C., Art. 33. The international agreements concluded by the Communities or by the Member States in connection with the treaties are also submitted to the control of legality exercised by the Court of Justice; indeed, the E.E.C., Art. 173 and Euratom, Art. 146 refer without limitation to " acts of the Council and the Commission other than recommendations or opinions."[36] The fact that the decisions of the representatives of the governments of the Member

[33] See E.E.C., Art. 228 and Euratom, Art. 101.
[34] See for instance E.E.C., Arts. 50, 220.
[35] J.O. 1217/60 and 1284/62.
[36] See case 22–70, judgment of 31 March 1971, wherein the Commission asked the Court of Justice to annul a decision of the Council concerning the conclusion of an international agreement, Rec. XVII, 264.

States meeting in Council are on the contrary not submitted to the Court's jurisdiction is only one of the many problems raised by these acts which are not explicitly provided for by the treaties.[37]

Since these decisions constitute agreements between the Member States they are in fact international " treaties " and should as such, depending on the national constitutional provisions, be submitted to national parliamentary control. Owing to the great variety of such decisions, it is impossible to give a general definition of these acts or to determine whether or not they are for instance binding not only for the Member States but also for the Community institutions or even for natural and legal persons. This must be established on a case by case basis.

Although these " decisions " provide a very flexible instrument in the hands of the Member States, they undoubtedly are not without danger, and not least for the institutional equilibrium provided by the European treaties. Beside immunity from the Court's control these acts which are not unimportant for the development of Community law do not require a Commission proposal or an opinion of the European Assembly. As long as they concern matters not provided for under the treaties they seem unavoidable but if they are used to escape the Community procedures they should be vigorously opposed by the Community and the national institutions alike.

[37] They are not to be confused with decisions of the Member States, such as the appointment of the members of the Commission (Merger treaty, Art. 11) or the judges of the Court (E.E.C., Art. 167): these decisions are taken " by common accord of the governments of the Member States " and " in accordance with the provisions of the Treaty."

FINAL REMARK

This book attempts to give a photograph of the present development of Community law (mid-1972). The reader should bear in mind that this law, more than any other, is in constant evolution since it aims at transforming several national economies (an evolutive matter by definition) into a single economy. Moreover, the accession of four new Member States is certain to have a profound impact on the future developments of Community law. If one adds to that the fact that the European Communities are, at the same time, faced with profound and dramatic choices as to their own future developments – economic and monetary union, institutional adaptations, political co-operation – it might appear foolhardy to present any description at all.

On the other hand it might be argued that it is precisely at such a time that the necessity to " take stock " is the most urgent; it makes it possible to assess whether or not the choices that were made nearly twenty years ago will ultimately lead to an " organized and vital Europe."* On the basis of past experience it appears that this objective can indeed be achieved with the present structure, provided the Member States, old and new alike, are willing to take the appropriate measures.

* Preamble to the E.C.S.C. treaty.

INDEX